7.95

EDUCATION FOR ADULTS
Volume I: Adult Learning and Education

Education for Adults

Volume I: Adult Learning and Education

Edited by
MALCOLM TIGHT
at the Open University

CROOM HELM
London ● Sydney ● Wolfeboro, New Hampshire
in association with
THE OPEN UNIVERSITY

Selection and editorial material
copyright © The Open University 1983

Croom Helm Ltd, Provident House, Burrell Row,
Beckenham, Kent BR3 1AT
Croom Helm Australia, 44-50 Waterloo Road,
North Ryde, 2113, New South Wales
Croom Helm, 27 South Main Street,
Wolfeboro, New Hampshire 03894-2069, USA
Reprinted 1987

British Library Cataloguing in Publication Data
Tight, Malcolm
    Education for adults.
    Vol. 1: Adult learning and education.
    1. Adult education
    I. Title.
    374   LC5215
    ISBN 0-7099-2449-6

Typeset by Leaper & Gard Ltd, Bristol
Printed in Great Britain by
Biddles Ltd, Guildford, Surrey

CONTENTS

Part Four: Group Learning

Part Five: Community Learning

to e

PREFACE

This Reader is one of two collections of material published in connection with the Open University course E355, 'Education for Adults'. The course is designed for all those interested in the education of adults, whether adult educators, trainers, teachers, administrators, voluntary workers or members of the general public.

It is not necessary to become an undergraduate of the Open University in order to take the course. Further information may be obtained by writing to: The Course Manager, E355 (Education for Adults), School of Education, The Open University, Walton Hall, Milton Keynes MK7 6AA, Bucks.

GENERAL INTRODUCTION

This Reader and its companion volume have been prepared with the interests of a large group of people in mind: namely, all those who have some concern with the education of adults, in whatever form this may take. Though the stimulus for its preparation came from the needs of students taking a particular Open University course, it is hoped and believed that these students will constitute only a minority of those to whom the Readers will be of interest.

The general title chosen for the Readers, 'Education for Adults', reflects their broad concern. In the United Kingdom, the education of adults is still very much an emerging field of study. There are few journals devoted to the field, the subject is not commonly studied in universities or in other institutions of higher education, and much of the literature has either not been published or is not widely available. A considerable proportion of specially commissioned or previously unpublished material has, therefore, been included in these Readers. It is hoped that this selection will in its own way contribute to the further development of the field.

The selection and organisation of material in Readers is always to some extent arbitrary. Many items which could have been included here have had to be left out, and some editing of the longer articles chosen has been necessary. Editorial interpolations and excisions are within square brackets.

The theme of this volume is adult learning and education. Following an opening section which considers definitions and patterns, for which a comparative international perspective has been adopted, the processes involved in the education of adults are considered. The three final sections are arranged in terms of the major settings for the education of adults — the individual, the group and the wider community. Both case studies and thematic articles have been included, selected so as to illustrate the breadth of the field along a number of axes: formal, non-formal and informal education; face-to-face and distance education; from basic levels of education to higher education; from highly deterministic to more 'open' or self-directed forms of education. It is felt that the study and practice of the education of adults can best be advanced by the adoption of such a broad view.

I would like to thank all those who have helped in the preparation of this volume, particularly June, Bob, Martine and the other members of the Education for Adults course team, as well as the contributing authors.

Malcolm Tight
Fenny Stratford
July 1983

Part 1

DEFINITIONS AND PATTERNS

The three chapters included in this part of the Reader examine the varied traditions, definitions and patterns of education for adults to be found in the Western World, in the Soviet Bloc and in the Third World.

Brian Groombridge, in the opening chapter, takes the bull by the horns in addressing the underlying problems of definition. He points out the different usages of the term 'adult education' in Britain and other parts of the Western World, and puts forward a broader view of education for adults, categorising different kinds of provision and education along a three-fold axis between prescriptive (e.g. traditional schooling), personal or popular (individual or group control of the educational process) and partnership (where teachers and learners meet on an equal and cooperative basis) modes of study. This simple but useful classification may be borne in mind when considering other chapters in this Reader and elsewhere, when terms like 'adult education' and 'education of adults' are often used almost synonymously.

The humanity that is apparent in the chapter by Groombridge, and the current marginal status of adults in the British educational system despite the long history of provision made for them, contrasts sharply with the position in Eastern Europe described by Jindra Kulich. The history of educational provision for adults in these countries is brief, yet it is currently of great importance and is carefully controlled and used by the state. The development of the study of adult education is also well advanced, though sometimes on narrowly focused lines, with much of the material that has been produced difficult to access in the Western World.

Lalage Bown's chapter on Third World patterns provides a further contrast. Here again the history of education for adults is relatively short, but the potential for development is great and is in part being realised, whilst the impact of Third World thinking and practice on the West is already apparent (see, for example, the chapters by Allman and Mezirow in this Reader).

ADULT EDUCATION AND THE EDUCATION OF ADULTS

Brian Groombridge

Source: Copyright ©The Open University 1983 (specially written for this volume).

The literature of adult education abounds in attempts to define it. One of the most succinct definitions is that pared down over a period of years by Edward Hutchinson, founder-director of the National Institute of Adult Education (England and Wales):

> Adult education is … all responsibly organised opportunities … to enable men and women to enlarge and interpret their own living experience.[1]

All such definitions are problematic, of course, and this terse attempt is no exception. The word 'responsibility' might seem now to have too institutional a connotation; and not everyone will respond to the subtle harmonics of 'living experience', as distinct from mere 'experience'.

Cyril O. Houle's definition is almost as economical. In this essay I shall not try to do better (although I might have substituted the more inclusive word 'change' for 'improve'):

> Adult education is the process by which men and women (alone, in groups, or in institutional settings) seek to improve themselves or their society by increasing their skill, knowledge or sensitiveness; or it is any process by which individuals, groups, or institutions try to help men and women improve in these ways.[2]

In this definition, the adult education process is not necessarily 'provided'. As Robert A. Carlson points out, in a combative chapter at the end of the American handbook *Redefining the Discipline of Adult Education*:

> Certainly some adult education is carried out by agencies and by

3

educational arms of existing institutions. But even more of it is carried out ... by ... peers, poets, propagandists, priests, peddlers, politicians, performers, publishers, pamphleteers, playwrights, publicans, and practitioners of the plastic arts.[3]

When undertaking to define adult education, writers are at least trying to hold the words steady so that their meaning may be clearly discerned, but when they are just being used the student of adult education will find that the words 'adult education' are often unstable. They have changed their meanings over time: they may even change their meaning within the span of a single text. Thinking systematically about adult education can be like trying to build with wet soap.

Some definitions or usages of 'adult education' are too broad. Writers who are properly anxious not to equate adult education with a narrow range of designated agencies sometimes go too far and seem to make education synonymous with all learning. The key words in Houle's definition are 'seek' (in 'seek to improve') and 'try' (in 'try to help'). Education is present when there is an *intention*, not necessarily to teach, but at least to accomplish or facilitate learning. Defending themselves against Carlson, Boyd and Apps, the editors of the handbook already quoted, insist that the term: '... *unorganised education* is, for us, a paradox'.[4]

On the question of who organises, however, their view is close to Carlson's. For them:

> Education is a plan for learning, and activities that are planned are not unorganised. Institutions and agencies, however, do not have a monopoly on organising learning activities. Any agency, institution, individual, group or community can organise adult education activities. Churches, museums, service clubs, groups of neighbours, party lovers and noontime joggers have the potential to provide adult education. It does not matter if a group is commonly thought of as an institution of adult education; nor does it matter if any of the participants are designated adult educators by training or experience. The criterion ... is whether the individual or group has developed a plan for learning.[5]

There is a grey area of importance. We are all 'educated', to a greater or lesser extent, by legislation, by publicity, by images in the mass media, and by other environmental forces, where there is not necessarily a 'plan for learning' as such, but where there is a socially diffused, semi-structured, more or less deliberate intention to shape attitudes and mould consciousness. The distinctions between 'educational' and 'educative', or between 'intended to educate' and 'tending to educate' are useful in differentiating phases in a continuum.

By contrast, some definitions or usages of 'adult education' are too narrow. Between the 1920s and 1950s, for example, it was common to identify 'adult education' with *movements* promoting liberal education for social reform, usually employing some characteristic teaching method, and thereby to equate it, in Britain, with the long courses of the Workers' Educational Association in tandem with University extra-mural departments; in Denmark, with the residential Folk High Schools; in Sweden, with Study Circles; and in the United States with community action and development. The British literature of the period constantly refers to 'the adult education *movement*', but a decade later practitioners began to debate whether it was a movement or a service. The dilemma arose in part from a modest but definite increase in the scale and quality of commitment by the local authorities.

Although the 1944 Education Act is dedicated to the education of the people (and not just the children) of England and Wales, the term 'adult education' does not appear in it. Legally speaking, 'adult education' is a relatively unprotected species of the genus 'Further Education' (which *is* named in the Act). By convention, it has come in England and Wales to mean the associated activities not just of the WEA and the Universities but, above all, the general, personal, cultural, recreative classes (so-called 'non-vocational' classes) run by local education authorities. This was the meaning of 'adult education' in the slogan, heard increasingly in the late 1970s, 'Save Adult Education'. At that time considerably *increased* sums of money, including state and public money, were in fact being spent on educational opportunities for adults through new forms of industrial training and through extensions to educational broadcasting (including programmes in liberal and cultural subjects). A distinction was being made, more or less overtly, and undoubtedly of great significance to the campaigners, between 'adult education' and the education of adults. (Other countries and other languages have been affected by the same uncertainties, with, for example, the distinction in French between *l'apprentissage des adultes, éducation des adultes,* and *l'éducation populaire,* alongside the broader concept of *éducation permanente* (lifelong education), which in turn seems often to be reduced in practice to *formation continue.*)

Categories

An internationally accepted distinction between Formal, Non-formal and Informal Education helps to make the domain comprehensible. Even these categories are not used uniformly or consistently, but broadly speaking:

1. Formal education is that provided by the education and training system set up or sponsored by the state for those express purposes;
2. Non-formal education comprises the many deliberate educational enterprises set up outside the education system, e.g. by other ministries or departments (health, agriculture and others), or by agencies with primary objectives to which education is subordinate (churches, trades unions and others);
3. Informal education (which undoubtedly slides into unplanned, incidental learning) is that vast area of social transactions in which people are deliberately informing, persuading, telling, influencing, advising and instructing each other; and deliberately seeking out information, advice, instruction, wisdom and enlightenment.

These categories have their uses. When confronted by a text or slogan about adult education, it may be relevant to check whether Formal, Non-formal or Informal is meant. Adult education may be part of the education system; or it may be an activity or process promoted by a non-educational body; or it may be a relatively spontaneous feature of social life. Recognising that adult education may be part of the education system underlies the more specific recognition that some forms of it are remedial and others are not. Although not so designated, some adult education is in effect adult primary education, adult secondary education, and so forth. Much education for adults in, for example, the Netherlands (the so-called 'Mother-school' for instance) and in Eastern Europe is in this form. There is a strong belief in Britain, however, reflected in the stress on maturity in E.M. Hutchinson's definition, that many kinds of adult education are by no means remedial, for which being a developing adult, having adult experience and responsibilities, is the essence of the matter.

Implications for Policy

The debate about resources for adult education has been in large part a debate about whether such adult education should be regarded as an integral part of the post-school sector of the Formal system. In Britain, there is a tendency sharply to distinguish the education of adults from the schooling of children, an antithesis which makes for pedagogical strengths in adult education but for its political weakness; in several European countries, by contrast, there is a tendency to treat adult education as remedial schooling for grown-ups.

These more-than-semantic matters have left their impression on the process of policy formation in Britain. They showed, for example, in the terms of reference and conclusions of two major committees of enquiry in the 1970s — the Russell Committee in England and Wales[6] and the Alexander Committee in Scotland.[7] Despite their positive and sometimes eloquent assertion of the value of personal, social and general education for adults (so that 'adult education' turned into 'community education' in Scotland and it became harder everywhere to use the feeble negative 'non-vocational'), both reports were weakened, conceptually and in their impact on politics, through the emasculating absence of any direct concern with education for economic well-being, technological adaptability and industrial productivity — matters as important to individuals (the good job as a passport to the good life and even as part of it) as to societies (needing to create wealth as well as dispose of it).

The Russell Report had some effect. It provided a rationale and created a climate for the adult literacy campaign and other cheap but worthwhile extensions of adult primary education. It helped the WEA find a new relevance and extra-mural departments to become of more interest and value to their parent universities. It correctly anticipated that the success of the Open University would lead to the creation of what Russell called 'analogues' (open and distance learning systems) operating at other academic levels and in non-academic fields. It also recommended that policy and practice would be improved by the creation of a national development council for adult education. What actually happened was better and worse: worse in that an *advisory* council was set up (in 1977), poorly financed and with no assurance of a long life; better in that it was called the 'Advisory Council for Adult and *Continuing* Education' (ACACE). The phrase 'adult and continuing education' was widely thought at the time to be a mere politically acute euphemism. In the event, the term 'continuing' became the more important, but without the liberal, reformist values connoted by 'Adult Education' being extinguished. ACACE's major report, avowedly a policy guide meant to last 20 years, was called *Continuing Education: From Policies to Practice.*[8]

In his Chairman's Preface to the report, Richard Hoggart is inevitably preoccupied with meanings. He clearly distinguishes 'adult education' and 'continuing education', construing the former mainly as a specialised service sector and the latter as a comprehensive system. 'Adult Education', which the report qualifies as 'adult general education' comprises 'all the varied opportunities offered to adults by local education authorities, university extramural departments, and voluntary bodies such as the Workers' Educational Association, in cultural, physical, basic, social and civic education, which have hitherto been negatively classified, and consequently often stigmatised, as non-vocational education'. 'Continuing Education' has a much wider 'institutional scope'. The report 'advocates adult learning in universities, polytechnics, institutes of higher education, further education colleges, schools, adult education and community centres, at home and at work, and wherever learning opportunities can be organised and provided — whether face-to-face or at a distance'. All these institutions — including institutions for industrial training — must 'consciously set about opening their doors and providing tuition with adults clearly in mind'.[9]

Hoggart guards against misunderstanding about this system. It is not, he writes:

> ... another education 'sector' to march beside the administratively distinct sectors of school, further and higher education. By 'system' we mean not an administrative division but a conjunction of policies, funding, provision and attitudes, which effect changes *in all the present educational sectors* to the

advantage of a rapidly growing number of adult learners.[10] (my emphasis)

In terms of the categories used internationally and already mentioned (Formal, Non-formal and Informal Education), therefore, the concern here is with a conjunction of enterprises within the Formal System. The ACACE Report nevertheless makes an important reference to forms of adult education outside the scope of Continuing Education:

> There are, for example, many organisations in the national training system, other than the Manpower Services Commission and the Industrial Training Boards, providing education and training for adults: the Confederation of British Industry, the employers' associations, individual firms, the Trades Union Congress, individual trades unions, the armed services, and many professional bodies. Similarly there are many public authorities providing continuing education outside the public education sector: the sponsors of cultural and leisure activities such as the Arts Council and the Sports Council, the public library services, the Health Education Council, the Department of Health and Social Security and the local Social Service Departments, and the broadcasting media. There are also many independent further education institutions, not to mention private tutors, providing opportunities to study music, languages, crafts, dancing, sport, driving, office skills, etc. There is the vast range of national and local voluntary organisations and community development associations with either a primary or secondary purpose in providing education for adults. There are large numbers of community arts centres and neighbourhood and community development projects with educational dimensions and innumerable local clubs and societies with the further education of their members among their aims.[11]

Clearly this range of activity could never be incorporated into some kind of amazingly compendious master-system, beyond the power or means of even the most managerially adroit of totalitarian states, but from the point of view of individual citizens, individual learners, the overall health of that panoply of enterprises can be as important as ACACE's express concern, access to the Formal System.

In his preface, Hoggart hopes the Report's 'broad definition of continuing education' will become common usage. Were ACACE to succeed in establishing such a definition it would be possible to reclaim the phrase 'adult education', not for the narrow, traditional concept but for the total domain, far wider than 'continuing education' itself because comprehending Non-formal and Informal as well as Formal education for adults. Such a comprehensive concept is needed not merely for philosophical cogency, but also for practical reasons. In many countries, some of the most interesting and urgent issues hinge on the relations *between* the Formal System and the other two.

Different Categories Distinguished and Exemplified

This vast field is in strong contrast, in its size and scope, to the schooling of children; yet it is the school which provides the model and the metaphor for most public thought about education. If sense is to be made of this immense and heterogeneous domain, then more analytical tools are needed. The three categories — Formal, Non-formal and Informal — relate to large systems and forms of social organisation. They matter to administrators. They also matter to groups and individuals wanting access to society's educational resources at their most concentrated, and to politicians, wanting a good return on the investment in those resources. From the many other categorisations available in the literature I shall select one from Houle's *The Design of Education* and offer one of my own.

Houle suggests eleven different categories of educational programme. He introduces the scheme by reference to an educational programme category with which almost everyone is familiar — classroom instruction. As he observes:

> Classroom instruction is, in fact, so commonly used in the schooling of young people from kindergarten through graduate instruction that many people carry over into their adulthood the belief that it is virtually the only possible learning situation. This view is shared by many educators of adults. An extension dean may believe that the only university-level instruction which is intellectually respectable is one in which an acknowledged master of a field of content teaches it to a group of well-prepared students. The dominance of classroom instruction is further

reinforced by both professional and lay discussions of education, most of which imply that it is the only form of learning and teaching which is worth consideration.[12]

Charles Wedemeyer notes that this prejudice leads to scepticism about the educational authenticity of institutions which do not use face-to-face classroom instruction as their chief mode.[13]

The evaluation and reputation of such institutions in Britain as the Open University or the National Extension College have no doubt been affected by this deep attachment to classroom instruction — subsumed, in Houle's actual scheme, into a wider category ('a teacher or group of teachers designs an activity for, and often with, a group of students'). The scheme, which is elaborated with illuminating examples and wise commentary in two substantial chapters, is summarised in the following table:

Table 1: Major Categories of Educational Design Situations

Individual

C-1   An individual designs an activity for himself

C-2   An individual or a group designs an activity for another individual

Group

C-3   A group (with or without a continuing leader) designs an activity for itself

C-4   A teacher or group of teachers designs an activity for, and often with, a group of students

C-5   A committee designs an activity for a larger group

C-6   Two or more groups design an activity which will enhance their combined programs of service

Institution

C-7   A new institution is designed

C-8   An institution designs an activity in a new format

C-9   An institution designs a new activity in an established format

C-10 Two or more institutions design an activity which will enhance their combined programs of service

Mass

C-11 An individual, group, or institution designs an activity for a mass audience

Source: Houle (1972), p. 44.

Houle's many examples include:

C1 — Malcolm X teaching himself to read in prison by transcribing the pages of a dictionary.

C2 — A department store supervisor tries systematically to help one of his sales staff to do better.

C3 — A church pastor organises a group to read and discuss the writings of Paul Tillich.

C4 — A home economist helps poor mothers choose and prepare food which is both cheap and nutritious.

C5 — A planning group works out a programme for the Cooperative Extension Service.

C6 — The presidents of a number of voluntary groups in a city neighbourhood form a council to identify common problems and study ways to deal with them.

C7 — A national association is formed to educate its members in foreign affairs.

C8 — a university extension programme designs a new curriculum to provide adults with access to a special baccalaureate degree.

C9 — An educational institution decides to enlist the help of a newspaper or radio station to achieve a community-based goal.

C10 — An extension organisation and a county library collaborate to foster each other's programmes.

C11 — A celebrated authority can share his or her knowledge with a mass audience through television.

I propose to take Houle's eleven categories and reduce them to three, by focusing on one central but fundamental question: who decides what is to be learned, what is worth learning? This connects with another important question: who decides when what was to be learned has been satisfactorily learned? Several truths are packed into the old aphorism, 'knowledge is power', so these are key questions. And if autonomy is meant to be a prime characteristic of the adulthood of free men and women, then they are particularly salient questions in relation to adult education. I shall suggest that all forms of adult education conform to one or other of three modes — (1) Mode One: Prescriptive; (2) Mode Two: Popular or Personal; and (3) Mode Three: Partnership.

Mode One

Almost everyone is familiar with the Prescriptive mode because it is characteristic of traditional schooling. In mode one, experts with authority decide what is to be learned and whether it has been learned satisfactorily. In the Formal System it is usual to speak of the curriculum. In mode one, therefore, the curriculum and the syllabuses are, as we say, laid down. The actual teaching methods may be more or less humane, more or less progressive, more or less effective. What matters at this point is that the student/pupil/ learner is dependent on others in this cardinal matter of what counts as knowledge (worth acquiring). Most schooling is of this kind, as well as most first degree work in most universities, and most industrial and military training.

It is often thought, especially by professionals who would identify themselves as adult educators, as well as by deschoolers and many critics of an unduly authoritarian, hierarchical society, that this mode is not only dominant — it is also counter-educational, socially regressive and morally wrong. This reaction, which, as a self-identifying adult educator, I tend to share, is almost certainly fallacious and over-simplified. If I were an industrial trainer, and so just as much an adult educator, I might not regard this mode as suspect. Some manifestations of the mode are vulnerable to criticism, but how would each of us assess the following examples of the mode in practice, especially when, as adults, we knowingly put ourselves in the hands of a Prescriptive regime? In all of the following situations the Prescriptive mode prevails, sometimes usefully, sometimes ineffectively, sometimes harmfully. We learn (or fail to learn) from experts; experts certify whether we have learned their knowledge to their satisfaction.

Prescriptive situations

— studying for O levels;
— studying for A levels;
— studying for an Open University degree;
— studying academic subjects and disciplines up to date;
— learning how to use a wordprocessor;
— learning languages through broadcasting or with a set of Linguaphone discs;
— learning how to monitor an atomic power station for criticality;

—   learning how to drive;
—   learning the catechism;
—   learning the rules of a new game;
—   learning the 'Knowledge' (London taxi drivers' knowledge
of routes and places);
—   learning etiquette in a foreign country.

Mode Two

In this mode, the individual (Personal) or group (Popular) decide
what they need, what is good for them, and whether they have
learned it to their own satisfaction. Autodidacts exemplify this
mode, as do groups undertaking learning projects on their own
terms (for the sake of education or for the sake of other personal
and social objectives). They may have recourse to experts (the
individual may buy a book or an audiocassette; the group may turn to
an authoritative resource person). There is no curriculum in the
formal sense (i.e. a body of knowledge to be learned in a certain
way, as defined by specialists in that knowledge). Satisfaction is
achieved when the individual feels satisfied, when the group has
succeeded, when the problem is solved. The only tests are pragmatic and subjective, though they may be based on long experience
through which standards are developed — we reckon we sang that
madrigal well and the audience liked it; our neighbourhood
cooperative has cracked the market for this particular product or
service. This mode is intrinsically more adult than mode one. No
doubt it often results in some of us not learning some things as well
as we need, even for our own well-being, but we tend to learn from
experience when we have not learned well enough. Adult educators, if invited, can help by giving individuals, groups and communities the self-confidence and the skills to pursue their own
learning.

The contemporary feminist movement provides a powerful
exemplification of this mode, through women of many kinds learning from each other, and through the deep dialectical examination
of the changing experience of women. In this mode the 'best'
educated may find themselves carried forward by a quite different
quality of energy than they would have encountered as providers in
mode one. To give one illustration: *Beyond the Fragments* (by Sheila
Rowbotham, Lynne Segal and Hilary Wainwright) was a key text
for this movement in 1979 and after. It can be read not only for the
interest of what it says but also as the product of a prolonged and

collective educational process — originally a pamphlet, it became a reworked book because of the authors' responsiveness to wide-ranging discussion throughout the movement.[14]

Other examples of the popular mode are abundant, especially in Britain where the associative tradition is so strong: hobby and interest groups ('educative societies', as they have been called); invisible colleges; single issue political lobbies; the members of Fircone (Friends-in-Retirement) providing an adult education programme for each other in Birmingham; members of the National Housewives' Register or of the Pre-school Playgroups Association planning a programme together; the complex community self-development schemes of the Craigmillar Festival Society; housing cooperatives in downtown Liverpool and elsewhere; learning exchanges of many kinds. This mode broadly overlaps with and is a major aspect of the Informal sector. It is clearly of major human, social, cultural and political significance.

Mode Three

In the Partnership mode, what is to be learned is decided by negotiation between those who wish to learn and those responsible for teaching. There is a curriculum, but it is not promulgated unilaterally. It may arise from the prompting of people who are not regarded as expert, as well as from the desire of experts to share what they know. The body of knowledge to be communicated may derive not only from scholarship but from the life experience of students, systematised and refined by them in association with instructors or tutors. Satisfaction is achieved when the learners or students feel, or know from experience, that they have progressed in insight, sensitivity or mastery, and when teachers recognise that they have taught not only subject matter, but something of the processes of study, so that learners may continue on their own. There may be tests, if both parties agree, so that learners may have the additional satisfaction of having their knowledge objectively and publicly assessed and accredited.

This mode is characteristic of 'adult education' in the narrow sense, the heartland of adult education, which the ACACE report already mentioned qualifies as 'adult general education'. For example, it is common for craft teachers employed by local education authorities to create a curriculum by combining their general knowledge of the crafts with the specific task-related needs and enthusiasms of their students; it is also common, in this mode, for university tutors to work out syllabuses with their students and for teachers and taught to learn from each other. This happens typically, or is at least supposed to happen, in much extension or 'extra-mural' work, but it may sometimes occur even in university first degree studies. Internal students at the School of Independent Studies, University of Lancaster, for instance, like students at the Empire State University, New York, work out Learning Contracts (agreements to follow negotiated syllabuses) with their tutors.

This mode can be seen in operation at the institutional as well as the tutorial level, as when a local authority class (e.g. in choral singing) turns into a voluntary society; or as when a voluntary society invites a local authority to supply it with tutors; or, as when university departments of adult education enter into some kind of concordat with districts of the Workers' Educational Association (WEA), or when the WEA itself provides courses for the trade union movement.

The strength of this mode lies in its recognition that knowledge can be generated in different ways (through scholarship and training, through experience), that it can be organised in different ways (for use by interested men and women, not only for elaboration within a disciplinary framework by scholars), and that it can be validated in different ways (formally or experientially).

Values

People in general and educators in particular put different values upon these modes, or specific manifestations of them. Different states do so by treating them differently in law and in practice. In Britain, the Prescriptive mode tends to be much the most generously financed; the Partnership mode less well; and the Popular mode hardly at all (the voluntary tradition in Britain is felt to imply independence of the state). Other countries with different histories have reached other conclusions. In the Nordic countries, for example, it is the Popular forms of adult education that attract generous funding, sometimes in ways that seem puzzling to other countries — the different political parties, for example, all undertake adult education work, and that is publicly subsidised.

These differences have been insufficiently examined for their philosophical implications and policy stimulus. They have a direct bearing on the diversity of reasons given to justify adult education. Different advocates — politicians, practitioners, learners — may be influenced by taking one mode, or one sector, to stand for the adult education enterprise at its most important. It is certain that the values attributed to adult education will largely reflect values at more fundamental levels — political, religious and philosophical.

For Unesco, adult education is important for the lifelong development of human beings and the diffusion in society of the values (peace, intellectual progress, democracy) for which Unesco itself stands. The Organisation for Economic Cooperation and Development (OECD) advocates adult education as an integral part of the political process in modern societies, whatever their political system. The International Council of Adult Education is not so neutral and regards adult education as an instrument of public liberation ('social mobilisation') against oppression. Official advocacy for adult education in Britain is often limited to those forms which contribute to economic regeneration and industrial adaptability. Practitioners of adult education themselves may be inspired by a dedication to personal growth, by a Christian conviction that their work cultivates God in everyman, by the hope that it will challenge the hegemony of capitalist ideas which hold back the march to socialism, or by a liberal sense that adult education is about enabling people to be more autonomous in their own lives and with their own values.

Such differences of value underlie conflicts in practice, whether, say, between the state and advocates of adult education, or between rival enthusiasts. The slogan from the 1970s already mentioned, 'Save Adult Education', meant in effect: save (provide more money for and strengthen the legal and policy basis of) that form of adult education in the Partnership mode which is locally available, informal and approachable in ambience, and flexibly designed for open access, because of its importance to individuals and families, and, more generally, as a significant contribution to a good quality of life. Whereas the state, at that time (and, it must be said, in most countries), tended to give preference to activities in the Prescriptive mode (for economic ends). More 'liberal' forms of education could, it was felt, be provided *en masse* by the mass media.[15]

There is a classic conflict based upon major differences of value in the history of British adult education, which has repercussions to this day. Between the two world wars, there was bitter conflict between the Workers' Educational Association (Partnership) and the National Council of Labour Colleges (Popular). Both agreed that adult education mattered because it was an adjunct to the movement for a more humane society in general and for the progress of the labour movement in particular. The WEA argued, in effect, that nothing but the best was good enough for the British working class; the best was to be found *par excellence* in Oxford University and to some extent in other such institutions; the WEA existed to make that knowledge available to working men and women (and to teach the universities a thing or two). The NCLC argued, in effect, that the universities were the think-tanks of a repressive State; that knowledge stemming from them was tainted and served the interests of the class enemy; that those dealing with them, however long the spoon, would find themselves co-opted and emasculated. These are but cartoon sketches of deeply significant, deeply felt, and continuing arguments.[16]

Not dissimilar, if less acrimonious, conflicts are at work between those who urge that Universities of the Third Age should be learning exchanges for older people, having no truck with institutions of higher education (Popular) and those who advocate the opening up to, and transformation of those institutions by, the hitherto dispossessed older generation (Partnership).

Underlying such conflicts is the difference (again a difference of values) between those for whom adult education is valuable in so far as it serves certain larger goals — social, political, religious — and those for whom it is valuable because it aids the very process of discovering and defining what those larger goals may be.

Notes

1. E.M. Hutchinson, Introduction to *Adult Education 35*, 5 (National Institute of Adult Education, Leicester, 1963), pp. 232-3.

2. C.O. Houle, *The Design of Education* (Jossey-Bass, San Francisco, 1972), p. 32.

3. R.A. Carlson, 'The Foundation of Adult Education: Analysing the Boyd-Apps Model' in R.D. Boyd, J.W. Apps, *et al.*, *Redefining the Discipline of Adult Education* (Jossey-Bass, San Francisco, 1980), p. 178.

4. J.W. Apps and R.D. Boyd, 'Response', ibid., p. 186.

5. Ibid., pp. 186-7.

6. The Russell Report, *Adult Education: A Plan for Development* (HMSO, London, 1973).

7. The Alexander Report, *Adult Education: The Challenge of Change* (HMSO, London, 1975).

8. Advisory Council for Adult and Continuing Education, *Continuing Education: From Policies to Practice* (ACACE, Leicester, 1982).

9. Ibid., pp. vii-viii.

10. Ibid., p. vii.

11. Ibid., pp. 44-5.

12. C.O. Houle, *The Design of Education*, p. 41.

13. C.A. Wedemeyer, *Learning at the Back Door: Reflections on Non-Traditional Learning in the Lifespan* (University of Wisconsin Press, Madison, 1981).

14. S. Rowbotham, L. Segal and H. Wainwright, *Beyond the Fragments: Feminism and the Making of Socialism* (Merlin Press, London, 1979).

15. See K. Berrill, 'Why Old Dogs Need New Tricks', *Learn Magazine, 1*, 18-20 (1979); and also the response in the following issue — B. Groombridge, 'You Are Wrong, Sir Kenneth!', *Learn Magazine, 2*, 26-7 (1979).

16. See, for example, J.F. and W. Horrabin, *Working-Class Education* (Labour Publishing Co., London, 1924); M. Stocks, *The Workers' Educational Association: The First Fifty Years* (George Allen & Unwin, London, 1953).

PATTERNS OF ADULT EDUCATION IN EAST EUROPE

Jindra Kulich

Source: Copyright © The Open University 1983 (specially written for this volume).

Introduction

Adult education in the East European countries is viewed very broadly. It includes not only the usual formal school-type provision at elementary, secondary and post-secondary levels, and the considerable training operations carried out by industrial enterprises, but also a widespread network of non-formal facilities and programs such as libraries, houses of culture, trade union and village level clubs, people's and workers' universities, societies for the popularization of science, political party organizations, amateur art, music, theatre and folklore groups, mass organizations for culture, education and physical culture and others. Adult educators are often referred to as cultural or cultural-educational workers. Consistent with the post-war ideological, political and economic system in East Europe, all forms of adult education and cultural work have to fit into the prevailing social system and into the planned economy, as well as being subject to Communist Party and state control.

Social, Political and Economic Background

Although the countries of East Europe (Albania, Bulgaria, Czechoslovakia, the German Democratic Republic, Hungary, Poland, Romania, the USSR and Yugoslavia) share some historical similarities and in recent years have all been part of the socialist camp, differences in their origins, ethnic composition and stages of economic development are important.

Before 1918 many of these countries were occupied or governed by foreign powers. As a result of the First World War new states emerged in East Europe. Czechoslovakia and Hungary broke away from Austria, and Poland was unified, while Yugoslavia was formed from several South Slav territories. Albania regained independence in 1920. Following the 1917 revolution, the Russian Empire became the Soviet Union (USSR) in 1922. Between the wars, only Germany and Czechoslovakia could be classed as highly developed industrial countries; the Soviet Union was developing rapidly, while Bulgaria, Hungary, Poland, Romania and Yugoslavia were predominantly agricultural countries in various stages of industrialization. Albania was a peasant feudal fiefdom. The level of literacy varied significantly among these countries from Albania with 83 per cent illiterates to Germany with only .05 per cent.

The destruction of the Second World War left East Europe in ruins economically, politically and spiritually. In the aftermath of the war far-reaching political, social and economic changes swept the region and by 1950 all the countries had governments in which the Communist Party played a dominant role. The post-war reconstruction and the new social order developing in East Europe had its impact on adult education.

Historical Roots of Adult Education in East Europe

The beginnings of adult education in Central and East Europe date back to the mid-nineteenth century, the period of national linguistic and cultural awakening amongst many of the ethnic groups in the region. At that time a number of literacy, reading and educational circles appeared in the cities, to be followed later by a similar development in the villages. The national awakening movements among the intelligentsia, burghers and peasants, and the struggle for ethnic renewal in the face of foreign cultural domination, were a crucial motivator for adult education in the nineteenth century, unequalled elsewhere in Europe except for Scandinavia.

As in most other parts of Europe, Sunday schools were the first formal institutions for adult education. Sunday schools were established in Germany as early as the eighteenth century, whereas in most other countries in Central and East Europe such schools were not in operation until the mid-nineteenth century. They were replaced at the turn of the century by evening adult schools, providing at first elementary education and later expanding in the 1920s to offer secondary education for adults as well. Private and public correspondence schools were also established throughout the region around the turn of the century.

The mechanics' institutes, which originated in the United Kingdom and spread to the British colonies, did not take root in East Europe. The vehicles for the education of artisans and workers in East Europe were the workers' reading and educational clubs, which originated in Germany in the 1860s and spread throughout the region. Unlike the mechanics' institutes, which came to serve the middle class soon after their establishment, the workers' clubs remained the preserve of the working class.

In the rural areas, the role played by village school teachers in the ethnic and cultural awakening of the nineteenth century and in adult education in the twentieth century was extremely important. The progress made in adult basic education, agricultural innovation, health education, cultural development and civic education throughout the region would have been inconceivable without the major contribution made by the village teachers.

The reading rooms and private and public libraries which were established by the mid-nineteenth century contributed significantly to the enlightenment of the people. These institutions were often part of, or worked in cooperation with, the many voluntary educational associations. Some of the most significant of the latter associations, which developed in Eastern Europe in the late nineteenth century, were the physical education associations, possibly the first example of lifelong educational provision. These associations, which organized activities for children, youths and adults, did not limit their activities to the health of the body, but were also active in civic education.

Unlike the mechanics' institutes, the university extension idea was successfully transplanted to many of the East European countries around the year 1900. The beginnings of popular university lectures in what is now Czechoslovakia were made at the Charles University in Prague. Such activities in Romania started at the University of Cluj around the same time and spread to other universities. Similar development occurred in the other East European countries. Following the establishment of popular lectures, many of the East European universities in the 1920s then made possible extra-mural and correspondence study leading towards degrees.

However, university extension in East Europe never grew into the important institution it did in the United Kingdom. (The only exception was the Soviet Union where, in the 1920s, workers' universities were established to accelerate changes in the composition of the intelligentsia by a massive infusion of the working class into higher education.) One of the reasons was that the East European universities were not as receptive to the extension idea. The other main reason was the parallel development of people's universities, which were doing very much the same work of popularization of the sciences and humanities, but without formal university affiliation. People's universities became the main adult education institutions in the region during the period between the two world wars. In addition to these primarily evening institutions, in Germany, Hungary and Poland adaptations of the Danish residential folk high schools, which provided general education to the peasant population, developed.

It was natural that, with the low level of literacy in many parts of East Europe, there were also attempts to eliminate or at least reduce illiteracy during the 1920s and 1930s. With the exception of the Soviet Union, where a major military-style campaign reduced illiteracy from 48.8 per cent in 1926 to 18.8 per cent in 1939, those early attempts produced only short-lived gains, and widespread relapses into illiteracy occurred among the peasant population.

Civic education was an important aspect of adult education in countries created largely as a result of the First World War, and struggling with various degrees of success with the democratization of their societies. Before this process was interrupted by the authoritarian regimes instituted in most of the East European countries in the 1930s, civic education for children and adults was among each state's priorities. It was carried out by schools, voluntary associations, popular movements and the armed forces.

Another aspect of adult education not equalled anywhere in Western Europe were the widespread amateur circles, clubs and ensembles fostering the preservation and enjoyment of folk art, music and dancing. These activities originated in the national awakening movements of the nineteenth century, and persist as vital elements of national life throughout East Europe to this day.

East European Concepts and Definitions of Adult Education

From the beginning of organized adult education activity in East Europe, the concept of adult education was different and much broader than that adopted in the United Kingdom. This undoubtedly had its cause in the need for national awakening which was so important in East Europe, as well as in the widespread belief among the progressive intelligentsia in the power of knowledge and the need for the enlightenment of the general population.

This conception is reflected in the terminology used throughout the region until the early post-Second World War period; 'enlightenment work', 'cultural-enlightenment work', 'popular education'. These terms encompassed the broad variety of adult education activities outlined in the preceding section, and thus included what in the United Kingdom would be subsumed under adult education and further education, as well as under other activities not generally considered as adult education.

The concept of self-education, of self-development as an important factor, has deep roots in East Europe. It found its manifestation, amongst other things, in the institution of 'external examinations', both at secondary and university levels, which enabled adults to advance by independently taking challenging examinations. Some theoreticians of adult education, particularly in Poland and Yugoslavia, believe that the ultimate aim of adult education is to enable all adults to become self-motivated self-learners; and thus eventually eliminate the need for organized adult education courses.

The development of adult education in the Soviet Union and in the rest of East Europe during the 1920s and 1930s was strikingly different. While the backbone of adult education in most of the countries was a variety of primarily voluntary associations, aimed at general adult education with a modicum of state support or involvement, the Soviet Union built up a system of elementary, secondary, higher and vocational education of adults, controlled by the state and the Communist Party, and charged with building up the underpinnings of the new, socialist society. Mass ideological work and political indoctrination became increasingly part of the daily life of the population and permeated all educational and cultural activities.

With the far-reaching political and social changes which occurred in East Europe in the late 1940s, and which made countries in the region part of the socialist camp under Soviet Union rule, most of the indigenous adult education institutions and associations were destroyed in the early 1950s (except for Yugoslavia), while the Soviet concepts and methods of mass political work were imposed on the populations.

After the end of the Stalinist era in 1956 and the relative liberalization which followed, many of the old indigenous institutions and associations began to reappear and flourish again, while some of the positive developments of the early post-war era, such as increased access to secondary and post-secondary education, remained equally strong.

The current prevailing concept of adult education in East Europe is that of a process of development of the new socialist man in all his social and individual aspects. The linking and intertwining of work and education is seen as an important method in the ongoing development of the personality. Adult education is considered as an integral part of a lifelong process of Communist education.

Current Organization of Adult Education

The current pattern of organization includes three sub-systems of adult education: (1) the school sub-system, (2) the out-of-school sub-system, and (3) the training at the enterprise level sub-system. Yugoslavia is the one country which does not have a clearly defined distinction between the sub-systems. Although there are some differences among the other East European countries, especially in the area of the out-of-school sub-system, the similarities seem to far outweigh the differences. And according to some writers, there is a trend to convergence in approaches to the provision of adult education, which is occurring not only among the East European socialist countries but among all industrialized countries. Let us now consider the three sub-systems as these exist in East Europe.

The School Sub-system of Adult Education

Among the East European countries the Soviet Union has the longest experience in the establishment of a school sub-system of adult education at elementary, secondary, vocational/technical and higher education levels. Such schools were established prior to the Second World War and were greatly expanded in the post-war period. After the initial thrust in the 1920s to create a new intelligentsia coming from the working class, which required full-time adult education schools and universities, the emphasis gradually changed to the provision of part-time evening, correspondence and shift schools at all levels, which enabled adults to continue their education and training without interruption of full-time employment.

With rapid technological and scientific development in the Soviet Union since the 1950s, the need for highly trained manpower resulted in the establishment of a widespread network of purely evening and correspondence faculties and universities. Study to first degree level in these faculties takes only one year longer than by full-time study. Part-time study is fostered and supported by the state and the Communist Party, and adults who engage in it are given both public recognition and tangible rewards, in the way of paid leave for consultation and for preparation for examinations, as well as improved chances of promotion.

During the 1950s, faced with the need to eliminate illiteracy (particularly in Albania, Bulgaria, Romania and Yugoslavia), to provide secondary education and vocational training to adults in order to increase the numbers of skilled workers, and to increase access to the universities and change the social composition of their students, the countries in East Europe adopted the Soviet Union adult schooling prototype.

Elementary schools for adults were established in all the countries, except for East Germany and Czechoslovakia where there was no need for schooling at that level. Separate general education secondary schools for adults, both of the full-time day type and the evening or correspondence type were set up. In Czechoslovakia, where there was not such a pressing need for separate day schools, these were almost exclusively evening and correspondence schools, while in East Germany the secondary general education function has been undertaken since 1956 by the reorganized folk high schools. In most of the countries ordinary youth schools were also used to provide adult education through evening classes. In Poland the secondary schools for adults cooperate very closely with factories, and often schedule classes in the enterprises. In Yugoslavia, following the introduction of self-management into factories and business enterprises in the 1950s and subsequent educational reforms, educational institutions and industrial and business enterprises cooperate closely in the provision of education for adults.

The East European countries also rapidly established vocational/technical secondary schools, needed for planned or ongoing industrialization. There were more differences in practice among the East European countries in this area than in elementary and general education secondary schools. In addition to the standard type of evening and day-release vocational schools, prevalent in all the countries, Bulgaria set up school centres for vocational education and rural agricultural schools, East Germany established enterprise academies and village academies, and Poland set up ten rural residential folk high schools.

At the higher education level, all the East European countries operate evening and correspondence courses for adults, where, as in the Soviet Union, the study usually takes only one year longer than in full-time attendance. In Czechoslovakia the stress is on distance education, encompassing independent study, assisted by regular visits to consultation centres. The magnitude of the part-time study provision in East Europe can be illustrated by the fact that in Poland approximately 40 per cent of the students in higher education are part-time adult students, whilst in Romania the figure is some 30 per cent.

As in the Soviet Union, adult part-time students at all levels of the school sub-system are accorded public social support as well as a variety of benefits, ranging from payment of full wages while studying to work release for examination preparation and visits to consultation centres. Throughout the region the school sub-system of adult education is considered a significant part of educational provision.

The Out-of-school Sub-system of Adult Education

Since the sovietization of adult education in Eastern Europe during the 1950s, institutional differentiation has again developed, especially in the out-of-school sub-system.

The reader should keep in mind that in all the East European countries, except in Yugoslavia, the state, governed by the Communist Party, has ultimate control over all forms of education, including informal and non-formal adult education. The state and its organs assumed full responsibility for, and control of, the adult education carried out by voluntary associations in the 1920s in the case of the Soviet Union, and in the late 1940s in the case of the other East European countries. This control is carried out by variously named local government committees at the regional, country and town or village level. Yugoslavia is the one significant exception to the centralist state pattern of East Europe, with its progress towards a self-management society which aims at the decentralization of decision making and at decreasing the role of the state in economic, social and educational areas.

The role of mass organizations, among these the trade unions, youth organizations, defence leagues and peace movements, in the ideological-political education of the citizen is considered of crucial importance in East Europe. This is even more intensified for party members of the ruling Communist Party. All of the countries have a widespread network of party schools and evening universities of Marxism-Leninism, with attendance compulsory for party members. This activity is unmatched anywhere in Western Europe.

During the 1950s many social and educational institutions, common in the Soviet Union, were transplanted to the other East European countries while indigenous institutions were disbanded. Among the transplants were the houses of culture. In the Soviet Union these institutions were prominent in serving the general education and cultural needs of the population, as well as the socializing needs of the state. In many Soviet cities they became major palaces of culture serving all age groups in the population. As a rule, the houses of culture contain the local library, and provide premises for extension courses, amateur groups, special interest and hobby circles, and music schools; many of the houses of culture also have cinemas and provide stages for theatre performances and concerts, as well as halls for art and other exhibits.

Other transplants were the societies for the dissemination of scientific knowledge, formed after the model of the 'Znanie' (Knowledge) society operating in the USSR. These societies are formed by scientists and other university educated specialists, who are expected to offer popularizing lectures in their speciality. The magnitude of the participation by intellectuals can be illustrated by the membership in the Hungarian society (TIT) of 20,000 and by the 37,000 plus in the Polish society (TWP). The total activity of these societies is considerable: for example, close to 320,000 lectures and lecture series with 11.1 million participants in East Germany, 100,000 lectures with 4.5 million participants in Poland, and 300,000 lectures and lecture courses with one million plus participants in Bulgaria. All of the societies have their own publishing houses with considerable outputs of periodicals and books. In recent years, several of these societies began to cooperate with the state broadcasting systems in televised educational programs.

People's universities are the other main provider of informal adult education throughout the region. Basically these are adult education institutions similar to the evening institutes. They are indigenous to all the East European countries, except for East Germany and Yugoslavia, having been abolished in the late 1940s and re-established in the late 1950s. Although these institutions now appear in all the countries, there are some differences. In East Germany, the folk high schools were re-established in 1945 and charged with political re-education; from 1953 to 1956 their task was general cultural education; and from 1956 on these institutions were converted to evening general and vocational schools for adults. In Romania the people's universities were re-established in 1954 as centres of humanistic culture and political education; in the 1970s their program was enlarged, through the addition of vocational subjects, with the absorption of the workers' universities which up to then had been attached to trade union clubs in factories. In Czechoslovakia, Poland and the Soviet Union the people's universities developed a considerable specialization into separate people's universities of science and technology, art and music, as well as into people's universities for special groups in society such as parents, older people, the army, etc. The Yugoslav people's and workers' universities, which have enjoyed uninterrupted existence and orderly development since 1944, are the best developed and functioning institutions for general adult education in East Europe.

As has already been mentioned, amateur activities in folk art, music and dancing have deep historical roots and are widespread in East European countries. Thus, for example, there are over 10,000 amateur folk music and dancing ensembles with some 200,000 members in Hungary. These activities are seen in the East European context as an integral part of cultural-educational work.

Physical education and culture activities for all ages are also much more widespread in East Europe than in other parts of the continent. In this respect Czechoslovakia has the oldest, most comprehensive and best developed system of physical education and culture.

Though there is a commonality among the East European countries in the adult education institutions established there during the period since the Second World War, there are some institutions which are specific to one or two of the countries and which do not seem to have counterparts elsewhere. Among these are the summer universities in Hungary. These offer non-credit general education courses concentrating on one topic; they usually run for one week and are residential programs. (The summer universities are very similar to the summer schools and courses offered in the United Kingdom.) The summer university institution did not spread to the other countries, except for Romania, where a summer school was established recently, based on a historical antecedent.

Another country-specific institution can be found in Poland in the residential folk high schools. These schools were first established around the turn of the century on the model of the Danish folk high schools. During the period between the two world wars these schools developed in a direction which combined the Danish model with Polish needs and ideas, and served the peasant population well. In another transformation in the 1960s and 1970s the schools became training schools for village cultural-educational workers. Although such schools also existed for a short time in the post-war period in Hungary, at present no other East European country has residential folk high schools.

The Training at the Enterprise Level Sub-system

Training of employees by industrial and business enterprises, and in the administrative apparatus, forms an integral part of the overall education system in most of the East European countries. Unlike the Western European countries and North America, where there is significant involvement by business and industry in vocational and technical training on the job, in many East European countries such training provision also encompasses elementary and secondary general education and political-ideological indoctrination. The close linking of work and education is stressed throughout the region, although the manifestations may vary somewhat from country to country. The countries which have achieved, each for its own reasons and in its own way, the highest degree of integration between work and education are Albania, Romania and Yugoslavia.

The Soviet Union does not have a sub-system of training at the enterprise level. It is assumed there that the well-developed school sub-system, with its courses for shift workers (often held in the factories), evening schools, and correspondence schools offering both general and vocational/technical education, adequately meets training needs and that a separate sub-system is not required.

In Yugoslavia, which is in the process of implementing the concept of social self-management by the workers and employees, the three sub-systems of adult education are beginning to mesh and merge in an increasing provision for close links between work and education, between labour collectives and educational institutions and social services. This development has been accelerated since the 1974 constitutional changes, which provide for a move away from full-time education after initial schooling, and for alternation between work and education.

Czechoslovakia and East Germany have the most developed sub-system of training at the enterprise level, aimed at vocational/technical upgrading, qualification and specialization. In Czechoslovakia this is carried out by a network of factory schools, technical schools and enterprise institutes, while in East Germany it is the task of well staffed and equipped enterprise academies and village academies.

Bulgaria, following previous practice in the Soviet Union, has relied for a long period on training through the brigade method. This method uses a skilled and highly motivated worker, whose skills and behaviour provide a model to emulate, to lead a group of workers in on-the-job training. A more systematic approach to training was not developed in Bulgaria until the early 1970s.

Hungary and Poland started to establish the beginnings of a sub-system of training at enterprise level in the late 1960s. The main task here is not yet comprehensive training but rather specialized training and the adaptation of general vocational education to the specific on-the-job requirements.

Romania has been engaged since the early 1970s in a process of industrialization which has created demands for intensive training. Since 1970 all ministries and other state organs have had direct responsibility for vocational/technical training in their areas. Legislation, directives and Communist Party declarations lay stress on the upgrading of the work force and on continuing professional development. Legislation passed in 1976 decreed the integration of higher education with production in industry and agriculture and with research; this will have far-reaching consequences for all three sectors.

Training of Adult Educators

In East Europe adult educators, active as volunteers, part-time or full-time employees, include many cultural workers and political propagandists. In their age composition adult educators in East Europe also differ markedly from other parts of Europe in that considerable numbers of them are in their twenties.

Adequate training of the many volunteer and professional adult educators is crucial to the effective provision of adult education and its further development in any country. Unlike many Western European countries, the training of adult educators in East Europe is well developed. It is provided at the university level as well as in specialized secondary technical schools. The exceptions are Albania and Bulgaria, where to date no provision for training has been made. Significantly, however, except for the training of party propagandists, there is still no systematic training provision for adult educators in the Soviet Union, where those active in the school sub-system are trained only as teachers of children.

Czechoslovakia is the only country in Europe with a comprehensive system of training of adult educators which provides for pre-service training as well as upgrading and in-service training, and for the training of volunteers. The pre-service training is organized at the university level and in specialized two-year secondary technical schools (these usually also train librarians and cultural-educational workers); it is available on a full-time or part-time basis. The upgrading and in-service training, and the training of volunteers, is conducted mainly by regional cultural houses.

Hungary, Poland and Yugoslavia, although they do not have a system of training at all levels, have well-developed training for adult educators and cultural-educational workers. In Hungary, as in Czechoslovakia, such training is available at university level and in specialized secondary technical schools on a full-time and part-time basis. In Poland several universities also offer training programs in adult education, and the folk high schools train cultural-educational workers for the villages, again on a full-time and part-time basis. The TIT society in Hungary and the TWP society in Poland both conduct courses on adult education techniques for their many volunteer lecturers. Yugoslavia has extensive university provision for adult education training, not only in faculties of education but also in faculties of arts, medical schools, military academies and other higher education institutions. Many of the workers' universities provide courses for volunteers, and the Andragogical Centre in Zagreb annually organizes extensive in-service training in its Summer School for Andragogues.

In Romania teacher training colleges have theory of adult education as a compulsory subject, while it is an elective subject at all technical training schools. Adult education training at the university level is a recent phenomenon; it is developed best at the University of Bucharest.

Even from this brief outline it can be seen that training is accorded an important place in most East European countries. Given the overall stance in these countries towards the need for technical and vocational training and the upgrading of their adult population, it is no surprise that work in the field of adult education is supported by extensive training provision.

Research in Adult Education

If training of adult educators is crucial to the development of adult education provision, broadly based theoretical and empirical research is equally crucial as a basis for both.

The ideological climate in East Europe in the 1950s was not conducive to social research. Such serious writing and publishing as has been done concerning adult education in the period from 1945 up to the late 1950s has been primarily in the areas of theory building, conceptualization, definition and ideological argument. With the consolidation of Communist Party rule in all the East European countries by 1950, all the theory building went along the lines of Marxist social theories.

The planned economy of the socialist East European countries also finds its expression in planned research in all sciences. Czechoslovakia, East Germany, Romania and the Soviet Union have each incorporated specific research tasks in the discipline of adult education into their comprehensive state research plans.

Theoretical and ideological studies in adult education in the USSR date back to the 1920s. This activity was, however, interrupted in 1936 by a Communist Party directive to concentrate exclusively on pedagogical questions. Research, especially empirical and sociological studies, in adult education did not occur in the Soviet Union again until the 1960s. The main research centre in the Soviet Union is the Leningrad-based Research Institute for

Adult Education (significantly this institute was formed overnight, by a decree, from a pedagogical institute) which employs some 160 researchers.

In Hungary and Poland research in adult education is broadly conceived and deals with psychological and didactical questions as well as sociological research. The areas of research stretch from school-type and industry-type provision to broad educational and cultural out-of-school activities. Yugoslavia is the East European leader in research in adult education. Broadly based research there developed during the 1960s and by now there is a considerable store of empirical research accumulated in Yugoslavia. The research findings in adult education in Hungary, Poland and Yugoslavia would be of interest and of benefit to adult educators in West European countries, but unfortunately the language barrier makes these findings inaccessible.

Much of the East European research in adult education is still influenced by the education of children and youth and conducted in a didactical vein. However, more and more researchers are beginning to question this approach and are turning from adult pedagogy (logically a contradiction in terms) to andragogy. This process started in Yugoslavia in the 1960s and has spread to Hungary and Poland to a significant degree, while lately it seems also to be making incursions in Czechoslovakia.

Envoi

The provision of adult education in any society is the product of historical as well as contemporary social forces and political and economic circumstances. It arises in response to social, societal and individual needs. Some of its manifestations are bound by the culture in which they are embedded and as such are difficult, if not impossible, to transplant to other cultures. Others are culture free and can take root elsewhere.

Those responsible for, or working in the field of, adult education in any society need to be aware not only of the wealth and variety of the provision of adult education in their own country, but also to have a broad awareness and overview of such provision in other societies with varying cultural, political and economic systems. In most modern societies adult education plays a role in the solution of educational, social, economic development and public health problems. The approaches employed may be the same or may vary from society to society. By being critically aware of approaches used elsewhere and comparing these with their own, social planners and adult educators can better assess and strengthen their own approaches, introduce appropriate innovations and resist inappropriate transplants.

This brief overview of the provision of adult education in East Europe, its historical roots, development and current situation, is an introduction to a better understanding of the forces which formed the particular types of provision common in that geographical-political region. It can serve as no more than just an opening of the windows. Hopefully the readers' curiosity has been aroused enough to induce them to pursue this further through the readings listed below.

Further Reading

East European Region

Jindra Kulich (ed.), *Training of Adult Educators in Europe* (Monographs on Comparative and Area Studies in Adult Education). Vancouver, Centre for Continuing Education, The University of British Columbia, 1977.
International Labour Office, *Training Systems in Eastern Europe.* Geneva, ILO, 1979.
Jindra Kulich and Wolfgang Krüger (eds.), *The Universities and Adult Education in Europe* (Monographs on Comparative and Area Studies in Adult Education). Vancouver, Centre for Continuing Education, The University of British Columbia, 1980.
Dušan M. Savićević, 'Adult Education Systems in European Socialist Countries: Similarities and Differences'. pp. 37-89 in *Comparing Adult Education Worldwide* (AEA Handbook Series in Adult Education), edited by Alexander N. Charters. San Francisco and London, Jossey-Bass, 1981.
Jindra Kulich, *Adult Education in Continental Europe: An Annotated Bibliography of English-Language Materials 1975-1979* (Monographs on Comparative and Area Studies in Adult Education). Vancouver, Centre for Continuing Education, The University of British Columbia, 1982.

Bulgaria

Kostadine Popov, *Cultural Policy in Bulgaria* (Studies and Documents on Cultural Policies). Paris, Unesco, 1972.
Pavlina Micheva, Georgia Bizhkov and Iordan Petkov, *Adult Education in the People's Republic of Bulgaria* (Adult Education in Europe, Studies and Documents No. 12). Prague, European Centre for Leisure and Education, 1982.

Czechoslovakia

Miroslav Marek, Milan Hromadka and Josef Chroust, *Cultural Policy in Czechoslovakia* (Studies and Documents on Cultural Policies). Paris, Unesco, 1970.
Jarolím Skalka and Emil Livečka, *Adult Education in the Czechoslovak Socialist*

36   Patterns of Adult Education in East Europe

Republic (ČSSR) (Adult Education in Europe, Studies and Documents No. 1.).
Prague, European Centre for Leisure and Education, 1977.
J.J. Andel, 'Leisure Education Czechoslovakia — Official Attitudes and Their
Theoretical Background', *Studies in Adult Education*, vol. 9, no. 1 (April, 1977),
pp. 49-57.

German Democratic Republic

Hans Koch, *Cultural Policy in the German Democratic Republic* (Studies and
Documents on Cultural Policies). Paris, Unesco, 1975.
Georg Schmelzer, Karl-Heinz Fleischhauer and Gerhard Pogoda, *Adult Education
in the German Democratic Republic* (Adult Education in Europe, Studies and
Documents No. 5). Prague, European Centre for Leisure and Education, 1978.

Hungary

Soós Pal, 'Training Adult Educationists in Hungary', *Adult Education*, vol. 39, no 4
(November, 1966), pp. 212-14.
Gyula Csoma, Joszef Fekete and Karoly Hercegi, *Adult Education in Hungary*.
Leiden: Leidsche Onderwijsinstellingen, n.d. (1968?).
Alan Bryan, 'Disadvantage and Participation — Hungarian Style', *Adult Education*,
vol. 48, no. 5 (January, 1976), pp. 330-4.
Györgi Fukász *et al.*, *Adult Education in the Hungarian People's Republic (HPR)*
(Adult Education in Europe, Studies and Documents No. 3). Prague, European
Centre for Leisure and Education, 1978.

Poland

Ryszard Janucik, 'The Television Agricultural Secondary School in Poland', *Adult
Education*, vol. 49, no. 3 (September, 1976), pp. 154-60.
Ryszard Pachocinski and Josef Połturzycki, *Adult Education in the People's Republic
of Poland* (Adult Education in Europe, Studies and Documents No. 6). Prague,
European Centre for Leisure and Education, 1979.

Romania

Ion Dodu Balan, *Cultural Policy in Romania* (Studies and Documents on Cultural
Policies). Paris, Unesco, 1975.
Jindra Kulich, 'Training of Cultural Workers, Political Educators and Adult
Educators in Romania', *Adult Education*, vol. 49, no. 1 (May 1976), pp. 34-7.

USSR

Nigel Grant, *Soviet Education*, Harmondsworth, Penguin Books, 1964.
Seymour M. Rosen, *Part-time Education in the USSR: Evening and
Correspondence Study*. Washington, US Department of Health, Education and
Welfare, Office of Education, 1965.
A.A. Zvorykin, N.I. Golubtsova and E.I. Rabinovich, *Cultural Policy in the Union of
Soviet Socialist Republics* (Studies and Documents on Cultural Policies). Paris,
Unesco. 1970.
Institute of Art Criticism, Ethnography and Folklore of the Academy of Sciences of
the Byelorussian SSR, *Cultural Policy in the Byelorussian Soviet Socialist
Republic* (Studies and Documents on Cultural Policies). Paris, Unesco, 1979.

Yugoslavia

M. David, *Adult Education in Yugoslavia* (Monographs on Education No. 1). Paris, Unesco, 1962.

Dušan M. Savićević, *The System of Adult Education in Yugoslavia* (Notes and Essays on Education for Adults, No. 59). Syracuse, Syracuse University Press, 1969.

Ana Krajnc and Ilja Mrmak, *Adult Education in Yugoslavia* (Adult Education in Europe, Studies and Documents No. 4). Prague, European Centre for Leisure and Education, 1978.

Ešref Delalić, *Workers' Universities in Yugoslavia: An Adult Education Modality* (Monographs on Comparative and Area Studies in Adult Education). Vancouver, Centre for Continuing Education, The University of British Columbia, 1979.

Stevan Majstorović, *Cultural Policy in Yugoslavia: Self-Management and Culture* (Studies and Documents on Cultural Policies). Paris, Unesco, 1980.

ADULT EDUCATION IN THE THIRD WORLD

Lalage Bown

Source: Copyright © The Open University (specially written for this volume).

Introduction: Towards Common Reflection

'We must go with lanterns
ahead of the sun
to beat tracks that lead away
from the dawn of disaster.
It is time
to share the hardships of the season
the pains and labours of the hour
now that the harvests of yesterday
are planting seeds again.'[1]

These lines by a Nigerian poet in his twenties are characteristically West African, but they have a universal message. We all have forebodings about the world's future and would all concede that the way to avert disaster must be by common action — within the nation and between nations. But what about common *reflection*? Those of us concerned with adult learning must, by the nature of our concern, be interested in reflection. But all too often, we still forge our concepts in isolation and then assume either that others share those idiosyncratic concepts or that common action is possible among people starting from a whole variety of different principles.

This paper is written in the belief that it is important to understand (and appraise) non-British concepts of adult learning and education in the interest of possible common action and also since our own concepts may be illuminated and perhaps enriched by those of others. It focuses on the Third World in the further belief that some of the most creative recent work in adult education has developed in some Third World countries.

It is realised that *Third World* is a vague term. It is used here for the developing countries, most of them in Africa, Asia and Latin

America, and most of them politically in the 'non-aligned' group. Their economic circumstances vary from an average GNP of less than $150 a head (e.g. Bangladesh, Ethiopia) to an average GNP of $1,400 (e.g. Brazil, Nigeria).[2] Altogether, these countries embrace some three-quarters of the world's population. Obviously, such a group will not be unanimous, on adult education or anything else, but they do have certain common concerns and interests.

The Broad Canvas
Third World Influences on International Thought About Adult Education

Third World thinking and practice have noticeably affected general international trends in adult education in the last quarter of a century. This may be instanced in the changing character and stances of international meetings to consider the nature, purposes and mission of adult education.

Early international conferences were heavily dominated by Europe. The World Association of Adult Education, bravely formed in 1919, held a 'world conference' in Cambridge in 1929. A remarkable outcome of the creative vision of the Czech statesman Jan Masaryk and the British adult educator Albert Mansbridge, it brought together over 300 people from 33 countries in what was still the steamship age. But there were few people present from outside Europe, North America and the white Commonwealth; and the proceedings concentrated on the problems of widening access to the high culture of Western Europe, largely through voluntary organisations.

Twenty years later, in 1949, Unesco held its first international conference on adult education at Elsinore and once again representation and conceptual assumptions were heavily Western. Only five out of 100 or so delegates came from what we would now think of as the Third World (one each from China, Egypt, India and Thailand and one Latin American). Its broad-based declaration that 'Adult Education has the task of satisfying the needs and aspirations of adults in their diversity' was rather vitiated by a failure to see the political implications, i.e. that *governments* needed to be involved if those were the task's dimensions.

The first signs of appreciation that there were other ways of perceiving adult education appeared at the second Unesco-sponsored international conference on the theme, held in Montreal in 1960. Among the 51 countries represented were eight from Africa, eight from Latin America and ten from Asia (and incidentally the USSR and six Soviet bloc states were also there for the first time since the emergence of the bloc after the Second World War). The conference met at a time when many ex-colonial countries were regaining political independence, when African and Asian countries in particular were trying out programmes of community development which depended on a wide range of adult learning activities from literacy to home improvement, and when Cuba was just launched on its crash campaign to eliminate illiteracy. Dialogue on such matters led inevitably to a broadening of view as to what adult education consisted of, and also to the conclusion that *governments* had to be involved in its facilitation, and that they 'should treat it as a necessary part of the educational provision of every country'.[3] Governments were also urged 'to treat Adult Education as a part of economic and multi-purpose development'.[4]

Concern with adult education as a part of public policy was manifested by the character of the delegations to the next Unesco world conference on adult education, held at Tokyo in 1972. National representation tended to be no longer by a few professionals in the field, but also by ministers and others in political or economic planning roles. Moreover the majority of the 84 countries officially attending were now from the Third World. Among the Tokyo terms of reference was: 'To consider the functions of adult education in the context of lifelong education'[5] — an indication that there had been a general shift away from the view of education as a preparation for life, with its implication that adult education was mainly a remedial exercise for those who had not received an adequate preparation. At the same time, one major theme which emerged at the 1972 conference was concern for the educationally underprivileged — termed in the Final Report 'the forgotten people'. The prescriptions laid down included:

> No groups or individuals in society should be denied access to education. Participation should be as broadly based as possible. This requires that the barriers to access should be removed and that the motivation for adults to learn be specially studied. It should be particularly noted that many adults lack the time and resources to participate in education. Paid study leave, day release and security of employment during study leave should therefore be guaranteed through appropriate legislation.

Unemployed workers should have the right to occupational training and to be paid during training. Workers' education and trade union and cooperative education should be promoted. The main thrust of adult education in the 1970s ... should be to meet the educational needs of groups traditionally underprivileged in many societies. Among these can particularly be mentioned unemployed youth, premature school leavers in developing countries, the rural population of many countries, migrant workers, the aged and the unemployed. Within these groups girls and women are often particularly disadvantaged.[6]

Such a set of recommendations bound together the interests of both 'developed' and 'developing' countries.

A result of all this international activity was the *Recommendation on the Development of Adult Education* adopted by the Unesco General Assembly of 1976, held in Nairobi (the first time it had met outside Europe). It includes a definition:

the term 'adult education' denotes the entire body of organized educational processes, whatever the content, level and method, whether formal or otherwise, whether they prolong or replace initial education in schools, colleges and universities as well as in apprenticeship, whereby persons regarded as adult by the society to which they belong develop their abilities, enrich their knowledge, improve their technical or professional qualifications and bring about changes in their attitudes or behaviour in the twofold perspective of full personal development and participation in balanced and independent social, economic and cultural development; adult education, however, must not be considered as an entity in itself; it is a sub-division, and an integral part of a global scheme for lifelong education and learning.[7]

Elements in Third World Influence

In sum, one can perceive new strands in international thought which (1) place adult education in the context of lifelong learning; (2) define it very broadly; (3) relate it to public policy, in particular to development policy; and (4) display a concern for positive action in favour of the educationally underprivileged. All these themes have emerged as a result of the appearance of Third World countries at the conference table. A similar process can be seen to have taken place in the smaller international forum of the Commonwealth.[8] The process of redefinition of adult education and of its linkages and objectives is significant in itself, but it has resulted in some forms of international action which would otherwise certainly never have been taken up. One example was the Experimental World Literacy Programme, launched in 1965, which over a ten year period tested methods of functional literacy based on a selective approach, in a dozen countries, building up necessary infrastructures and training large numbers of adult educators.[9]

In a short paper, it is only practicable to concentrate on the wider international canvas. It must also be mentioned, however, that specific countries have produced interesting innovations which have also claimed outside attention. One is India, which embarked on a massive National Adult Education Programme aimed at 100 million people between the ages of 14 and 35, and which allocates 10 per cent of its education budget to adult education (this may seem small, but it is a larger allocation than is made by any other country outside Scandinavia).[10] Another is Tanzania, which has linked adult education closely to an attempted restructuring of its economy.

Moreover, there are individual Third World publications which have been widely read and have also affected perceptions of the nature of adult education. Perhaps the best-known writer is Paulo Freire. His distinction between education for domestication and education for liberation and his insistence on 'the transformation of the learner from a passive being to an active, critical, creative one' have provided goals for adult educators in Britain as well as in many other countries. Another widely-noted Third World writer is Julius K. Nyerere, the President of Tanzania. In a famous statement, he relates education to development and also warns against false types of education:

> Man makes himself. It is his ability to act deliberately, for a self-determined purpose, which distinguishes him from the other animals. The expansion of his own consciousness, and therefore of his power over himself, his environment, and his society, must therefore ultimately be what we mean by development.
>
> So development is for Man, by Man and of Man. The same is true of education. Its purpose is the liberation of Man from the restraints and limitations of ignorance and dependency. Education has to increase men's physical and mental freedom — to increase their control over themselves, their own lives, and the

environment in which they live. The ideas imparted by education, or released in the mind through education, should therefore be liberating ideas, the skills acquired by education should be liberating skills. Nothing else can properly be called education. Teaching which induces a slave mentality or a sense of impotence is not education at all — it is an attack on the minds of men.[11]

Perhaps it should be said that the word 'liberating' is not rhetorical in the mouth of a nationalist leader who brought his country to independence.

Some Highlights
The Third World Context

Having indicated in broad terms how ideas on the nature of adult education have been affected by the involvement of the Third World in international fora, by the spread of knowledge of Third World innovations and by the writings of Third World thinkers, let us now pick up some specific issues in adult education which have been highlighted by Third World experience. In order to make sense of that experience and judge its degree of relevance to Britain, it is necessary to provide a brief context. That context determines the preoccupations of Third World educators and policy-makers.

First, there is the fact of poverty, leading to a concern for basic human needs. It was rapidly seen that if such needs were to go beyond the animal, and their satisfaction to go beyond the paternalistic, development policies had to emphasise participation, to stress citizens being subjects not objects of change and thus to provide for popular mobilisation — only possible if all kinds of learning take place.

Secondly, as words like citizen and mobilisation remind us, development has a political dimension, and many Third World countries are grappling with political change, often having returned to political independence in the past few decades. A classic exhortation on the importance of adult learning for political change was made by the late Chairman Mao:

No political party can possibly lead a great revolutionary movement to victory unless it possesses revolutionary theory and a knowledge of history and has a profound practical grasp of the movement ... Complacency is the enemy of study ... Our attitude towards ourselves should be 'to be insatiable in learning' and towards others 'to be tireless in teaching'.[12]

Thirdly, many of the countries do not have universal compulsory schooling of the Western type (most would undoubtedly wish to, but do not have sufficient resources). Past traditions of education remain quite strong, and are mostly less formal and not solely attached to childhood; 'seekers after knowledge' in Islamic countries, for instance, may be of any age.[13] This is one factor in an interest in lifelong education. Limited access to compulsory schooling results in large-scale illiteracy in the adult population and to a general interest in the nature and consequences of literacy. It also leads to mass campaigns to make adults literate. Some are of the short sharp mobilisation type. For instance in Cuba, all schools were closed for a year and all pupils sent out to teach their elders to read and write; the army was also brought in to assist. As a result, from an estimated literacy rate of less than 50 per cent, illiteracy was virtually wiped out and current World Bank figures show Cuba with 96 per cent literacy. Other countries which have made similar efforts include the Republic of Somalia, which also closed schools, for *two years* (1973-5), and Nicaragua, which had a five-month Literacy Crusade in 1980, during which basic illiteracy was reduced from 50 per cent to less than 13 per cent, through the action of some 85,000 volunteers. More measured campaigns include the Nigerian one; with a population very much larger than Cuba, Somalia or Nicaragua, it embarked in 1982 on a ten-year pro-gramme to abolish illiteracy.

A further consequence of limited access to schooling has been a resort to the mass media, as a way of reaching the non-literate. The most famous examples include the use of the radio in Tanzania in a series of public education campaigns on specific issues and India's rural television education by satellite.[14] Again, in such circum-stances, education is easily viewed as lifelong.

In consequence, Third World concepts of adult education tend to be broader than those of Europe and less concerned with doc-trinal differences between what is vocational and non-vocational; they tend to be more closely defined by objective (economic and social development, satisfaction of basic needs); they are often preoccupied with literacy; and they have encouraged experi-mentation, particularly in the use of the media.

Key Issues in Third World Adult Education

Underlying adult education policies and objectives are assumptions about human beings and human behaviour. Freire and other Third World thinkers insist that the individual human being is the author of his or her own and society's development, and have emphasised adult education as a mode of liberation. (In some ways this is reminiscent of the original interests of European liberalism before it became bound up with the concept of bourgeois high culture.) Also underlying, though, are views of society and social and economic development. President Nyerere and others have re-emphasised the relation of adult education to change and have pointed out that adult education is not only a preparation for but also a process of development.

Because of urgent development needs, made glaring by contrast with industrialised countries and in particular by the very limited access of the Third World to all kinds of technology (which gives the great powers, especially the USA and the USSR, a position of dominance), Third World countries also have a sense of urgency about various types of adult education, and it is a common theme among their policy-makers that the quickest road to economic and technological change is to educate adults already at work. Resources are readily allocated to the provision of training institutions and to all kinds of in-service and study-leave facilities.

Interest in a nation-building and development role for adult education has led to some interest in the Third World in lifelong education structures. This is partly to do with the provision of basic support services for adult learning (e.g. the provision of reading rooms, as in Zimbabwe, and the removal of tax on radio and television sets, as in Tunisia), but it is also to do with the conceptual relationship of adult education with other cognate activities, such as community development, agricultural extension and library work. Where is the dividing line between community work, community development and adult education, for instance?

Besides structures, there has been an interest in adult educational processes and delivery systems. There seems to be difficulty in applying Freirean methods on a large scale. After the Portuguese revolution and the full independence of Guinea-Bissau, an effort was made along these lines and Freire himself assisted in training the literacy workers,[15] but what evidence has emerged indicates little success. Are there alternative ways of reaching large masses of people? We have already raised the issue of political mobilisation and of the use of mass media for educational purposes. It has become of concern to distinguish between education and propaganda, and also to become aware of sophisticated techniques of 'disinformation', which may be used by some Third World governments on their own populations or by outside governments aiming at another country's population.

These are key issues in Third World adult education. One other key concept should be mentioned here. The existence in parallel of 'traditional' pre-colonial learning systems and formal Western-type schooling has often meant that the content of one is learnt by means of the other. Traditional apprenticeship systems have, for instance, been adapted to train bicycle repairers or motor mechanics, while the indigenous organisations through which traditional birth attendants acquired their lore and skills may now convey the messages of modern midwifery. This has resulted in the development of the concept of *non-formal education*. To quote Paul Fordham:[16]

> The non-formal idea is ... part of a widespread search for alternatives in education which is itself intimately bound up with changing conceptions of development. The term 'non-formal' was given currency by development planners rather than educators. Existing terminology was seen as too narrow — while many of the more important programmes (e.g. farmer training) were sometimes not seen as education at all, even by practitioners themselves. What was needed was an all-embracing term for ... 'educative services'. As it gained currency, the term also came to include provision for the school-age dropouts and left-outs of the formal system.

It is to be noted that non-formal education is thus not confined to adults.

Questions for the United Kingdom

Our starting-point was the premise that Third World ideas and practice might help to illuminate our own studies of the nature of Adult Education. Several questions of relevance to our own situation may be raised.

First, do we take sufficient account of the re-emphasis on lifelong learning and 'the entire educational potential outside the educational system'? That is, do we have a clear idea of adult education's relation to the school system and have we in this country really taken on board the concept of *recurrent education* — of persons moving in and out of education at intervals throughout their lives?

Secondly, do we need, against the backcloth of lifelong learning, to re-examine the concept of adulthood? In the Third World, this has been made necessary because many young persons are faced with full social and economic responsibilities regardless of their physiological or legal status. Would it be useful to us to be less legalistic in our own approach to definition?

Thirdly, our approach to all forms of education tends to be institutional. Even in adult education, we talk of *students*, of *provision*, of *teaching*. Third World usage has a vocabulary of *learners*, *participation* and *learning*. Should we not follow this example?

Fourthly, and following from this, would it not be helpful to us to follow Third World interest in participatory processes of adult learning? Some thinkers and adult educationists in Britain have long worked along these lines, but the current vogue for training and instruction may push them to one side.

Fifthly, we have discovered a literacy problem in our midst, partly owing to the 'unfinished business of the schools' and partly owing to immigration. Would it help us to look at reinterpretations of literacy developed in the Third World? Such reinterpretations relate to its impact on individuals and its connection with political power. They also remind us of alternatives to literacy, and of the educational service role of the broadcast media.

I believe that these are all important questions. They are particularly important to us in the 1980s because our own circumstances are becoming closer to those prevailing in developing countries. We, like them, face the problems of poverty and great unevenness in access to formal education. We still have unemployment levels much lower than theirs, but they are still dislocatory and destructive of human dignity. Thus we too are forced to consider adult education in relation to economic and social development.

Conclusion: Ahead of the Owls

Since some of our human and social problems are not dissimilar,

there would seem to be real value in the broad vision and innova-
tory approaches which we can gain from the Third World.

Above all, perhaps we ought to take account of the common
Third World emphasis on having a *rationale* for what we do in adult
education. We study the nature of the activity because pragmatism
has proved insufficient. As Freire says: 'The action of persons
without objectives ... is not praxis'.[17] We may then be equipped to
follow our Nigerian poet:

'We must go with lanterns
ahead of the owls
sowing dreams to spurn
the fears that check
our struggle
for a better day.'

Notes

1. Odia Ofeimun, 'We Must Go with Lanterns'.
2. IBRD/World Bank, *World Development Report 1982* (Oxford University Press, New York, 1982). See section on 'World Development Indicators'.
3. From *The Montreal Declaration*, 1960.
4. From the resolution on Adult Education passed at the Montreal Conference.
5. Unesco, *Third International Conference on Adult Education Final Report* (Unesco, Paris, 1972).
6. *Ibid.*
7. For a fuller description of the development of international ideas see John Lowe, *The Education of Adults: A World Perspective* (Unesco/OISE Press, Paris and Toronto, 1982), 2nd edn.
8. See especially Paul Fordham, *Participation, Learning and Change — Commonwealth Approaches to Non-Formal Education* (Commonwealth Secretariat, London, 1980).
9. Unesco/UNDP, *The Experimental World Literacy Programme: A Critical Assessment* (Unesco, Paris, 1976).
10. India, Ministry of Education and Social Welfare, *National Adult Education Programme: An Outline* (MESW, New Delhi, 1978).
11. J.K. Nyerere, 'Declaration of Dar es Salaam: Liberated Man, the Purpose of Development' in *Convergence*, 9, 4 (1976), 9-10.
12. Mao Tse-Tung, 'The Role of the Chinese Communist Party in the National War' in *Quotations from Chairman Mao Tse-Tung* (Foreign Languages Press, Peking, 1967).
13. There are generalisations on this theme in Faure *et al.*, *Learning to Be* (Unesco, Paris, 1972). More particular evidence is to be found in, for example, Godfrey Brown and Mervyn Hiskett, *Conflict and Harmony in Education in Tropical Africa* (Allen and Unwin, London, 1975).
14. See, for example, Madu G. Mailafiya, 'The Mass Media, Distance Teaching and the Individual Learner' in Lalage Bown and S.H. Olu Tomori, *A Handbook of*

Adult Education for West Africa (Hutchinson, London, 1979), pp. 143-58.

15. See Paulo Freire, *Pedagogy in Process: the Letters to Guinea-Bissau* (Writers' and Readers' Publishing Cooperative, London, 1978).

16. Fordham, *Participation, Learning and Change.*

17. Paulo Freire, *Cultural Action for Freedom* (Penguin, Harmondsworth, 1974).

Part 2

PROCESSES

The inclusion of three chapters by North Americans (Knowles, Kidd and Mezirow) in this part of the Reader is indicative of the more developed nature of the study of education for adults in North America, when compared with the United Kingdom and other parts of the English-speaking world.

The first two chapters deal with the general processes involved in the education of adults. Malcolm Knowles advocates the use of the term 'andragogy', as distinct from pedagogy, to denote the art and science of helping adults learn (interestingly, as Kulich points out in this Reader, Yugoslavia is the main centre for the study of andragogy). He stresses the distinctions to be drawn between education for adults and for children, and points to a series of implications for the conduct of adult learning. The chapter by Roby Kidd provides an examination of the stages and processes of adult learning — the assessment of the needs of the learner, the development of a curriculum to meet those needs, its implementation, evaluation, and the effects of the evaluation on further learning.

The next two chapters serve to focus the discussion whilst keeping the coverage of different kinds of educational provision for adults broad. Thus, on the one hand, Kenneth Lawson's short chapter seeks to resolve any possible confusion between education, which is intentional and involves both learner and teacher (even though the 'teacher' may take the form of self-instructional material), and learning, which may be both unintentional and trivial. The chapter by Mike Smith, on the other hand, serves to remind us that educational institutions are not the only institutions dealing in education for adults. The stages which Smith identifies in the typical industrial training programme are, however, directly analogous to those noted for a generalised learning transaction by

Kidd — the identification of objectives and requirements, the identification of training tasks, task analysis, preparing instructional schedules, conducting training, evaluation.

The final two chapters in this part of the Reader are rather more theoretical and speculative. Paula Allman seeks to provide a firm psychological basis for the separate study of education for adults. She indicates some of the strengths and limitations of competing psychological theories in this field, and looks towards the development of a theory of andragogy which will take into account the potential for learning and growth which has been shown to exist throughout the adult years. Jack Mezirow's concern is also with those aspects of learning which are peculiarly adult. He examines, in particular, the concept of perspective transformation, an emancipatory process involving fundamental change and growth in the adult's self-understanding, and the adult's capacity for critical reflection, and looks at the implications of these for the practice and theory of adult education. Finally, he puts forward a charter for andragogy, which he defines as 'an organised and sustained effort to assist adults to learn in a way that enhances their capability to function as self-directed learners'.

ANDRAGOGY: AN EMERGING TECHNOLOGY FOR ADULT LEARNING

Malcolm Knowles

Source: Reprinted from *The Modern Practice of Adult Education: From Pedagogy to Andragogy*, copyright 1970 by Malcolm S. Knowles. Reprinted with the permission of the publisher, Cambridge Book Company.

Farewell to Pedagogy

Most of what is known about learning has been derived from studies of learning in children and animals. Most of what is known about teaching has been derived from experience with teaching children under conditions of compulsory attendance. And most theories about the learning-teaching transaction are based on the definition of education as a process of transmitting the culture. From these theories and assumptions there has emerged the technology of 'pedagogy' — a term derived from the Greek stem *paid-* (meaning 'child') and *agogos* (meaning 'leading'). So 'pedagogy' means, specifically, the art and science of teaching children.

One problem is that somewhere in history the 'children' part of the definition got lost. In many people's minds — and even in the dictionary — 'pedagogy' is defined as the art and science of teaching. Even in books on adult education you can find references to 'the pedagogy of adult education', without any apparent discomfort over the contradiction in terms. Indeed, in my estimation, the main reason why adult education has not achieved the impact on our civilization of which it is capable is that most teachers of adults have only known how to teach adults as if they were children.

Another problem with pedagogy is that it is premised on an archaic conception of the purpose of education, namely, the transmittal of knowledge. As Alfred North Whitehead pointed out a generation ago, it was functional to define education as a process of transmittal of what is known so long as it was true that the time-span of major cultural change was greater than the life-span of individuals. Under this condition, what a person learns in his youth will remain valid for the rest of his life. But, Whitehead emphasized,

53

'We are living in the first period of human history for which this assumption is false ... today this time-span is considerably shorter than that of human life, and accordingly our training must prepare individuals to face a novelty of conditions.'[1]

Up to the early part of the twentieth century the time-span of major cultural change (e.g., massive inputs of new knowledge, technological innovation, vocational displacement, population mobility, change in political and economic systems etc.) required several generations, whereas in the twentieth century several cultural revolutions have already occurred and the pace is accelerating. Under this new condition, knowledge gained by the time a person is 21 is largely obsolete by the time he is 40; and skills that made him productive in his twenties are becoming out of date during his thirties. So it is no longer functional to define education as a process of transmitting what is known; it must now be defined as a lifelong process of discovering what is not known.

Skillful adult educators have known for a long time that they cannot teach adults as children have traditionally been taught. For adults are almost always voluntary learners, and they simply disappear from learning experiences that don't satisfy them. So the practice of adult education has in fact been departing from traditional pedagogical practices for some time. And often this deviation has been accompanied by misgivings and guilt feelings over the violation of long-established standards, for adult educators have not had a coherent theory to justify their treating adults as adults.

Figure 1: The Relationship of the Time-span of Social Change to Individual Life-span

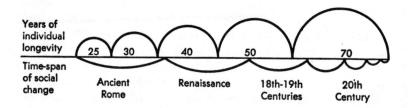

This lack is now on the way to being remedied. For adult-education theorists in both Europe (especially in Germany and Yugoslavia[2]) and in North America are rapidly developing a distinctive theory of adult learning. And from this theory is evolving a new

technology for the education of adults. To distinguish it from pedagogy, this new technology is being given a new name: '*andragogy*', which is based on the Greek word *anēr* (with the stem *andr-*), meaning 'man'. Andragogy is, therefore, the art and science of helping adults learn. [...]

Some Assumptions of Andragogy and their Technological Implications

Andragogy is premised on at least four crucial assumptions about the characteristics of adult learners that are different from the assumptions about child learners on which traditional pedagogy is premised. These assumptions are that, as a person matures, (1) his self-concept moves from one of being a dependent personality toward one of being a self-directing human being; (2) he accumulates a growing reservoir of experience that becomes an increasing resource for learning; (3) his readiness to learn becomes oriented increasingly to the developmental tasks of his social roles; and (4) his time perspective changes from one of postponed application of knowledge to immediacy of application, and accordingly his orientation toward learning shifts from one of subject-centeredness to one of problem-centeredness.

Each of these assumptions will be described briefly and some of its implications for the education of adults will be explored.

Self-concept

Children enter this world in a condition of complete dependency. Their every need, except for purely biological functions, must be taken care of by someone else. The first image a child gets of himself as a separate entity is that of a dependent personality whose life is managed for him by the adult world.

This self-concept of dependency is encouraged and reinforced by the adult world. In fact, society defines the normal role of a child as that of learner; this is his full-time occupation, the source of his rewards and self-fulfillment. And on the whole, this role is defined as the more or less passive one of receiving and storing up the information adults have decided children should have.

As the child's self-identity begins to take shape, he begins to see himself as having the capacity to start making decisions for himself, at first experimentally and in small matters that don't impinge on the adult world. But increasingly, as he matures, the child's self-concept moves in the direction of greater self-direction, and during adolescence his need to take significant responsibility for managing his own life becomes so strong that it often puts him in open rebellion against control by the adult world. [...]

But something dramatic happens to his self-concept when an individual defines himself as an adult. He begins to see his normal role in society no longer as being a full-time learner. He sees himself increasingly as a producer or doer. His chief sources of self-fulfillment are now his performance as a worker, a spouse, a parent, a citizen. The adult acquires a new status, in his own eyes and in the eyes of others, from these non-educational responsibilities. His self-concept becomes that of a self-directing personality. He sees himself as being able to make his own decisions and face their consequences, to manage his own life. In fact, the point at which a person becomes an adult, psychologically, is that point at which he perceives himself to be wholly self-directing. And at that point he also experiences a deep need to be perceived by others as being self-directing.

For this reason, adults have a need to be treated with respect, to make their own decisions, to be seen as unique human beings. They tend to avoid, resist, and resent situations in which they feel they are treated like children — being told what to do and what not to do, being talked down to, embarrassed, punished, judged. Adults tend to resist learning under conditions that are incongruent with their self-concept as autonomous individuals.

Often there is another ingredient in the self-concept of an adult that affects his role as a learner. He may carry over from his previous experience with schooling the perception that he isn't very smart, at least in regard to academic work. This fact about the adult psyche has several consequences for adult education. In the case of some adults the remembrance of the classroom as a place where one is treated with disrespect is so strong that it serves as a serious barrier to their becoming involved in adult education activities at all. If these adults are to be enticed back to systematic learning, the rewards of learning must be made so great that they outweigh the anticipated pain of learning. But even adults who overcome this barrier typically enter an educational activity expecting to be treated like children, and this expectation is frequently so strong that adult students often put pressure on their teachers to behave toward them in this way. Once a teacher puts adult students into a dependent role, however, he is likely to experience a rising resistance and resentment.

On the other hand, when adult students are first exposed to a learning environment in which they are treated with respect, are involved in mutual inquiry with the teacher, and are given responsibility for their own learning, the initial reaction is usually one of shock and disorganization. Adults typically are not prepared for self-directed learning; they need to go through a process of reorientation to learning as adults — to learn new ways of learning. Once an adult makes the discovery that he can take responsibility for his learning, as he does for other facets of his life, he experiences a sense of release and exhilaration. He then enters into learning with deep ego-involvement, with results that are frequently startling both to himself and to his teachers. Teachers who have helped their adult students to achieve this breakthrough report repeatedly that it is one of the most rewarding experiences of their lives.

Technological Implications

Several implications for the technology of andragogy flow from this difference in assumptions about the self-concept of the child and the adult.

1. The Learning Climate. Certainly it has a strong implication regarding the nature of the environment in which adults learn. It suggests that the physical environment should be one in which adults feel at ease. Furnishings and equipment should be adult-sized and comfortable; meeting rooms should be arranged informally and should be decorated according to adult tastes; and acoustics and lighting should take into account declining audio-visual acuity.

Even more importantly, the psychological climate should be one which causes adults to feel accepted, respected, and supported; in which there exists a spirit of mutuality between teachers and students as joint inquirers; in which there is freedom of expression without fear of punishment or ridicule. A person tends to feel more 'adult' in an atmosphere that is friendly and informal, in which he is known by name and valued as a unique individual, than in the traditional school atmosphere of formality, semi-anonymity, and status differentiation between teacher and student. [...]

The behaviour of the teacher probably influences the character of the learning climate more than any other single factor. The teacher conveys in many ways whether his attitude is one of interest in and respect for the students or whether he sees them essentially as receiving sets for his transmissions of wisdom. The teacher who takes the time and trouble to get to know his students individually and who calls them by name (especially by first name) obviously conveys the first set of attitudes. But probably the behaviour that most explicitly demonstrates that a teacher really cares about a student and respects his contribution is the act of really listening to what the student says. [...]

2. Diagnosis of Needs. The adult's self-concept of self-directivity is in direct conflict with the traditional practice of the teacher telling the student what he needs to learn. Indeed, it is even in conflict with the social philosophy that society has a right to impose its ideas about what he needs to learn on him. Of course, an adult will learn what others want him to learn if their power to punish him for not learning is strong enough. But he is more deeply motivated to learn those things he sees the need to learn.

In andragogy, therefore, great emphasis is placed on the involvement of adult learners in a process of *self-diagnosis* of needs for learning. This process consists of three phases: (1) Constructing a model of the competencies or characteristics required to achieve a given model of performance; it is in this model-building phase that the values and expectations of the teacher, the institution, and society are amalgamated with those of the learner into a composite picture. (2) Providing diagnostic experiences in which the learner can assess his present level of competencies in the light of those portrayed in the model. (3) Helping the learner to measure the gaps between his present competencies and those required by the model, so that he experiences a feeling of dissatisfaction about the distance between where he is and where he would like to be and is able to identify specific directions of desirable growth. This experiencing of self-induced dissatisfaction with present inadequacies, coupled with a clear sense of direction for self-improvement, is in fact a good definition of 'motivation to learn'.

3. The Planning Process. Every individual tends to feel committed to a decision (or an activity) to the extent that he has participated in making it (or planning it). Teachers of adults who do all the planning for their students, who come into the classroom and impose preplanned activities on them, typically experience apathy, resentment, and probably withdrawal. For this imposition of the will of the teacher is incongruent with the adult's self-concept of self-directivity.

Accordingly, a basic element in the technology of andragogy is the involvement of the learners in the process of planning their own learning, with the teacher serving as a procedural guide and content resource. When the number of students is small enough, they can all be involved in the planning directly; when the number gets much over 30, adult educators make use of representative councils, committees, task forces, teams, or other devices through which the learners feel that they are participating in the planning by proxy.

The function of planning consists of translating diagnosed needs into specific educational objectives (or directions of growth), designing and conducting learning experiences to achieve these objectives, and evaluating the extent to which these objectives have been accomplished. In andragogy, responsibility for performing this function is a mutual one between the learners and the teacher.

4. Conducting Learning Experiences. In traditional pedagogical practice the function of the teacher is defined as 'to teach'. The teacher is expected to take full responsibility for what happens in the teaching-learning transaction. The learner's role tends to be that of a fairly passive recipient of the teacher's instruction.

In contrast, andragogical practice treats the learning-teaching transaction as the mutual responsibility of learners and teacher. In fact, the teacher's role is redefined as that of a procedural technician, resource person, and co-inquirer; he is more a catalyst than an instructor, more a guide than a wizard. Andragogy assumes that a teacher can't really 'teach' in the sense of 'make a person learn', but that one person can only help another person learn. [...] An andragogical learning situation, whether it be a course, an institute, a training program, or a conference, is alive with meetings of small groups — planning committees, learning-teaching teams, consultation groups, project task forces — sharing responsibility for helping one another learn.

5. Evaluation of Learning. Probably the crowning instance of incongruity between traditional educational practice and the adult's self-concept of self-directivity is the act of a teacher giving a grade to a student. Nothing makes an adult feel more childlike than being judged by another adult; it is the ultimate sign of disrespect and dependency, as the one who is being judged experiences it.

For this reason, andragogical theory prescribes a process of self-evaluation, in which the teacher devotes his energy to helping the adults get evidence for themselves about the progress they are making toward their educational goals. In this process, the strengths and weaknesses of the educational program itself must be assessed in terms of how it has facilitated or inhibited the learning of the students. So evaluation is a mutual undertaking, as are all other phases of the adult learning experience.

In fact, what is happening in practice is that precisely the same procedures that are used for the diagnosis of learning needs are being employed to help the learner measure his gains in competence. For instance, by comparing his performance in solving a critical incident at the end of a learning experience with his performance in a similar critical incident at the beginning of the experience, a learner can quite precisely measure the changes produced by the experience. Because of the similarity of these two processes, I find myself now thinking less and less in terms of the evaluation of learning and more and more in terms of the *rediagnosis* of learning needs. And I find that, when my adult students perceive what they do at the end of a learning experience as rediagnosing rather than evaluating, they enter into the activity with more enthusiasm and see it as being more constructive. Indeed, many of them report that it launches them into a new cycle of learning, reinforcing the notion that learning is a continuing process.

This shift from evaluation to self-evaluation or rediagnosis places a heavy burden on the teacher of adults. He must set the example of himself being open to feedback regarding his performance. He must be skillful in establishing a supportive climate, in which hard-to-accept information about one's performance can be looked at objectively. And he must be creative about inventing ways in which students can get comprehensive data about their performance. [...]

Experience

Every adult enters into any undertaking with a different background of experience from that of his youth. Having lived longer, he has accumulated a greater *volume* of experience, but he also has had different *kinds* of experience.

There is, it seems to me, another rather subtle difference between children and adults as regards their experience. To a child, an experience is something that happens to him; it is an external event that affects him, not an integral part of him. If you ask a child who he is, he is likely to identify himself in terms of who his parents are, who his older brothers or sisters are, what street he lives on, and what school he attends. His self-identity is largely derived from external sources.

But to an adult, his experience *is* him. He defines who he is, establishes his self-identity, in terms of his accumulation of a unique set of experiences. So if you ask an adult who he is, he is likely to identify himself in terms of what his occupation is, where he has worked, where he has traveled, what his training and experience have equipped him to do, and what his achievements have been. An adult *is* what he has *done.*

Because an adult defines himself largely by his experience, he has a deep investment in its value. And so when he finds himself in a situation in which his experience is not being used, or its worth is minimized, it is not just his experience that is being rejected — he feels rejected as a person.

These differences in experience between children and adults have at least three consequences for learning: (1) Adults have more to contribute to the learning of others; for most kinds of learning, they are themselves a rich resource for learning. (2) Adults have a richer foundation of experience to which to relate new experiences (and new learnings tend to take on meaning as we are able to relate them to our past experience). (3) Adults have acquired a larger number of fixed habits and patterns of thought, and therefore tend to be less open minded.

Technological Implications

Several implications for the technology of andragogy flow from these differences in experience:

1. Emphasis on Experiential Techniques. Because adults are themselves richer resources for learning than children, greater emphasis can be placed on techniques that tap the experience of the adult learners, such as group discussion, the case method, the critical-incident process, simulation exercises, role playing, skill-practice exercises, field projects, action projects, laboratory methods, consultative supervision, demonstration, seminars, work conferences, counseling, group therapy, and community development. There is a distinct shift in emphasis in andragogy away from the transmittal techniques so prevalent in youth education — the

lecture, assigned readings, and canned audio-visual presentation —
toward the more participatory experiential techniques. Indeed,
'participation' and 'ego-involvement' are boldfaced words in the
lexicon of the adult educator, with the assumption often being made
that the more active the learner's role in the process, the more he is
probably learning.

2. Emphasis on Practical Application. Skillful adult educators have
always taken care to see that new concepts or broad generalizations
were illustrated by life experiences drawn from the learners. But
numerous recent studies on the transfer of learning and the
maintenance of behavioral change indicate the desirability of going
even farther, and actually building into the design of learning
experiences provision for the learners to plan — and even rehearse
— how they are going to apply their learnings in their day-to-day
lives.

3. Unfreezing and Learning to Learn from Experience. A growing
andragogical practice is to build into the early phases of a course,
workshop, conference, institute, or other sequential educational
activity an 'unfreezing' experience, in which the adults are helped to
look at themselves more objectively and free their minds from pre-
conceptions. Many diagnostic exercises help to serve this purpose,
but the most effective technique of all is probably a sensitivity-
training 'microlab', in which participants experience a short,
intensive period of feedback on their behavior. For one of the
almost universal initial needs of adults is to learn how to take
responsibility for their own learning through self-directed inquiry,
how to learn collaboratively with the help of colleagues rather than
to compete with them, and especially how to learn by analyzing
one's own experience.

Readiness to Learn

It is well accepted in our culture now that children learn best those
things that are necessary for them to know in order to advance from
one phase of development to the next. These have been dubbed
'developmental tasks' by developmental psychologists:

> A developmental task is a task which arises at or about a certain
> period in the life of the individual, successful achievement of
> which leads to his happiness and to success with later tasks, while

failure leads to unhappiness in the individual, disapproval by the society, and difficulty with later tasks.[3]

Each of these developmental tasks produces a 'readiness to learn' which at its peak presents a 'teachable moment'. For example, parents now generally accept the fact that they can't teach a child to walk until he has mastered the art of crawling, his leg muscles are strong enough, and he has become frustrated at not being able to stand up and walk the way everybody else does. At that point, and only then, is he able to learn to walk, for it has become *his* developmental task.

Recent research suggests that the same phenomenon is at work during the adult years. Adults, too, have their phases of growth and resulting developmental tasks, readinesses to learn, and teachable moments. But whereas the developmental tasks of youth tend to be the products primarily of physiological and mental maturation, those of the adult years are the products primarily of the evolution of social roles. Robert J. Havighurst, one of the pioneers in this area of research, divides the adult years into three phases — 'early adulthood', 'middle age', and 'later maturity' — and identifies ten social roles of adulthood: worker, mate, parent, homemaker, son or daughter of aging parents, citizen, friend, organization member, religious affiliate, and user of leisure time. The requirements for performing each of these social roles change, according to Havighurst, as we move through the three phases of adult life, thereby setting up changing developmental tasks and, therefore, changing readiness to learn.

For example, in a person's role of worker, his first developmental task is to get a job. At that point he is ready to learn anything required to get a job, but he definitely isn't ready to study supervision. Having landed a job, he is faced with the task of mastering it so that he won't get fired from it; and at that point he is ready to learn the special skills it requires, the standards that are expected of him, and how to get along with his fellow workers. Having become secure in his basic job, his task becomes one of working up the occupational ladder. Now he becomes ready to learn to become a supervisor or executive. Finally, after reaching his ceiling, he faces the task of dissolving his role of worker — and is ready to learn about retirement or substitutes for work. [...]

Technological Implications

At least two sets of implications for the technology of andragogy flow from these differences in readiness to learn:

1. The Timing of Learnings. If the teachable moment for a particular adult to acquire a given learning is to be captured, it is obvious that the sequence of the curriculum must be timed so as to be in step with his developmental tasks. This is the appropriate organizing principle for an adult education program, rather than the logic of the subject matter or the needs of the sponsoring institution. For instance, an orientation program for new workers would not start with the history and philosophy of the corporation, but rather with real-life concerns of new workers: Where will I be working? With whom will I be working? What will be expected of me? How do people dress in this company? What is the time schedule? To whom can I go for help? [...]

2. The Grouping of Learners. The concept of developmental tasks provides some guidance regarding the grouping of learners. For some kinds of learnings, homogeneous groups according to developmental task are more effective. For instance, in a program on child care, young parents would have quite a different set of interests from the parents of adolescent children. For other kinds of learnings, heterogeneous groups would clearly be preferable. For instance, in a program of human relations training in which the objective is to help people learn to get along better with all kinds of people, it would be important for the groups to cut across occupational, age, status, sex, and perhaps other characteristics that make people different. In my own practice, I have adopted the policy of making provision in the design of any adult learning activity for a variety of subgroups so as to give the students a flexibility of choice; and I find that they quickly discover colleagues with similar developmental tasks.

Orientation to Learning

Adults enter into education with a different perspective from children, which in turn produces a difference in the way they view learning. Children tend to have a perspective of postponed application on most of their learning. For example, most of what I learned in elementary school I learned in order to be able to get into high school; and most of what I learned there I learned to prepare me for college; and most of what I learned in college I hoped would prepare me for a happy and productive adult life. To a child, education is essentially a process of the accumulation of a reservoir of subject matter — knowledge and skills — that might be useful later in life. Children tend, therefore, to enter any educational activity in a *subject-centered* frame of mind.

Adults, on the other hand, tend to have a perspective of immediacy of application toward most of their learning. Education is a process of improving their ability to deal with life problems they face now. They tend, therefore, to enter an educational activity in a *problem-centered* frame of mind.

Technological Implications

Several implications for the technology of andragogy flow from this difference in orientation to learning.

1. The Orientation of Adult Educators. Where the youth educator can, perhaps appropriately, be primarily concerned with the logical development of subject matter and its articulation from grade to grade according to levels of complexity, the adult educator must be primarily attuned to the existential concerns of the individuals and institutions he serves and be able to develop learning experiences that will be articulated with these concerns. Andragogy calls for program builders and teachers who are person-centered, who don't teach subject matter but rather help persons learn.

2. The Organization of the Curriculum. [...] Because adult learners tend to be problem-centered in their orientation to learning, the appropriate organizing principle for sequences of adult learning is *problem areas,* not *subjects.* For example, instead of offering courses on 'Composition I' and 'Composition II', with the first focusing on grammar and the second on writing style, andragogical practice would put in their place 'Writing Better Business Letters' and 'Writing Short Stories'. In the adult courses, matters of grammar and style would be treated in the context of the practical concerns of the learners.

3. The Design of Learning Experiences. The problem orientation of the learners implies that the most appropriate starting point for every learning experience is the problems and concerns that the adults have on their minds as they enter. Whereas the opening session of a youth education activity might be titled 'What This Course Is All About', in an adult educational activity it would more appropriately be titled 'What Are You Hoping To Get out of This Course?' Early in the session there would be a problem census or a diagnostic exercise through which the participants would identify the specific problems they want to be able to deal with more adequately. This is not to suggest that a good adult learning experience ends with the problems the learners are aware of in the beginning, but that is where it starts. There may be other problems that the teacher or institution are expecting to be dealt with, and these are put into the picture along with the students' problems for negotiation between teacher and students.

Some Assumptions About Learning and Teaching

The critical element in any adult education program is, of course, what happens when a teacher comes face-to-face with a group of learners. As I see it, the andragogical approach to the learning-teaching transaction is premised on three additional assumptions about learning and teaching:

1. Adults Can Learn

The central proposition on which the entire adult education movement is based is that adults can learn. One of the great moments in the history of the movement occurred at the annual meeting of the American Association for Adult Education held in Cleveland in 1927, when Edward L. Thorndike reported for the first time his findings that the ability to learn declined only very slowly and very slightly after age twenty. Until that moment adult educators had based their whole work on blind faith, in direct opposition to the prevailing belief that 'you can't teach an old dog new tricks'. But now their faith had been vindicated; there was scientific proof that adults can learn. [...]

The research to date on adult learning indicates clearly that the basic ability to learn remains essentially unimpaired throughout the life-span and that, therefore, if individuals do not actually perform as well in learning situations as they could, the cause must be sought in such factors as the following:

(a) Adults who have been away from systematic education for some time may underestimate their ability to learn, and this lack of confidence may prevent them from applying themselves wholly.

(b) Methods of teaching have changed since most adults were in school, so that most of them have to go through a period of adjustment to strange new conditions.

(c) Various physiological changes occur in the process of aging, such as decline in visual acuity, reduction in speed of reaction, and lowering of energy levels, which operate as barriers to learning unless compensated for by such devices as louder sound, larger printing, and slower pace.

(d) Adults respond less readily to external sanctions for learning (such as grades) than to internal motivation.

2. Learning is an Internal Process

In our inherited folk wisdom there has been a tendency to look upon education as the transmittal of information, to see learning as an almost exclusively intellectual process consisting of the storing of accumulated facts in the filing drawers of the mind. The implicit assumption underlying this view of learning is that it is essentially an external process in the sense that what the student learns is determined primarily by outside forces, such as the excellence of the teacher's presentation, the quality of reading materials, and the effectiveness of school discipline. People holding this view even today insist that a teacher's qualifications be judged only by his mastery of his subject matter and clamor against his wasting time learning about the psychology of learning. For all practical purposes this view defines the function of the teacher as being to teach subject matter, not students.

A growing body of research into what really happens when learning takes place has put this traditional conception of learning in serious jeopardy. Although there is not yet agreement on the precise nature of the learning process (in fact there are many theories which seem to explain different parts of it), there is agreement that it is an internal process controlled by the learner and engaging his whole being — including intellectual, emotional, and physiological functions. Learning is described psychologically as a process of need-meeting and goal-striving by the learner. This is to say that an individual is motivated to engage in learning to the extent that he feels a need to learn and perceives a personal goal that learning will help to achieve; and he will invest his energy in making use of available resources (including teachers and readings) to the extent that he perceives them as being relevant to his needs and goals.

The central dynamic of the learning process is thus perceived to be the experience of the learner, experience being defined as the interaction between an individual and his environment. The quality and amount of learning is therefore clearly influenced by the quality and amount of interaction between the learner and his environment and by the educative potency of the environment. The art of teaching is essentially the management of these two key variables in the learning process — environment and interaction — which together define the substance of the basic unit of learning, a 'learning experience'. The critical function of the teacher, therefore, is to create a rich environment from which students can extract learning and then to guide their interaction with it so as to maximize their learning from it.

The important implication for adult education practice of the fact that learning is an internal process is that those methods and techniques which involve the individual most deeply in self-directed inquiry will produce the greatest learning. This principle of ego-involvement lies at the heart of the adult educator's art. In fact, the main thrust of modern adult educational technology is in the direction of inventing techniques for involving adults in ever deeper processes of self-diagnosis of their own needs for continued learning, in formulating their own objectives for learning, in sharing responsibility for designing and carrying out their learning activities, and in evaluating their progress toward their objectives. The truly artistic teacher of adults perceives the locus of responsibility for learning to be in the learner; he conscientiously suppresses his own compulsion to teach what he knows his students ought to learn in favour of helping his students learn for themselves what they want to learn. I have described this faith in the ability of the individual to learn for himself as the 'theological foundation' of adult education, and I believe that without this faith a teacher of adults is more likely to hinder than to facilitate learning. This is not to suggest that the teacher has less responsibility in the learning-teaching transaction, but only that his responsibility lies less in giving ready-made answers to predetermined questions and more in being ingenious in finding better ways to help his students discover the important questions and the answers to them themselves. [...]

3. There Are Superior Conditions of Learning and Principles of Teaching

It is becoming increasingly clear from the growing body of knowledge about the processes of adult learning that there are certain conditions of learning that are more conducive to growth and development than others. These superior conditions seem to be produced by practices in the learning-teaching transaction that adhere to certain superior principles of teaching as identified below:

CONDITIONS OF LEARNING

The learners feel a need to learn.

The learning environment is characterized by physical comfort, mutual trust and respect, mutual helpfulness, freedom of expression, and acceptance of differences.

The learners perceive the goals of a learning experience to be their goals.

PRINCIPLES OF TEACHING

(1) The teacher exposes students to new possibilities for self-fulfillment.
(2) The teacher helps each student clarify his own aspirations for improved behavior.
(3) The teacher helps each student diagnose the gap between his aspiration and his present level of performance.
(4) The teacher helps the students identify the life problems they experience because of the gaps in their personal equipment.
(5) The teacher provides physical conditions that are comfortable (as to seating, smoking, temperature, ventilation, lighting, decoration) and conducive to interaction (preferably, no person sitting behind another person).
(6) The teacher accepts each student as a person of worth and respects his feelings and ideas.
(7) The teacher seeks to build relationships of mutual trust and helpfulness among the students by encouraging cooperative activities and refraining from inducing competitiveness and judgmentalness.
(8) The teacher exposes his own feelings and contributes his resources as a co-learner in the spirit of mutual inquiry.
(9) The teacher involves the students in a mutual process of formulating learning objectives in which the needs of the students, of the institution, of the teacher, of the subject matter, and of the society are taken into account.

The learners accept a share of the responsibility for planning and operating a learning experience, and therefore have a feeling of commitment toward it.

(10) The teacher shares his thinking about options available in the designing of learning experiences and the selection of materials and methods and involves the students in deciding among these options jointly.

The learners participate actively in the learning process.

(11) The teacher helps the students to organize themselves (project groups, learning-teaching teams, independent study, etc.) to share responsibility in the process of mutual inquiry.

The learning process is related to and makes use of the experience of the learners.

(12) The teacher helps the students exploit their own experiences as resources for learning through the use of such techniques as discussion, role playing, case method, etc.

(13) The teacher gears the presentation of his own resources to the levels of experience of his particular students.

(14) The teacher helps the students to apply new learnings to their experience, and thus to make the learnings more meaningful and integrated.

The learners have a sense of progress toward their goals.

(15) The teacher involves the students in developing mutually acceptable criteria and methods for measuring progress toward the learning objectives.

(16) The teacher helps the students develop and apply procedures for self-evaluation according to these criteria.

Notes

1. Alfred N. Whitehead, 'Introduction', Wallace B. Donham, *Business Adrift* (McGraw-Hill Book Co., New York, 1931), pp. viii-xix.

2. See Dušan Savićević, 'Training Adult Educationists in Yugoslavia', *Convergence*, vol. 1 (March 1968), p. 69.

3. Robert J. Havighurst, *Developmental Tasks and Education* (David McKay Co., New York, 1961), p. 2.

THE LEARNING TRANSACTION

Roby Kidd

Source: Reprinted from *How Adults Learn*, copyright 1973 by J. Roby Kidd. Reprinted with the permission of the publisher, Cambridge Book Company.

[…] John Dewey often wrote about learning as a transaction. He said that active perception, interpretation, or understanding comes as a result of a transaction in which are linked the interpreter and the interpreted, the observer and the observed. In the market-place, unless both the buyer and the seller bring something of value, there is no transaction. So it is with learning. Many students of learning over many centuries have also used this term because they have been acutely aware of both process and *continuity* — continuity between the learner and his past, the learner and his environment, the learner and the content, the learner and his teacher.

Learning involves change and growth in the individual and in his behavior. 'You don't change,' said Eduard Lindeman, 'until you do something. You don't change by listening. You don't change by talking. You actually change when something happens to your muscles. When you step or move in a new way, then the change becomes really significant'.[1] What may be involved is cognitive learning or motor learning, or affective learning — or all in the same process — but always there is change and growth. […]

Sometimes learning is an individual act, sometimes it happens in a group or social situation where the transaction has at least five elements:

(i)   the learner
(ii) the teacher
(iii) the group (usually)
(iv) the setting or situation
(v)   the subject matter

But the main protagonists in the transaction are still the learner and the teacher. This is often true even in self-directed learning because self-directed learners frequently seek helpers or teachers for particular goals.

Let us ask ourselves what the learner brings to the transaction. What are his perceptions about the need for change? How deep is his uneasiness, his dissatisfaction with the present or his desire for the new? What are the inhibitions to learning that he brings, his ambivalence, his resistance to change, his refuge in the present? What does he know about his own capacity for learning? Does he perceive the content as abstract and irrelevant? Does he expect understanding and helpfulness from the teacher or some kind of threatening behavior? Does he feel a part of, or rejected by, the group?

Learning may be an adventure, but for the learner it may also pose unknown difficulties or raise images of past failures. Does the learner perceive the situation as it is or are his perceptions distorted? Is he likely to protect himself by verbalizing about the subject matter without internalizing or reorganizing it within himself? Whitehead has warned that passive learning of 'inert ideas' may be not only wasteful but actually harmful, since the result is a decrease in satisfaction gained from learning and probably an increase in resistance to further learning.

What does the teacher bring? Like the learner, the teacher also brings a great deal to the transaction, much more than his mastery of a skill or his knowledge of subject matter. Does he have awareness of the continuity or the interaction that is involved? Does he look on it as an encounter with another self, or perceive himself simply as a transmission system for presenting certain material? Nothing is more deeply belittling than the self-image that some teachers have of themselves as being but a repository of facts or ideas, ready to display them before others, but themselves taking little part except as transmitters.

How well is the teacher aware of the delicacy of his role, of the need that the learner has to be both dependent upon, and independent of, him? How well does he understand his own needs, his need to control people, or his need for affection, or his fear of hostility from the learner? How well is he able to accept the learner, not just as pupil but as a person?

Within the group, its experience, its skill in supporting the learner, its encouragement to him to stretch out, its capacity for obtaining assistance from the teacher, and so on, are factors of considerable consequence. [...]

A three-step time sequence is usually present in any learning transaction — that is, planning the curriculum, establishing the learning situation, and evaluating. [...]

One of the essential differences between adult education and the curricula often planned for children is that the adult learner, far more than the child, may expect to take a more active part in the consideration and selection of what he is to study. With children the amount of choice, and the degree of participation in the choice of learning materials and experiences will usually be limited. But with adults there can be a very wide range from dependence upon the teacher to the stage where the choice of learning objectives and the curriculum are made by the learners. Where examinations are set by some authority, or where the readings are already established, choice may be considerably restricted, but even in these cases there may be considerable opportunity for variety of illustrations or applications of principles. Whatever the limits, it is clear that where the learner does take part in the development of the curriculum, this act leads to a learning experience that is markedly different in quality. However, the learner may not have had any previous practice in choosing what to study. This may at first be a strange and perhaps even forbidding task for him, and he may need guidance in trying it.

Ralph Tyler[2] identifies three general sources for learning objectives:

(i) The learner himself
(ii) Contemporary life and the society in which the learner lives
(iii) The subject matter fields such as history and literature

Since we are concerned with cognitive, systematic, and effective learning, and since in some cases the main decisions about curriculum are made by the learner himself, in others by the students sharing in curriculum planning, and in still others by the teacher, there will be many variations in practice, but the same general procedure can usually be employed.

Needs of the Learner

[...] A study of the needs and wants of the adult learner is one means of beginning the development of a curriculum. Needs are so many and so varied that one must have some way of bringing them into order. One rough classification is (1) health (2) family and friendship relations (3) socio-civic relations (4) consumer aspects of life (5) occupation (6) recreation, and (7) religion and philosophy.

Many ingenious ways have been used to identify both needs and interests, employing questionnaires, interviews, and similar devices.

Objections have sometimes been raised to the employment of such information in developing a curriculum. It is claimed, for example, that information about interests may give the *range* of interest but not the intensity. It is also possible that adult students may come with mixed, or twisted, or unworthy interests and goals.

A further question is that placing too great a reliance on individual 'interests' may result in the slighting of information gained from community surveys and the analysis of social patterns and social groupings which, in practice, have been the source of many useful ideas for educational activities for adults.

The most frequent criticism is that an interest-based curriculum will result in reinforcing what may be a degraded level of taste. It is clear that some producers of the mass media in 'giving the people what they want' are not only underestimating what people really want, but are themselves modifying wants and interests.

The errors here are threefold. The first is to assume that people have had enough experience to know all that will interest them. One way to help people discover an interest is to expose them to a range of experiences. As William Hocking once said, 'There is many a horse which does not know it is thirsty and which, when led to water, finds that it wants to drink.' This is often true of the adult student whose horizons of experience have been restricted. How can he know how fascinating some of the 'unknown countries' may be? The only way he can discover this is by exploration which sometimes may be difficult and unrewarding, but may also prove a great adventure.

A second error is putting undue reliance upon superficial interest-finders of the questionnaire type, using inadequate sampling procedures. Results of such measures usually are very limited. On the other hand, well-conducted interviews, or thorough investigations, have revealed a surprising range and depth of interest among adults. One study of radio listeners in England by Joseph Trenaman[3] reports that there are desires for learning among 'ordinary people' of a kind that are seldom supplied in the daily run of broadcasting. The large numbers of people that have not enrolled but 'listen in' to the Open University is another example.

A third error can arise in the decision about a course of action based on what has been found out about the interests of learners. Supposing one discovers that men in a certain work gang read nothing but comic books. One then has the choice between supplying them with even more comic books or continuing the search for an interest or need around which other forms of reading or study may take place. [...]

The main reason, of course, for the concentration on interests as a source for educational objectives is the close relationship that this seems to bear with gaining the attention of people and having them participate in educational endeavors. Considerable study has been given to those adults in society who are infrequently or never found in educational activities. Despite recent growth in enrollment in adult education, the number of men and women who never take part in formal or informal activities must still be very large. Many who have studied nonparticipation believe that if more adults are to be brought into educational activities, not only must the curriculum be modified to accommodate other interests but also many of the traditional forms of organization may have to be revised.

Curriculum

Those devising a curriculum may search contemporary life for clues to the selection of learning experiences. Here, just as much as in analyzing interests, the amount of material is so vast and complicated that some categories or other organizing devices are required. [...]

An excellent source of learning objectives is in the established fields of study, such as mathematics and history. This has long been recognized in adult education, and not much comment is necessary. But there have been curious gaps. For example, although we live in an age that is often described as the 'scientific era', the time allotted to science in the curriculum for adult education has been only a tiny fraction of the whole. Moreover, the use of subject matter has been for learning objectives that have been surprisingly narrow. Often it has included little more than the acquiring of information. [...]

By seeking the aid of the subject matter specialist in developing a curriculum, not only can important fields be covered, but they can be opened up in the depth and breadth that they deserve.

In these ways far more educational objectives will be identified than can possibily be followed up by any single educational agency. How can selection be made of those of greatest worth? Tyler proposes two main 'screens' for selection — one's educational philosophy and the understanding that one has of what learning is or can do. [...] It is essential that one's educational philosophy be stated lucidly and the main implications for educational objectives may have to be spelled out.

The second screen is made up of what we know about the educational process. There are some learning objectives that are potential only, there are some that are possible only with years of application, there are others than can be accomplished in a single course, or a single presentation. [...]

From our knowledge of learning we can more readily organize material in time sequences. Some content may come first because it can be mastered more easily or because it provides necessary background, or a system for understanding what is to follow. It may seem an odd remark to make but another useful guide is our knowledge about 'forgetting'. A college student, for example, may forget as much as 50 per cent of what he learns in one year, or as much as 80 per cent in two years. But if he practices or uses the new he is not so inclined to lose it. It is desirable therefore, to choose learning sequences which the adult student is in a position to practice and apply. Moreover, things that are learned that are consistent with each other tend to reinforce and those that are inconsistent tend to interfere. This understanding can also guide us in selection of subject matter. Material which is inconsistent with the learner's view of the self is likely to be rejected or distorted. Where such material is a necessary part of the curriculum it ought to be introduced with some care and in ways by which the learner may be aided to face up to the implications squarely.

Some decisions may need to be made about the objectives that are 'educational' and those that require some other form of behavior. For example, some of the problems faced by an unemployed laborer with five children may be dealt with through education; others may require action through welfare, therapy, or politics.

Two final actions are required in the development of the curriculum: a careful statement of objectives and selection of the actual learning experiences. [...]

The important thing about learning has to do with changes in the learner; it is not behavior by the teacher, or kinds of subject matter. Accordingly educational objectives ought to be stated in a form which identifies the expected changes in the student. It is not enough to state that a learning objective is history or shopwork, or even in some generalized form such as 'History develops an historical point-of-view'. Two elements should be included in the statement — the kind of behavior change expected and the subject matter to be employed. Examples:

(i)   To prepare a clear and well-organized newspaper article about the reorganization of city government.
(ii) To develop an appreciation of modern architecture.
(iii) To achieve familiarity with dependable sources of inform-ation about the teaching of mathematics.

In this way there is clarity about the selection of specific learning experiences. Moreover the objectives are stated in a form that is required if there is to be any satisfactory form of evaluation. [...]

The learning experience must be one in which the learner gains the kind of satisfaction set out in the objectives. We have all suffered occasions where this has not happened. If, in a course in musical appreciation, in the way that musical examples and musical form are analyzed the learner comes to hate music, there has been a disastrous error both in selection of the learning experience and probably in the methods employed. The learning objective needs to be gauged as being within the possible range of accomplishment by the learner at his present level of experience. Discomfort will be produced if it is too elementary just as it will if there is too great difficulty. [...]

To summarize: choosing a curriculum for adults means several things. It means understanding the needs and interests of the learner, understanding the situation in which he lives, and the kinds of content that may serve his needs. It means a careful statement of objectives in a form that sets out the desired changes as well as the subject matter. It means selection of the precise learning experi-ences that may best accomplish these objectives. It assumes the fullest possible participation by the learner in curriculum building.

Moreover, it is now clear that devising suitable curricula for adults, though a fascinating enterprise, is somewhat complicated. If the learner is himself to play a large part in this, it is essential that more assistance be provided to him. Houle, in his survey of adult education in the armed forces, and in his books since has reiterated that counseling, both in the development of curriculum and in the selection of studies, ought to be provided in every educational situation for adults. He and others have maintained that since in adult education the possibilities of choice are usually greater than in most schools or colleges, it is even more essential for the adult student to be able to secure counsel in making an effective choice.

The Learning Situation

With the curriculum chosen we can look at the second phase or aspect of what is really a continuous process.

Whether the learning occurs through individual effort or in some kind of educational or training institution, the key concept is the same. It is best expressed in the world *engage* (particularly in the French *engager* for *gage*, or pledge) meaning 'to bind oneself, to pledge oneself, to become engrossed, to become involved.' Learning happens as the result of engagement, and the task of those guiding learning is to bring about engagement.

Naturally this does not happen by chance or by luck. It must be carefully planned. We say naturally, but it is not always deemed so. Since there is often considerable stress put upon informality in the learning of adults, it has been assumed by some that the learning transaction can proceed as an improvisation. But improvisation is possible, just as in music, only where there is a *mastery* of all the principles that must be brought into some harmonious arrangement. It requires planning and practice, even if it might appear artless.

There are a number of related aspects to this plan and practice:

  (i)   Exploring needs for, and resistance to, the learning objectives.
  (ii) Making decisions and taking action about the learning environment, i.e., physical arrangements, selection of forms, and devices.
  (iii) Achieving helping characteristics within the group if it is a social and not an individual project.
  (iv) Exploring the content.
  (v)   Testing and applying.

[...]

Exploration of Needs

If he is to become deeply engaged, the learner must perceive his needs and the relationship that the subject matter has to them. It may be useful for him to have some verbal discussion of this. Some teachers make the exploration of needs, as seen by the learners, the central core of the opening session of a course. It may also be useful to have some open discussion of blocks and limitations to learning that may be expected. Sometimes it is useful to have some expression of anxieties, that one is too old, or 'rusty', or has been unsuccessful in such kinds of situations before. Sometimes it may help if the teacher warns the members what to expect. For example, they may be told that the subject matter may be difficult until a certain stage is achieved, and that perseverance will be required.

It ought not to be expected that this exploration will take place without incident or some difficulty. People who have been used to governing their own learning will take part in such a preliminary as a matter of course. But what of the adult student whose previous experience has been of a very different kind? Perhaps in any previous educational situation he was *told* how and what to study. Now you are expecting him to assume some responsibility for his own learning. He may feel somewhat puzzled, or frustrated, or even threatened by a situation unlike anything experienced before. [...]

In all cases the individual may need encouragement. The principle is simple enough to understand and even to state as a generalization, but it is endlessly variable and fascinating in practice. If the learner has never had the experience of sharing in the planning of his own study, then the first occasion when he is confronted with the opportunity for greater participation is likely to be difficult. There may be the emergence of negative feelings, perhaps very strong ones. [...]

Naturally, unless these negative feelings can be expressed, there is little chance of the development of much understanding of what has produced them, or acceptance by the learner of a greater degree of responsibility. But if the learner finds that he can express feelings without being condemned, if he can take action or try out ideas that will not lead to his rejection by the teacher or by the class members, he has little need for a brittle defensiveness. [...]

One more point: the student not only needs to be prepared to handle his own difficulties but also may need the incentive of some forward view of the results.

Selection of Specific Forms and Devices

In any field where there is richness of opportunity the process of *selection* becomes more important and correspondingly more difficult. A teacher or leader of adults today best demonstrates his competence by his understanding and skill in the selection and use of an astonishing range of alternative resources and forms.

It is essential to make sure that all arrangements are in accord with what we know about learning. This will include at least the following:

(i)   Planning the environment in line with the program objectives.
(ii) Having all equipment in excellent condition, set up for immediate use, or available for practice at the time when needed.
(iii) Applying the suggestions devised to help overcome some of the sight and hearing limitations of older people.
(iv) Arranging the learning sequences in time units that challenge but do not fatigue or dull the interest of the adult learner.
(v)   Taking care that the pace of presentation is not too rapid, particularly for the older adult.

Characteristics of the Group which Supports Learning

At least three characteristics need to be present in the group if effective learning is to take place:

(i)   *A realization by the members of the group* that genuine growth stems from the creative power within the individual, and that learning, finally, is an individual matter.
(ii) The acceptance as a *group standard* that each member has the right to be different and to disagree.
(iii) Establishment of a group atmosphere that is free from narrow judgments on the part of the teacher or group members.

Exploration of the Subject Matter

The presentation of the subject matter can take many forms, such as reading, lectures, observation and experiment. If the attention of the learner is fully engaged he will want, in increasing measure, to experience the subject matter in all its fascination, or its difficulty, even its bewilderment. He may want or need the information or opinion of an 'expert'. Or he may be prepared for frank exchange of views. [...]

This exploration can and should go on, in depth. But there are also endless possibilities for breadth. With so much experience among the group members to start from, the possibilities of generalizing and of perceiving new relationships are many. Possibilities for the curriculum associated with travel and field trips, as well as education as part of community development and social action, open the field wider still but make all the more necessary a firm grasp on what are the learning objectives.

In the case of a skill, or motor learning (like learning to play tennis), little result can be anticipated without opportunity for practice. Actually this principle is valid not only for motor learning, but it is not so well recognized in other fields. Along with the presentation, exploration, and relating of subject matter must go the practice of ideas and skills, the try-out and testing of assumptions and hypotheses, checking them against alternatives, and counter-claims, estimating their validity with respect to inner logic or in application in real life.

If the learning has to do with the acquiring of new skills and attitudes, an essential part of the learning process will be imaginative applications in the home setting. The learner may want and need help in diagnosing the forces that may be resistant to change, in measuring his own strengths and weaknesses, and in seeking to re-establish himself back in his own situation.

The learner may also need help in developing a 'continuing system' of learning. If he has attained satisfaction in learning, already he has a 'bent' for more. What he may also need is to improve his skill in learning, to use more scientific methods of observation and analysis, to become more sensitive and under-standing of his own inhibitions to learning (and through under-standing reduce these resistances), to become more self-accepting, and, through gaining more security and becoming less defensive, freer to perceive without distortion.

This entire learning transaction proceeds most effectively if it is guided by 'feed-back' and evaluation.

Evaluation

[...] The function of evaluation was stated succinctly by a national committee of the Adult Education Association:

The primary purpose of evaluation in education is to find out how much change and growth have taken place as a result of educational experiences. One evaluates a total program or major parts of it to find out how much progress has been made toward program objectives.[4]

In some cases, measurement of results is relatively simple. An agricultural extension worker does not have to guess about outcomes: he either can or cannot find actual changes in practice. So can a political organizer. The test of some educational programs in social action is how many improved conditions were brought about. [...]

Evaluation should also be carried out with respect to specific learning objectives. Indeed, one of the principal reasons for being sharp and clear in the statement of one's objectives is so that appraisal can be conducted in a meaningful way. [...] Evaluation should be carried on as a *regular, ongoing* part of the total learning process.

If the objective of the learning program were merely the reproducing of information supplied by the teacher, or giving back the opinions of the teacher, evaluation might be expressed as some measure of facts or opinions committed to memory.

Usually, however, the objectives have to do with *changes* in observing, identifying, analyzing, understanding, organizing, applying, and testing information as well as the development of certain work habits, skills, and attitudes. Some way must therefore be found for measuring the changes, directly or by inference.

It is well to stress a variety of measures because it has often been assumed that evaluation means the use of pencil-and-paper tests. Obviously written tests have a part in evaluation. So do tests of performance in certain skills (for example, typing, gymnastics, welding, dissecting, leading discussion). So also does appraisal of samples of performance, such as selections from a student's writing. So do oral examinations of many kinds.

Not only does evaluation mean the measurement of changes in behavior but it usually signifies more than one test, more than a final examination. If evaluation is to mean much there must also be pre-examination, so that there is a base from which growth can be measured. There is also systematic ongoing evaluation or 'feedback.' There is testing at the conclusion of the program. And there is further assessment at some point in time afterwards, to note any application of the learning. [...]

In his book, *Informal Adult Education*[5], Malcolm Knowles

reports that 'to most adults the words "test", "quiz" and "examin-ation" call forth such unpleasant memories that it is often difficult to use them in voluntary adult groups.' This seems to be true, and thus far there have not been devised many satisfactory substitute methods. Various kinds of written 'objective' tests have been adapted from schools and universities. These are the sort in which the learner indicates whether he thinks the statement is true or false, or in which he makes a choice among several statements.

But little attention has yet been directed toward developing these for adult purposes. In adult education in England, particularly in the classes of the Workers' Educational Association, it is expected that every student will write a number of essays and much of the effort of the tutor in guiding the adult students comes in connection with this written work. Essays and projects are not unknown but are much less common in North America.

Some attempts have been made to use projective tests, in which the learner constructs an imaginary story or describes how he feels or what he sees when certain unstructured shapes are presented to him. Analysis by a trained psychologist of his responses can give a good deal of information about his attitudes, social adjustment, and personality structure. But such use is rarely possible except in psychological clinics and institutions; it is not at all for general purposes unless highly trained professional staff are available.

Some teachers have made use of studies of attendance, and of 'drop-outs', in evaluating their program. However, such statistics by themselves do not reveal very much unless it is possible to follow them up with interviews with a selected number of individuals. Studies of participation are becoming more common. Each teacher can and does make some subjective assessment of the performance and growth of the learners. But that is rarely satisfactory in furn-ishing data for any kind of comparisons.

Kropp and Verner[6] have developed an attitude-scale technique for evaluating the changes that occur in a single meeting or con-ference, which they feel will provide results that can be compared. The scale is based on the feelings and judgments that the learner has about the experience in which he has just participated.

The *agent* of evaluation may be very important. If the learning objective is simply reproducing what the teacher has taught, the result may just as well be measured by the teacher. But if a primary learning objective is for the learner to become increasingly auton-omous, to begin to take over direction of his own learning, then it is highly important that he take a large share, if not the complete control, of the evaluation. Now that it is better understood how much self-directed learning goes on, a major task of education will be to equip individuals with the attitudes and the skills required for curriculum planning and evaluation of their own programs of study.

In many learning situations, the participation by the learner in the evaluation is difficult to manage. Where there is a standard program of teaching skills, such as lifesaving, there is usually a fixed examination system. A factory, a school or university may also have an established examination procedure which is required by law for licensing, or to receive the payments of grants, or because it is backed by some other sanction. What can be done in the face of such rigidities?

First of all, it should be repeated that the measuring of performance against certain objective standards is an excellent way to obtain knowledge about oneself if the learner is himself making these comparisons, and if the process is carried out without some form of punishment for poor performance. Films or tape recordings by which he can observe good work, and appraise his own performance against what is excellent, provide one means of doing this. It is also important for him to measure his performance against his own previous performance and against his learning objectives. Again, the use of tape recordings, particularly videotape recordings, makes this possible in many fields. Motion picture film is regularly used for appraisal in sports like football.

In the classroom many teachers, obliged by the institution to give some test, have experimented with various means of testing that are also conducive to the development of self-appraisal. One practice is to have the class members themselves prepare the test form. Contrary to what might be anticipated, the resulting test is often more rigorous than that which would have been devised by the instructor. Another variation is where the students are asked to state a dozen or so major propositions in regard to their subject, bring them to class, and then be examined critically on their understanding and application of a selection of these propositions.

But where academic credit is not an issue, the number and variety of 'examinations' used in surprising. Often the test is some form of application of the subject matter and principles learned. [...] Two- or three-day exercises which feature the direct applications of principles have been devised in projects of in-service training for the staffs of national organizations. Participation in a political party or in social action respecting urban renewal have been the forms of evaluation and application of some political science courses. In a one-week-long intensive seminar on Shakespeare, the participants read, hear lectures, and attend performances of the plays. For their examination, the entire seminar group utilize the knowledge they have gained about the stage, the actors, design, costumes, and Elizabethan music and apply it in the design of a production of a different Shakespearian play. In this case, the seminar participants themselves decided upon the form of examination. They also identified the criteria to be used and methods to be followed in appraising their own performance.

The important factor of course, is not just interest in the activity, but how much engagement of the person can be attained in the process of measuring and understanding his own progress. [...]

When a message is being communicated from one person to another, if there is an opportunity for the recipient to report back what he is receiving, a great deal of error is eliminated.

Feed-back is the process by which, in any communication, or any learning process, the recipient or learner is able to state what is his perception of the situation at any given time.

Examples of this are many. The members of a class, at the end of a lecture, may state what they understood from the lecture. Feelings they have about what has transpired may be identified as well as facts. Much of the value of the feed-back is to discover with what feelings the activity or content is being received, and this can be used to guide both teacher and learner. At the conclusion of the first day of a conference the members may indicate to what degree the sessions are meeting the objectives that had been established for the conference, as well as some of the personal objectives that each of them had. They may also state what is lacking; what issues or emphasis ought to be included, or what has been unclear. The use of such material in planning subsequent lectures or sessions is obvious.

There are other by-products. The practice of regular assessment of what is occurring leads to improved performance in self-appraisal. Moreover, being able to measure his own success is perhaps the strongest motivating force for an adult to continue or to put fresh energy into the chosen study. [...]

Effect of Evaluation

It seems to be clear from all the evidence that adults, even more than children, are interested in the application of what they learn.

Adults seem to be more interested in the directions in which their learning is taking them. The motivation of adults, since they engage in most activities from free choice and not by law, is dependent upon their being convinced that progress is being made toward some goal. For all these objects evaluation is essential.

Adults want to know in what ways they have been changed. Several years ago the late Eduard Lindeman reported that a class of trade union members, studying international affairs with him, wanted to know if their study had changed them in any of the following respects:

(i) Has it increased my usable fund of reliable information? (The principal feature of their concern appeared to be (a) the relationship between different bodies of facts and (b) ways of distinguishing the various grades of reliability of information.)

(ii) Have I changed my vocabulary? Have I, in other words, learned how to make use of some *new concepts*?

(iii) Have I acquired any new skills? (e.g. learning how to interpret statistical tables and graphs).

(iv) Have I learned how to make reliable generalizations?

(v) Have I learned how to sort out the moral ingredients in the various situations considered by this study group? Have I learned to think in terms of values?

(vi) Have I altered any attitudes?[7]

It is quite clear from this list of questions that Dr Lindeman was assisting his class to learn how to evaluate, as well as how to read and study. [...]

One final word: we have seen that most adult learners have both educational and what might be called noneducational motives. For example, belonging to cohesive social groups may affect the amount of growth or educational change. But many of the instruments presently used for evaluation take no account of factors such as this. Evaluation in its full sense is a more subtle complex process than is yet represented in the techniques that are usually employed. Accordingly, any results of these devices should be interpreted with some care.

Notes

1. Eduard C. Lindeman, *The Meaning of Adult Education* (Harvest House Ltd., Montreal, 1962).

2. Ralph W. Tyler, *Basic Principles of Curriculum and Instruction* (University of Chicago Press, Chicago, 1950).

3. Joseph Trenaman, *Education in the Adult Population* (Oxford University Press, Oxford, 1959).

4. Adult Education Association, *Program Evaluation in Adult Education* (AEA, Chicago, 1952).

5. Malcolm Knowles, *Informal Adult Education* (Association Press, New York, 1954).

6. Russell P. Kropp and Coolie Verner, 'An Attitude Scale Technique for Evaluating Meetings', *Adult Education* (AEA, Chicago, 1957), vol. 7, no. 4.

7. Eduard C. Lindeman, 'Adults Evaluate Themselves', *How to Teach Adults* (AEA, Chicago, 1956).

2.3

LEARNING SITUATIONS OR EDUCATIONAL SITUATIONS?

Kenneth Lawson

Source: *Adult Education* (National Institute of Adult Education, Leicester, 1974), 47, pp. 88-92.

What is a Learning Situation?

One frequently hears adult educators claim that they are concerned with 'learning situations' not 'teaching situations' and when this view is seen as a reaction against certain forms of teacher centred situations it is understandably a popular view.

Clearly, learning is a major component in our thinking about education but I question the validity of characterising adult education in terms of learning situations and of isolating the concept of a 'learning situation' from the concept of 'teaching'. In this article therefore I am concerned with a conceptual study of learning situations rather than learning theory and I suggest that it might be more helpful to discuss adult education in terms of teaching and educational situations.

The Concept of Learning

A very distinctive feature of human beings is their ability to acquire new patterns of behaviour and to modify their responses to situations. This process of modification is going on practically all the time and we commonly call it 'learning' when the modification of response is not brought about by physiologically based maturation. I am not aware of any adequate definition of learning and most writers on the subject do not provide a definition of learning as such. Instead we are given a criterion of learning having taken place. Conventionally learning is said to have occurred when there is an observable change in behaviour which is the result of something other than maturation.

88

The learning process may in turn be defined as a series of events which lead up to a change in behaviour and which are thought to be causally related to the change. The specific activities which are identified as part of the learning process will depend upon the theories of learning currently held and our description of the learning process will derive from theory and from experimental data. At various times, for example, problem solving, repetitive practice, stimulus and response may each be regarded as features of the learning process depending upon the view of learning adopted.

The Learning Situation

On this view any activity which is demonstrably associated with a change in behaviour could be regarded as contributing to the learning process and many situations of quite varying character could be regarded as learning situations because the latter would be quite tautologically defined as a situation in which learning processes took place. Most situations could be regarded as potential learning situations and we recognise this in practice by talking in the ordinary way about people learning by experience, by falling off buses, by talking in bars as well as in classrooms and on courses. *How* we learn in these situations may be explained by learning theory but the simple requirement *that* we learn is all that is needed to define a learning situation.

Is such a concept helpful? As it has been presented here the answer must surely be no. The notion of a 'learning situation' is so general as to be of little or no value as a guide to educational practice or as an indicator of the kind of situation that is educationally relevant. Clearly an understanding of how we learn will inform and perhaps improve teaching but the definition of a learning situation offers no guidance as to the kind of learning, or the mode of learning with which an educational institution should be concerned. No educator can claim to be concerned with all learning in all types of situation because our concept of education implies that value judgments are made about the kinds of learning and the methods of learning which are to count as educationally valid. Education is concerned with *some* kinds of learning, not all kinds and with certain kinds of learning situation but not others.

The first task of the educator is to clarify more precisely the characteristics of the learning situations which he is prepared to handle because only then can we move on to the improvement of the ways in which they are handled. The limits of our *educational* concern and the nature of our *educational objectives* must first be established before we can improve performance.

Learning Situations — A Narrower View

There is a narrower conception of a learning situation which might be more useful for our present purpose and it can be exemplified in the following way. The question 'has he learned x?' can be quite neutral in respect of how he has learned. It is concerned only to elicit whether or not 'x' has been acquired. The question can however be put with a different emphasis, meaning 'has he *learned* x?' where *learn* is given a rather special meaning. I am not sure how far in practice this usage is employed but a number of writers interpret the verb 'to learn' in such a value judgmental way. Vesey[1] explicitly uses the two ways of emphasising the question 'has he learned' in order to distinguish 'learned' behaviour from 'conditioned' behaviour. Both satisfy the condition that other things than maturation are responsible for the change in behaviour but some methods of inducing change count as learning while others do not.

Oakeshott also makes the point that 'by learning I mean an activity possible only to an intelligence capable of choice and self-direction in relation to its own impulses and to the world around him. These are pre-eminently human characteristics and as I understand it only human beings are capable of learning'.[2] He further claims that 'a learner is not a passive recipient of impressions ... or one who attempts nothing he does not know how to accomplish'. On the contrary man sets out to do many things which he has to learn how to accomplish. Oakeshott is therefore putting learning into a range of activities which are conscious and goal orientated. A learner is someone who *wants* to achieve something and who is prepared to *do* something in order to achieve it.

Such a view of learning might be thought to be far removed from our usual ways of conceiving it but surely we do often imply an 'active' concept of learning when denoting various methods of learning. To learn by repetition, by solving problems and so on is different from 'unconsciously' learning to avoid bumping one's head on a low beam. The psychologist too employs an activity view: for example, N.L. Munn refers to learning as 'the modification of behaviour which results from activity, special training or observation'.[3] 'He learned x' therefore can be taken to imply that 'he did something to acquire x' as well as 'he acquired x'.

Hirst and Peters claim that learning has two logically necessary conditions. 'First, learning always has an object. One is necessarily learning a particular x and the process is therefore always related to some kind of mastery of x, to a particular success or achievement. To have learnt is always to have come up to some standard: for example to know what one previously did not know or to have mastered a given skill.'[4] Peters further adds that learning must be based on experience which means that we must be conscious of what we are doing. Sleep learning, or learning while under the influence of drugs is not a conscious acquisition of behaviour, so although something happens to us it is not an 'experience' and we do not learn in the Peters and Oakeshott sense.

Some Educational Implications

The implications for educators now begin to emerge. A learning situation is conceived in terms which involve the identification of *what* is to be learned. Goals have to be specified as do standards of attainment which count as *having learnt*. Appropriate strategies for learning which involve the active conscious participation of the learner also have to be worked out so we are moving into the realm of teaching conceived as a system of planning objectives, setting standards and devising methods which will help the learner to realise the goals set for him or which he sets for himself. In other words, we have arrived at a learning situation which is an educational situation, and it is only in such a situation that it makes sense to talk, for example, about improving standards because it is only in an educational situation as here set out that standards related to goals are built into the concept.

The next task therefore is to decide on what precisely we are prepared to teach, what demands for learning we are prepared to meet, what areas of knowledge, what range of skills we are able to pass on and develop in others. Exactly how we are to identify our educational objectives is a complex issue about which little can be said here because it involves a consideration of our whole educational philosophy. In general terms however the criteria by which we establish our objectives will depend in part upon the context in which we operate, but our conception of what education is, and what it is for, will define the limits within which teaching and learning objectives may be established. In other words, our educational values, derived from our philosophy, will be used as criteria for judging what it seems appropriate to do in a given context. Thus we might consider whether suggested objectives satisfy the criteria and that there be cognitive learning as well as the development of skills and that there should be the development of understanding and not more 'know-how'. On the basis of the present argument we should also expect that any learning objectives would be shared by both teacher and learner and that the latter would intentionally and consciously engage himself in learning.

This does not mean that adult education must confine itself to academic forms of knowledge or eschew practical skills. The decision might be taken to teach writing, reading or how to prepare a case for presentation to a local council. The emphasis may move from formal courses to informal situations but the improvement of standards will depend on our ability to identify educational objectives and to sharpen teaching techniques and on our ability to engage in conscious learning those with whom we choose to work. On this view therefore it follows that what is acquired accidentally in casual encounters or in social work or community work situations does not satisfy an essential educational criterion. It is therefore arguable that such situations are not the educator's concern although this is not to say that community work situations cannot be converted into educational situations by introducing intentional teaching and learning. It should perhaps be stressed however that if the learner is not made fully aware of what is happening to him we run the risk of developing something approaching an indoctrination situation.

Summary

It is suggested that the unqualified idea of a learning situation is so general as to be of little use in discussion about adult education. We need to concentrate on educational situations with an emphasis upon teaching. This involves the establishment of fairly specific objectives for both learner and teacher to aim at and this implies the 'engineering' of quite explicit learning situations in which exercises, problem solving, explanation, analysis of performance and criticism, together with all the other activities associated with teaching are included. In other words, learning in an educational context requires effort and planning.

Of course learning can go on in places like coffee bars and on committees but I question whether generalised learning situations which do not satisfy some minimum criteria of the kind set out above can meaningfully characterise what is meant by adult education. To be meaningful concepts such as 'education' have to be restrictive in the sense that some things have to be excluded by the term. We need to know what does *not* count as education in order to identify what does.

If all learning, in any circumstances, is regarded as education it is impossible to order priorities and meaningless to talk of educational methods and standards because 'learning situations' in the un-qualified sense develop regardless of priorities, methods or standards; they simply happen.

Notes

1. G. Vesey, 'Conditioning and Learning' in R.S. Peters (ed.), *The Concept of Education* (Routledge & Kegan Paul, London, 1967).

2. M. Oakeshott, 'Learning and Teaching' in R.S. Peters (ed.), *The Concept of Education* (Routledge & Kegan Paul, London, 1967), pp. 156-7.

3. N.L. Munn, *The Evolution and Growth of Human Behaviour* (Houghton Mifflin, Boston, 1965), p. 218.

4. P.H. Hirst and R.S. Peters, *The Logic of Education* (Routledge & Kegan Paul, London, 1970), p. 75.

2.4

ADULT LEARNING AND INDUSTRIAL TRAINING

Mike Smith

Source: Michael Howe (ed.), *Adult Learning: Psychological Research and Applications* (John Wiley, London, 1977), pp. 187-202.

The Context of Industrial Training

In theory at least, the *sine qua non* of adult learning in industry is the contribution it can make towards increasing the efficiency of the workforce. In practice, the situation is not so clear. One of the complicating factors is that training is only one of a whole variety of interchangeable ways of achieving this objective of increasing the efficiency and range of a workforce. Industrial trainers are sometimes apt to forget that improved selection, improved equipment design and even judicious poaching of the more able employee of a competitor may be solutions which are more cost-effective than increased training. In a nutshell, the point is that training must be kept in its context as *one* management tool. Another complicating factor is the complexity of organizational goals. These goals will have a crucial bearing on the amount of adult learning which is planned and carried out. Traditionally, the only goal of industry is considered to be the maximization of shareholders' profit. In today's conditions this view may be naive: in certain situations social and political objectives can be more important. Training may, for example, be politically expedient in times of unemployment because it is one easy action which politicians can be seen to be taking. In other situations, perhaps in a small family firm, or in certain departments of larger firms, the overriding organizational goal may not be efficiency but to provide a pleasant and congenial pastime for the proprietor and long-serving employees during their declining years. In such situations, the quantity and quality of adult learning required may be somewhat circumscribed.

In spite of these necessary qualifications, it would be difficult to underestimate the amount of industrial training which is undertaken by a multiplicity of different bodies. Most obviously, training is undertaken by the organizations themselves. The organizations need not be industrial organizations in the strict sense. The police force, health authorities, the armed forces and large catering organizations are good examples of non-industrial concerns which have to make a substantial training effort. If there is a geographical concentration of firms with similar training interests, they may pool their training effort in some form of group training scheme. These group schemes are particularly suitable where the individual firms are too small to justify their own training facilities, or where the training need is very specialized. Other types of training may be organized at the level of a whole industry, by the appropriate Industrial Training Board or the appropriate trade association. Still other types of training may be organized at national level by the government agencies such as the Training Services Agency, whose own Skill Centres aim to provide occupational training in basic skills such as bricklaying, computer programming or typing. Or the resources of the educational system may be used to provide day-release courses, block release courses or evening classes.

A General Training Paradigm?

In a field as complex as industrial training, where the 'special' situation is the rule rather than the exception, it is impossible to outline an approach which has universal generality. However, probably most industrial training specialists would accept an idealized paradigm containing six steps, which could be adopted as a basic model that could be modified to suit particular situations. The six steps are: identifying objectives, analysing training needs, analysing tasks, preparing training, conducting training and finally, evaluation and modification of training.

Step 1: Identifying Objectives and Requirements

The initial stage of identifying objectives is often overlooked in the haste of getting a training course off the ground. This first stage requires close and clear communication between the policy-making bodies and the training department. The training department needs to know both the organization's immediate plans for the next year and the longer-term plans. It will need to know whether the organization is to expand, contract or change its 'product' or location in any significant way. It will also need to know if there is impending legislation, such as metrication or decimalization, which might affect the operation of the company and its workforce.

Step 2: Identifying Training Tasks

The second stage is to identify those objectives and requirements which are best met by training techniques rather than other management techniques. If the tasks which are identified are very complex, it may be necessary to formalize this stage into a coherent plan whereby the tasks are broken down into smaller units and time-scheduled in the best sequence.

Step 3: Task Analysis

Once the objectives have been operationalized into training tasks, some form of task analysis will usually be undertaken. The exact form of task analysis will depend entirely on the parameters of the actual situation. Blum and Naylor (1968) offer a relatively comprehensive overview of the methods available, while Annett and Duncan (1967) and Duncan (1974) discuss some of the basic issues involved. A practical example of the role of task analysis in the adult retraining of gasmen is described by Dodd (1967).

Probably the most widely used techniques of task analysis are the critical incident approach pioneered by Flanagan (1954) and the skills analysis propounded by Seymour (1968). In essence, the critical incident approach adopts the view that while a job requires many activities such as memo-writing, clocking in, form-filling, only a few activities have a critical impact in so far that a substandard performance of these activities will be reflected in a substandard outcome. Identifying these critical incidents and specifying how they should be performed can be highly technical, but in a practical setting they will often be determined by systematically asking groups of competent and skilled workers or their supervisors. Once the critical tasks have been established, methods of performing them are devised after observation, analysis and interpretation of the way they are performed by a skilled worker.

Seymour's approach is directly relevant to this latter stage. The skills analysis propounded by Seymour (1968) divides job content into two main areas, *knowledge* content and *skill* content. The *knowledge* content may be further subdivided into (1) workplace knowledge — the knowledge of the workplace that the worker needs to have in order to get to his workbench and be ready and able to perform his work, the names of machines, tools, materials and processes; and (2) quality knowledge — the tolerances and production standards to be met. The *skills* content focuses on *how* a worker *does* his job. By observation, analysis of videotapes or slow-motion cine film, each action will be broken down into the actions of the right hand and those of the left hand. In addition, the visual cues, the tactile and kinesthetic cues and unusual or difficult movements or sensory discrimination will be identified. Seymour's approach was developed for operatives, largely in the knitwear industry, but it is surprising to see how, with some modification, it may be applied to more recent concerns such as social skills training.

Step 4: Preparing Instruction Schedules

Once the tasks to be learned have been identified and adequately described, the next step is to prepare instruction schedules which will efficiently impart knowledge and skill to the trainees. Only at this step are the range of learning factors encountered, including knowledge of results, massed versus distributed practice, sequence of learning and motivation. A good review of these factors in learning efficiency is offered by Gagné and Bolles (1959), and Glaser's (1965) approach adds emphasis on 'entering behaviour', i.e. the state of the trainee when he starts training. This emphasis is a welcome reminder that trainees are individuals who vary according to their abilities, knowledge and skills. Often, choosing the right 'learning method' is difficult.

One of the most useful guides is the CRAMP training design algorithm (Pearn, 1975). The acronym CRAMP was developed by R.M. Belbin (1969) as a mnemonic for *five major types of learning* commonly encountered in adult learning situations:

*C*omprehension-type learning or understanding theoretical subject matter;
*R*eflex-skills learning of skilled movements such as sewing, machining;
*A*ttitude development, say towards the public whom the trainees have to encounter;
*M*emorization; and
*P*rocedural-type learning of a series of simple instructions.

The algorithm incorporates the advantages and disadvantages of about *twenty different training techniques*, ranging from the magnification method, cueing and fading, to the progressive part method or the cumulative part method of learning.

The two major elements, the types of learning and the training techniques, can be connected by a flow diagram which starts with the different types of learning, and, taking into account other task characteristics and characteristics of the trainees, traces a path of the most appropriate training technique for the circumstances. For example, if training is essentially a substantial memory task and the trainees are aged over 30, the path might lead to the cumulative part method. On the other hand, a substantial memory task involving trainees under the age of 30 might lead to the progressive part method. In still different situations, discovery learning or case studies, or role-playing or T-groups, might be recommended.

Granted that any algorithm designed to assist the identification of the most suitable training method must have its limitations, it is unfortunate that the CRAMP training design algorithm pays scant attention to the social behaviour of trainees during training. Indeed, it is probably symptomatic of a more general neglect of social factors, which is surprising since the attitudes of the trainee, the interpersonal relations in the training situation and inter-group relations between trainees, experienced workers and management can nullify courses of action which appear to be perfect as far as the learning factors are concerned.

Step 5: Conducting Training

Discussions of training design often take for granted the obvious step of conducting the training. Indeed, in practice the training itself sometimes seems to get lost among the administrative chores of arranging instruction, timetabling and record-keeping. At this stage the skills of the instructor, the efficiency of equipment and the adequacy of accommodaticn are crucial. For example, problems arise concerning selection and training of instructors, availability of accommodation and adapting it to provide a suitable training environment, and providing sufficient learning aids in the right place at the right time.

Step 6: Evaluation

The final stage in the generalized training paradigm is evaluation to check if the training has achieved its objective. At operative level, this stage is relatively simple. The performance of trainees in terms of quantity and quality is measured and compared to experienced worker standard — which will have been previously established by pragmatic procedure. Evaluation of other levels of training presents more problems. In management training in particular, where timespan of discretion — the time-lag between a decision and its consequences — may be many years, evaluation is very difficult.

In other cases, where the primary aim of training is a change of attitude, a variety of attitude measurement techniques may be required. One promising technique for use in this area is the repertory grid, based on Kelly's personal construct theory (Kelly, 1955). The repertory grid method is statistically very complex, but it has the advantage of allowing each individual to construct a measuring instrument which is uniquely relevant to himself. In essence, the trainee is asked to name the elements (usually the people such as 'my boss', 'a subordinate', 'a colleague') which are relevant to him. He is then presented with random triads of the elements he has nominated and asked to say which of the three is the odd man out, and why. In this way the constructs (that is, the way the elements are thought about, for example, old fashioned, good, ambitious) are elicited. The elements and constructs are cast in a grid, with the elements along the top and the constructs down the side. The subject is then asked to rate each of the elements on each of the constructs. From the results it is possible to gauge a subject's cognitive complexity in a given area and to build a model of his construct system and one of the relationships between the different elements.

To measure the attitudinal learning resulting from training, the models obtained before and after training can be contrasted and, if possible, compared with the models obtained from the grids of control groups. Unfortunately, promising though it is, the technique has a number of limitations: it is time-consuming and sometimes difficult to use in a group-testing situation and, because the initial stages are very unstructured, it may place a strain on the rapport between the trainer and the trainee. One good example of the use of repertory grids in the evaluation of management training is given by Smith and Ashton (1975).

Evaluation of some kind is an essential step in developing a system for adult learning in industry which is both relevant and effective. Ideally, evaluation and the development of criterion measures should be considered as soon as the training objectives have been defined. In practice, however, training evaluation is a hard row to hoe. In an industrial setting, where production is paramount, evaluation may give rise to pressures on staff, time and resources, and it is often difficult to obtain adequate control groups, or to set aside 10 per cent of the training budget for evaluation programs.

Selection for Training

An element which is so far missing from the generalized training paradigm is the selection of trainees. There are, of course, situations where selection is either unnecessary or impractical. If the skills are simple and can be learned by the vast majority of people, the interposition of a selection procedure for trainees merely represents an additional cost with a very small yield. Similarly, in a period of labour shortage and of buoyant demand, employers may be happy to engage anyone who in the words of some employers 'is still warm and has the strength to work the doorbell'. In most situations, however, the cost of trainees who either leave before the end of training or fail to reach experienced worker standard is sufficiently high to justify a selection procedure designed to detect and eliminate the most likely of these cases.

The array of procedures used to select trainees is vast and ranges from the humble five-minute interview to careful psychometric testing or the use of special tests to measure trainability *per se*. Psychometric tests of personality such as Cattell's 16 PF test or the Guilford-Zimmerman test are most useful at the level of management training. Multiple regression equations exist which attempt to predict characteristics such as the ability to 'grow' into a new job, scholastic aptitude or likely professionalism (Cattell *et al.*, 1970). Attainment tests can be used at the level of technician training to establish if intending trainees have the background knowledge necessary in order to benefit from further training. At operative level, tests of practical abilities such as manual dexterity have been found useful. For example, the Purdue pegboard, a test which requires pins to be placed in holes using a pair of tweezers, has been used in the knitwear industry to select trainees for delicate jobs such as 'linking' where the stitches from the neck of the garment have to be picked up and matched with the stitches of the collar.

In recent years there have been attempts to measure training *per se*, and a number of these trainability tests have been developed at the Industrial Training Research Unit, Cambridge (Downs, 1970). The essence of 'trainability tests' is that the potential trainee is shown how to perform a typical sample of the job she will have to learn. This job sample is chosen according to three main parameters: (1) it is based on the key elements in the job, (2) it involves only those elements which can be imparted in the short learning period of the test, i.e. under 30 minutes, and (3) it is difficult enough to discriminate between capable and incompetent applicants. The instructors then demonstrate the task to the trainees and after a short practice the trainees are asked to produce the item by themselves. The amount they have learnt is gauged by checking off the mistakes they make against a checklist of errors. On the basis of this 'score' and other observations, the instructor comes to a conclusion regarding the trainees' trainability potential.

When all the steps of the generalized training paradigm are considered as a whole, they can be taken to form a training subsystem which resides within the wider system of an industrial organization. An overall appreciation of this subsystem is more easy to obtain when it is stated in diagrammatic form. With systems diagrams such as Figure 1 or similar diagrams produced by Eckstrand (1964), Tilley (1968) and Dodd (1967), the causal relationships between the interlocking parts can be made explicit. The timing and nature of the consequences of disturbances in various parts of the system can be predicted with greater ease and precision.

One final point to consider before leaving the topic of the generalized training paradigm is the assumptions it makes about organizational structure. Generally it assumes that business is organized

Figure 1: A Generalized Training Paradigm

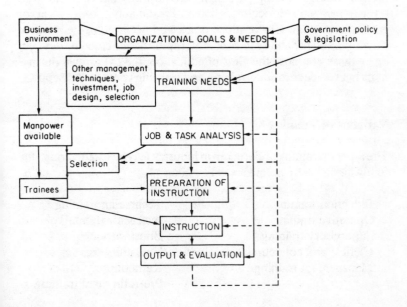

according to the Weberian bureaucratic model, with considerable role specification and clear lines of authority based on logic and rational 'laws'. This type of organizational structure, epitomized by the organizational chart that pervades many companies in both the industrial and service sectors of the economy, was perhaps a reasonably good approximation to large business organizations in the first half of this century. But it has been increasingly criticized by organizational theorists. Merton (1952) and Argyris (1974), for example, claim that this type of organization leads to dysfunctions. Furthermore, Toffler (1972) suggests that an accelerating rate of change will be *the* characteristic of the future. Business organizations will need to adapt to new problems by quickly forming *'ad hoc'* groups of individuals whose pooled experience and knowledge would seem likely to find a solution. Once the particular problem has been solved the group would be dissolved. Thus Weber's bureaucracy will be replaced by forms of *'ad hocracy'*. If this development occurs, it will clearly have great implications for the organization of adult learning in industry. Learning in the form of training for the performance of clearly prescribed roles will be useless. By the time all the stages of the generalized training paradigm have been followed, and some allowance made for evaluation and feedback, the situation may have changed and the training been abandoned. The problem of replacing the generalized training paradigm with another that can cope with these stresses is difficult to solve. Presumably, some form of generalized training to produce quick and accurate perceptions of situations and the ability to cope with rapid change could be devised. Since these are more the aims of education, the overdrawn distinctions between education, training and learning could well disappear.

Varieties of Training

The types of training undertaken in industry may be listed, though the following list is by no means exhaustive:

Induction training	Technician training
Operative training	Instructor training
Supervisory training	Booster training
Clerical and commercial training	Versatility training
Management training	Retraining
	Pre-retirement training

Most of these categories are fairly self-explanatory and simply take their name from the category of personnel involved, shedding little light on the actual training undertaken.

Induction training is a fairly familiar concept inspired by the need to reduce the high rates of labour turnover which are commonly experienced among new recruits. Usually, it consists of two main elements: providing essential information such as the location of the wages office, lavatories and canteen, and instructing in essential procedures such as safety routines or how to make out a work docket; in addition, as Morea (1972) points out, induction training can help the socialization of the trainee into a new workgroup.

Booster training and versatility training are less common. *Booster* training is used when the level of operative performance has fallen below some acceptable limit. The operatives are then given some extra training designed to improve either the quality or the quantity of output. Usually the emphasis is on improving the speed of performance while still maintaining quality standards. One useful device involved in booster training is the pacing machine (Toye, 1973). The operative's task will be broken down into its constituent segments. The operative will then sit at the machine for short periods of about 30 minutes each day and, while she is performing her job, auditory signals will be given to mark the point when she should have completed each particular segment of her task. Initially the timing of the signals will be generous, so that she can easily complete each segment in time. On subsequent days the timing will be gradually speeded up until the required speed of performance is obtained. Various types of pacing machine are available. Some merely give a signal at the end of each segment, while others give continuous information by using a signal of increasing pitch or volume during each segment.

Versatility training simply involves learning to do more than one job. It is particularly important in small firms who employ only a few workers on each process. Eventualities such as absence and illness of staff happen infrequently, but when they do arise the absence of one person can create a bottleneck in the production process, because that one worker may represent 50 per cent of productive capacity at that point. Few small firms can afford either supernumeraries to give cover in these situations or the alternative of holding large stocks. The most practical answer is to train a few workers up to an acceptable standard in several skills so that they can be redeployed to avoid bottlenecks building up. Both versatility training and booster training are distinctive in that the trainees are almost invariably long-term employees who have a great deal of background knowledge about the firm, its products and its methods.

Another dimension to the training process is the place where training is carried out. Here, the main alternatives can be listed as:

(a) on-the-job training (the sit-by-Nellie method)
(b) vestibule training
(c) training centres
(d) training in educational centres.

On-the-job training has been the backbone of apprenticeships since before medieval days. On starting work the recruit is told to 'sit by Nellie' and watch what she does. Sit-by-Nellie training has the advantage of being realistic, and is widely accepted as the 'proper' method of training. Unfortunately, it has a number of powerful disadvantages. The success of 'sit-by-Nellie' training depends largely on the characteristics of Nellie herself. She may pass on inefficient working methods and restrictive attitudes. Furthermore, Nellie has her own job to do. Even though she may be paid a small premium for taking a trainee under her wing, it may not be considered adequate compensation for the trouble of having the trainee under her feet, and she may not be prepared or able to devote time and thought to the learning processes of the trainee. The selection of Nellie as the trainee's mentor raises other issues. In all probability, Nellie will not have been trained in the essential skills of job analysis and communication. Indeed, she may have been chosen because she is the 'best' or fastest worker, but it is risky to assume that the fastest worker is the best instructor. The consequence of these disadvantages is that on-the-job training usually takes a long time. Contrary to first impressions, when the trainee's wages, Nellie's wages and factory overheads are included, on-the-job training can prove very costly indeed.

In an attempt to overcome these drawbacks, the Government's TWI (Training Within Industry) scheme includes Job Instruction in one of its modules. The course takes about ten hours and is usually split into two five-hour sessions. It is given to Nellie within the factory itself by qualified training officers. The aim of the course is to impart the basic skills of operative training which can then be used in the on-the-job, sit-by-Nellie situation.

Vestibule training, which takes place in a special area — either a training school or an area of the workshop that has been set aside — is generally more efficient at getting trainees up to experienced worker standard in a short time. It may even be possible to arrange an ideal learning environment. There may, however, be acute problems at the end of training when the trainee is moved from the seclusion of the training school to the rigours of the factory floor.

In principle, *training in training centres* such as the Government Skill Centres is much the same as vestibule training but with the disadvantages writ large. Because training centres may have to cater for the needs of several firms, the training has to be more general, so that the specific modes of working have to be gained after starting work with a specific employer. This, and other considerations, can make the transition from the training centre to the factory floor quite traumatic.

It is perhaps at the level of technical training and clerical training that *training in educational establishments* is most important. Evening classes are almost universally accepted as the means by which employees can better themselves. Indeed, among the older generation of supervisors and lower management, evening classes were probably the main and perhaps the only form of formal training they received, and they usually look back on their recollections with great affection. After 20 or 30 years of technical change, it is doubtful if the night school system is, on its own, an adequate means of transmitting the complex or involved and intricate technological skills needed today. Other trainees may be fortunate enough to be granted day releases for one day a week from their firm in order to attend the local 'technical college'. A slightly different pattern, useful in cases where the daily journey from work to technical college is too long, is the block release system where trainees will go to college, perhaps having accommodation found for them, for a two-or three-week concentrated course. Unfortunately, block release courses are sometimes unpopular because it can place a great strain on the factory floor if one individual is absent for prolonged periods. Another disadvantage is that some trainees have difficulty in assimilating such concentrated instruction. [...]

References

Annett, J. and Duncan, K. (1967) 'Task Analysis and Training Design', *Occupational Psychology, 41*, 211
Argyris, C. (1974) *Applicability of Organizational Sociology*, Cambridge University Press
Belbin, R.M. (1969) *The Discovery Method in Training*, HMSO, London
Blum, M.L. and Naylor, J.C. (1968) *Industrial Psychology*, Harper & Row, New York

Cattell, R.B., Eber, H.W. and Tatsuoka, M.M. (1970) *Handbook for the 16PF*, NFER, Windsor, Berks

Dodd, B. (1967) 'A Study in Adult Retraining: The Gas Man', *Occupational Psychology, 41*, 143

Downs, S. (1970) 'Predicting Training Potential', *Personnel Management*, 26 (September)

Duncan, K. (1974) 'Analytical Techniques in Training Design' in E. Edwards and F.P. Lees (eds.), *The Human Operator in Process Control*, Taylor & Francis, London

Eckstrand, G.A. (1964), 'Current Status of the Technology of Training', *AMRL Document Technical Report, 64*, 86 (September)

Flanagan, J.C. (1954) 'The Critical Incident Technique', *Psychological Bulletin, 51*, 327

Gagné, R.M. and Bolles, R.C. (1959) 'A Review of Factors in Learning Efficiency' in E. Galanter (ed.), *Automatic Teaching: The State of the Art*, Wiley, New York, pp. 21-48

Glaser, R. (1965) 'Psychology and Instructional Technology' in R. Glaser (ed.), *Training Research and Education*, Wiley, New York

Kelly, G.A. (1955) *The Psychology of Personal Constructs*, Norton, New York

Merton, R.K. (ed.)(1952) *Reader in Bureaucracy*, Free Press, New York

Morea, P.C. (1972) *Guidance, Selection and Training*, Routledge & Kegan Paul, London

Pearn, M. (1975) CRAMP *A Guide to Training Decisions: A User's Manual*, ITRU Research Paper, Industrial Training Research Unit, Cambridge

Seymour, D.W. (1968) *Skills Analysis Training*, Pitman, London

Smith, M. and Ashton, D. (1975) 'Using Repertory Grid Technique to Evaluate Management Training', *Personnel Review, 4*, 15

Tilley, K. (1968) 'A Technology of Training' in D. Pym (ed.), *Industrial Society*, Penguin, Harmondsworth

Toffler, A. (1972) *Future Shock*, Pan Books, London

Toye, M. (1973) *Pacing and Pacing Machines: An Evaluation*, ITRU Research Paper TR4, Industrial Training Research Unit, Cambridge

THE NATURE AND PROCESS OF ADULT DEVELOPMENT

Paula Allman

Source: Copyright © The Open University 1983 (specially written for this volume).

Introduction: The Plasticity Model of Adult Development

By the end of the 1970s most developmental psychologists were acknowledging a new body of descriptive and experimental evidence which indicated that cognitive (i.e. thinking) decline was *not* a necessary consequence of ageing. This evidence and the research methodology which produced it constituted an effective challenge to a much larger body of psychological evidence which had supported the socially persistent stereotype of inevitable and irreversible decline with advancing age. In the 1960s psychologists had formulated more complex and sophisticated research designs, in order to correct recognised biases in the designs which were normally used to produce descriptive evidence on development. What they found was that whether or not individuals' cognitive or thinking abilities decline, remain stable or continue to develop over the years of adulthood 'depends' on the interplay of many factors. Psychologists began to recognise that development, or the lack of it, during adulthood was inextricably linked to the degree and quality of individuals' inter-actions with their social and historical contexts. Since such inter-actions could fluctuate the pattern of development could as well. This model of development has been called the 'plasticity' model.

Though the evidence of the 1970s may complicate our thinking about adult development, it does make it quite clear that people have a 'potential' for continuing development across the entire life-span, and this idea has revolutionised our thinking about adults. To say that the 'potential' of adults is for lifelong cognitive development contradicts the prevailing view that adulthood is a stable period of life at least until what was believed to be 'the inevitable consequences of ageing' cause decline in cognitive functioning. This non-developmental concept of adulthood was the only one available to adult educationalists until the mid-1970s. Directly and indirectly it has affected the practice of education for adults. If we expect adult learners to have fully mature and stable cognitive structures, then it is quite reasonable to define the developmental objectives of an educational experience within a somewhat limited framework. This is why adult educators have thought of development as either the further elaboration or accumulation of knowledge or the growth of self-knowledge and understanding. Both of these functions focus upon types of content or knowledge and assume that the processes and thought structures which deal with the content are unchanging. The revolution in our thinking about adults' potential for lifelong cognitive development requires that we re-examine our practice of adult education and discuss whether it is fulfilling its role in enabling this potential for continuing development to be realised.

When viewed together, our reconceptualisations regarding the nature of development during adulthood hold profound implications for adult educationalists. To me it seems indisputable that whenever in life there is potential for development the function of education is to enable it; and to achieve this function the educationalist must understand both the nature of what might be realised as well as the process by which development proceeds. However, it is worth noting that there is a fundamental difference between enabling the development of youth and the development of the adult. The teacher of children and adolescents will be enabling the learner to develop competencies, ideas and cognitive structures which the teacher has already developed. The enabling process where adults are involved demands a different perspective of development, because enabling in this context pertains equally to teacher and student. This difference alone would appear to require essentially different relationships between teachers and learners.

The evidence which has emerged from new, sequential research designs indicates that adults of all ages exhibit a 'plasticity' or fluctuation over time in their intellectual or thinking competencies. For example, on standard measures of intelligence some people between the ages of 70 and 84 showed gains and others showed losses (Schaie, 1975) and this was also true for other age groups. In addition, Huppert's comparatively recent British study (1982) indicates that if we look at individual performance, certain individuals in the oldest age group perform as well as, and a few outperform, the best scoring younger subjects. Nevertheless, even the evidence from these studies indicates that there is a tendency for the mean or average score of the younger age group to be higher than that of the older age groups; but, rather than attribute this to age *per se*, this tendency is now attributed to a whole range of contextual factors, such as changes in the quality and amount of education which these age groups, on average, have experienced. However, regardless of whether we look at individual or group performance, there remains the problem that we are looking at performance on standard measures of intelligence and these were derived from theory based on the study of child and adolescent development (Labouvie-Vief, 1980).

Not all intelligence tests are based on the same theory of child and adolescent development but all are designed to measure intellectual functions that human beings have the potential to develop by the age of 16. For example, according to Piaget's theory, which is the most widely accepted theory of child and adolescent development, the development of thinking proceeds towards and culminates some time during adolescence in the stage of formal operations, which involves the ability to apply abstract formal logic. Because we assumed adulthood to be a non-developmental period, our model of adult thought was the same as our model of fully matured adolescent thought. We hadn't bothered to ask the very important question which has only recently become the focus of adult developmental psychology, namely, *is* the nature of fully mature or effective adult thinking the same as the nature of fully mature and effective adolescent thought? It is of great credit to Piaget (1971, 1972) that, even though he never studied adults, he was one of the first psychologists to ask this question. In some of his last writings, Piaget predicted that certain changes would take place in formal reasoning during adulthood because adult experiences in work and social relationships would necessitate adaptations in adults' thinking processes. This concept of thought becoming progressively adaptive through interaction with adult life experiences is central to a great deal of the theory and research which has emerged in the study of adult development.

Dialectical Operations: An Integrative Framework

In my opinion, the most important recent theory regarding the nature of adult thought is the theory of 'dialectical operations' (Riegel, 1973). Though Riegel proposed this theory more than a decade ago, it was not until the 1980s that it began to have a concerted and widely acknowledged effect on psychologists' thinking about adult development. This theory is firmly grounded within the 'contextualist' framework or paradigm rather than the 'mechanistic' or 'organismic' paradigms in which psychological research and theory prior to the late 1970s had been couched. The 'contextualist' paradigm assumes that what people think and how they think emerges from people's transactions or interactions with their social and historical contexts. Since these contexts are dynamic, it is impossible to predict the most adaptive competencies which humans can develop or to predict an end stage in the developmental process. The mechanistic paradigm reflected the assumption that man was determined by internal and external factors, whilst the organismic paradigm placed an emphasis on people as the active agents in their own development which was seen to unfold according to some inherent predisposition of our species.

In explaining his theory of 'dialectical operations' Riegel reminds us that Piaget's theory was based on the model of formal logic, and that we might have to look to other systems of logic if we want to formulate a fully comprehensive model or theory of mature adult thought. One of the most important contributions of Piagetian theory was the realisation that the child's thought was qualitatively different from the mature adolescent's. The stages of cognitive development identified by Piaget demonstrated a progression from pre-logical or pre-operational thought through to formal operational thought, the processes of which conform to the model of formal logic. Child cognitive development therefore is not simply a process involving further accumulations of knowledge but a process entailing qualitative transformation in the structures of thought and modes of thinking.

The most essential principle of formal logic is 'identity' or the concept that an object may retain certain characteristics, such as quantity, mass or volume, even when it undergoes observable change. When individuals are using formal operational thought, they are seeking to resolve contradictions between what they see or perceive and what they think or know. The resolution of contradiction in formal thinking necessitates the development of hypotheses to test the variables involved in a given situation and deduce their cause-effect relationships. Riegel accepted that formal logic constituted a model for certain types of adult thinking or even stages in the adult's thinking with reference to certain types of problems, but argued that the nature of adult thinking was potentially more complex. This is why he suggested that we consider other systems of logic to cull a more comprehensive model of adult thinking, and to explain the more complex and adaptive forms of thinking that adults have the potential to develop as they interact with adult life experiences, and the complex problems which arise from those experiences.

Riegel's theory draws on a system of dialectic logic (i.e. reasoning) wherein 'contradiction' rather than 'identity' is the most essential feature. The principle of contradiction implies that an object or some entity has a given quality and at the same time does not have that quality or has another quality, the presence of which contradicts the first. For example, a person's self-concept might define that person as being a tolerant person whilst recognising and even tolerating the fact that certain circumstances influence them to react in an intolerant manner. According to Riegel, the most effective adult thinking and thinking which causes advancement whether in scientific pursuits or personal and social relationships, is not that which provides immediate answers but that which first discovers the important questions and/or poses the important problems. Therefore, it is not primarily a matter of eliminating contradiction but of tolerating it and thus allowing for new questions and problems to emerge. This does not mean that mature or dialectic thought never reaches a state of equilibrium but when it does it is a resting point, a temporary resolution, rather than an immutable structure.

Riegel also pointed out that formal operational thinking involves a separation of thought from reality, i.e. thought becomes increasingly abstract and therefore alienated from the subject or content of thought. Riegel contends that effective adult thinking entails a reuniting of thought with reality. Only when the processes of thinking are applied and adjusted in terms of concrete reality can complex problems be explored effectively. Ulric Neisser (1982) has also reached much the same conclusion in his critique of psychological research into memory and learning:

In short, the results of a hundred years of the psychological study of memory are somewhat discouraging. We have established firm empirical generalisations, but most of them are so obvious that every ten year old knows them anyway. We have made discoveries, but they are only marginally about memory; in many cases we don't know what to do with them, and wear them out in endless experimental variations. We have an intellectually impressive group of theories, but history offers little confidence that they will provide meaningful insight into natural behaviour ... because they say so little about the everyday uses of memory, they seem ripe for the same fate that overtook learning theory not so long ago. (pp. 11 and 12)

Neisser is arguing that theories about memory are meaningless because they pertain to 'esoteric laboratory tasks' rather than to the use of memory in terms of people's concrete reality. Riegel is simply extending this idea a bit further by saying that real thinking and effective thinking processes, including memory, must be reunited with concrete reality, and that to understand the nature of adult thought we must observe it in this process of reunion.

There are several reasons why I think Riegel's ideas are of extreme importance. They introduce the hypothesis that mature adult thought, or the type of thought which adults have the potential to develop, is qualitatively different from the thought of adolescents or very young adults. This hypothesis has led to a more serious study of the potential for cognitive development and the nature of thought during the adult years. Riegel's theory also provides a framework which, in my opinion, links or integrates several other findings and theories regarding adult development which may previously have appeared to be unrelated. This integration — of ideas from cognitive development research, ego development, moral development, the development of learners' concepts of learning and knowledge, and other areas — provides a foundation of theory and research from which we can begin to draw implications about the most appropriate approach for supporting and facilitating adult development through learning or educational experiences.

To view this research within the parameters of contextualism is slightly problematic; because some of it, like that which produced the 'plasticity model', is caught in transition between organicism and contextualism.[1] Even Riegel's theory could be easily misinterpreted as a stage theory, i.e. one which predicts a known sequence of stages with definable outcomes. Psychologists, whose work derives from the contextualist paradigm, would dispute the basic assumptions of stage theories because contextualism assumes that thought emerges from the human being's interaction with a constantly changing, social-historical context. To interpret Riegel's as a stage theory is incorrect, to my way of thinking, because of the very nature of dialectical thought. Whereas, when someone is thinking according to formal logic, we can give them a problem and predict very accurately what answer they will give, we cannot predict the results or consequences of dialectical thought. By this I mean that we cannot know what questions will emerge or what problems will be discovered when another person engages in thinking dialectically about their reality. Nor can we set limits on the degree or quality to which one can come to 'know' something as this will be developing in interaction with the dynamics of the social-historical context. Furthermore, we cannot predict an end state or stage in the development of human thinking because new and progressively adaptive forms of thinking may result as a consequence of dialectical thought as well as from the interaction of thought with social and historical change. Therefore, though some of the research and theory we will be discussing does not fall entirely within the contextualist paradigm, it is my opinion that Riegel's theory of dialectic operations does.

Arlin (1975) hypothesised that formal operations were not the final stage of cognitive development. In confirmation of this hypothesis, she found that the ability to ask or discover important questions emerged subsequent to the stage of formal operations. Arlin's work is widely quoted in the literature on adult cognitive development, but has received neither considerable challenge nor support from repeated studies. This is equally true of Sinnot's (1975) study of the formal operational ability of adults. Sinnot designed a series of tasks which demanded formal operational thought with reference to the types of problem content adults confront in everyday living. Previously, researchers had assessed the extent of formal operational thinking in adults with the same types of problem content Piaget had used to assess adolescents. Whereas little evidence of adults' formal operational ability had been found in those studies, Sinnot's study showed a far higher percentage of adults to be capable of formal operational thought. Arlin's work testifies to the importance or developmental superiority of question asking and/or problem posing, and Sinnot's emphasises the importance of reuniting formal thought with problems which emerge from the reality of adult life. As such, neither of the studies is fully supportive of Riegel's theory but each touches upon and offers support for certain aspects of the theory of dialectic operations.

Though Riegel does not emphasise this point, it is my contention that one of the basic structures of dialectic thought is reflectivity. Neugarten (1977) in her research into the salient features of middle age reported that reflective thinking became increasingly prevalent during the middle years of adulthood. And Piaget (1967) suggested that the reflective processes in formal operational thinking during adolescence only reach equilibrium or maturity when the adolescent stops using reflection to oppose experience and begins to use these processes to interpret and predict experience. In other words, Piaget is suggesting that the reunion of reflection with concrete reality produces a more mature type of reflection. I suspect that what Neugarten is referring to as an increase in reflectivity is, in fact, the use of a qualitatively altered form of reflectivity.

It may be that this type of reflective thought is a basic thought structure which emerges during the adult years and which allows for the development of the more advanced forms of thinking, such as dialectic thought. If so, it would be similar to the basic structures which develop in the child's thought, such as concept formation and conservation. Moshman (1979) has demonstrated that meta-theoretical thought — thinking about one's own theories — develops subsequent to formal operational problem solving. Whether this ability is necessary to, or follows from mature reflection, as I have defined it, and whether it is necessary to Arlin's stage of question asking or to dialectic operations, and therefore precedes the development of these forms of thinking, is not clear but would seem to be probable. Reflecting on how we think about the content of our environment and experiences may be a necessary prerequisite to asking questions, discovering problems and to contradiction becoming a basis for thought.

In the study of the continuing development of ego or identity during the adult years, I have argued elsewhere (Allman, 1982) that Erikson's theory of psychosocial ego development can be reinterpreted at least to some extent according to a dialectical model or within a contextualist perspective. Erikson (1959) proposes that the dynamic of ego development is the interaction of the individual's psychological processes with their social context, though he tends to ignore the dynamic nature of that context. Erikson suggests that the interaction with the social context introduces crucial issues with which the individual must deal if development is to proceed. Each issue is embodied in a dialectical tension between two polar or opposite ways of resolving the issue. For example, the establishing of identity is the most crucial issue of the adolescent years but will often re-emerge as a crucial issue in the course of adult life experiences, because interaction with experience enables the development of identity to be a lifelong process. Surrounding this issue is a creative dialectical tension between identity at one pole and role confusion at the other. The healthiest resolve is not to establish such a firm identity that the person's thinking or reflection becomes closed when interacting with new experiences; therefore, the questions which arise from the dialectical tension between role confusion and identity help to create a sense of identity which is open to change and development. Erikson's theory is usually described as a stage theory but to do so ignores some of the basic complexities of his theory, which allows that what is gained can be lost, and that what is not gained in the first instance can be gained later due to the interaction of psychological processes with social experience.

Also in the field of ego development, Loevinger (1976) has proposed a stage theory which depicts increasing complexity in the person's way of thinking as well as in the ways in which the person relates to others. The last three stages, to which adults can potentially progress, involve tolerance for ambiguities and would appear to demand that the persons can think in terms of contradiction or with at least some degree of dialectical thought. Even though Loevinger's theory conforms to the assumptions of a stage theory, I have placed it along with Erikson's within this framework because both of these theories differ in a fundamental way from other theories about the development of ego, identity, personality and self-concept (i.e. theories of personal development). When careful attention is paid to what these theories say, and especially when we consider Erikson in terms of the qualifications which Marcia (1966) has added, we can infer that ego development cannot proceed without the type of cognitive development depicted in the theory of dialectic operations. According to these theories, ego development is not simply the natural unfolding for which human beings have an inherent predisposition, which is the notion conveyed by theories which lie solidly within the organismic paradigm (Rogers, 1961; Maslow, 1970), but is underpinned and made possible by increasingly complex ways of thinking or a willingness to engage in thinking about complex issues.

If we now turn to the study of moral development, we find that Kohlberg (1976) has had an influence on theory and research which is comparable to Piaget's influence on the study of cognitive development. Kohlberg's theory is a stage theory which can be depicted briefly as moving from pre-conventional to conventional and finally post-conventional forms of moral reasoning. The development of operational thinking is a prerequisite to, but not a guarantee of, higher stages of moral reasoning. Pre-conventional responses to moral dilemmas are egocentric and/or absolutistic predeterminations of right and wrong. Conventional responses are aligned to the legal and moral codes of a given society; whereas post-conventional responses appeal to universal moral principles which may be in conflict with a particular society's legal or moral codes.

Various studies have revealed that the majority of adults resolve moral dilemmas or problems according to conventional moral reasoning. However, Gilligan and Murphy (1979) suggest that many of these adult responses which have been coded as conventional may actually entail advanced transformations of thought. In a longitudinal study, they asked adults to reflect upon post-conventional responses to moral problems which the same adults had given seven years earlier. In response to their earlier post-conventional thinking, these subjects were critical of the simplicity in their reasoning. They were able to see that they had not considered the consequences of their judgements because they had ignored the interdependence of their solutions with the social context. Gilligan and Murphy concluded that:

> These transformations arise out of the recognition of the paradoxical interdependence of self and society, which overrides the false simplicity of formal reason and replaces it with a more encompassing form of judgement. (p. 97)

These researchers are saying that adults may have been incorrectly assessed as conventional because the majority of researchers did not observe their development over a period of time, and did not delve thoroughly enough into the complexity of the adult response. These advanced transformations in moral reasoning involve the principle of contradiction and conform more appropriately to the model of dialectic rather than formal operations.

Gibbs (1981) reports several interesting studies regarding the development of learner's concepts of learning and knowledge. The most comprehensive theory to emerge from this work was offered by Perry (1970). He found that in the early stages of college or university study, students were dominated by a blind acceptance of authority and academic expertise and therefore tended to seek absolute and unchallengeable truths. Later, however, they move away from this form of thinking towards understanding that knowledge and authoritative explanations are relative. In the final stages of development, while continuing to accept the relativity of knowledge, many learners will form a commitment to particular explanations rather than others. If this progression were not studied longitudinally, and the learner's concepts of knowledge and learning comprehensively explored, a researcher could easily mistake the final stage as the first. However the difference is paramount. The final stage involves a recognition of and tolerance for contradiction, and therefore it appears to involve the development of dialectic operations.

This selection of theory and research offers a tentative yet much clearer and more comprehensive picture of the types of thinking which should be enabled when adults engage in educational or learning experiences. This tentative picture or description of the adult's developmental potential includes several factors. As adults we have the potential to develop the ability to think both formally and dialectically or to both solve and discover problems. In employing dialectic operations we have the ability to tolerate ambiguities and contradictions and perhaps even be excited by them. We also have the potential to form commitments to particular theoretical stances or explanations but only after engaging in considerable reflection and mental struggle with respect to the issues involved. The reunion of thought with reality may allow for continued qualitative refinements in both cognitive structures and identity or self-understanding. The ability to reflect upon and analyse the way we think about or theorise about experience should be a natural consequence of the development of mature reflection, which may well underpin many of the other developments in adult thought. As we continue to study the nature of adult thinking, and especially when we extend that study to cultures other than our own, we will no doubt be able to further elaborate this description of the adult's potential. However, we must also accept the tentative nature of the description, if we acknowledge the interdependence of adult thinking and the social historical context and thus the dynamic nature of both the relationship and the types of adult thinking which result from it.

To this tentative description of the potential nature of adult thought, we also need to add a concept of the process of development during adulthood. Stage theory concepts, which may be entirely appropriate when applied to childhood and adolescence when biological maturation is still taking place, led to the notion that the last competencies acquired in the stage sequence would be the first to be lost in the process of intellectual decline during adulthood (Coombs and Smith 1973). Therefore, stage theories are aligned to the maturational model of development. Labouvie-Vief (1980) reviews several studies which indicate that, like the maturational model, the last in/last out concept of the developmental process may not be appropriate when applied to adults. Instead, it has been proposed that a first in/first out or 'trade-off' model offers a more appropriate description of the process of development in adulthood. Labouvie-Vief and others have tested this hypothesis with reference to the study of memory. They found that older adults were not as competent as younger ones when the task required memory of detail. In psychological experiments most tasks do require memory of detail. However, if the researcher also introduces tasks calling for more advanced forms of memory, such as the memory of propositions or principles, then they find that older adults perform as well and often better than younger adults. In examining further the lost competence in memory of detail, Labouvie-Vief also found that older adults tended to adjust the detail they did recall so that it conformed with their past experiences.

If these studies are repeated and the 'trade-off' model — that certain competencies must be lost if more adaptive ones are to be gained — is found to be a more accurate description of the process of development with reference to other cognitive competencies, then we will have to add a further dynamic element to our concept of adult development. And as a result, adult educationalists will have to recognise that the types of thinking competence they encourage in young adults may be quite different from the competencies of which the adult is capable in middle and later life. Therefore, the nature of learning during the adult years may alter several times as a consequence.

Towards a Theory of Andragogy

Earlier in this article I made the assertion that most of the current practice in the education of adults must be grounded in a non-developmental view of adulthood because this was the only view available to us until quite recently. I would hope that this discussion of the revolutions in our thinking about adult development underlines both the necessity and the urgency of evaluating our current practice. Over the past two years a group of adult education colleagues and I have attempted to formulate a comprehensive theory of andragogy based on a consideration of this theory and research on the adult's developmental potential.

We began by studying what Knowles (1978) had to say about andragogy and by considering Mezirow's (1981) charter for andragogy. We agreed with a great deal of what they had to say, but continued to feel that andragogy was a term in search of a more comprehensive theory. At this point we discovered that a particular concept linked much of the work which had led to our tentative description of adult developmental potential. This was the concept that, in all aspects of adult development, the movement appeared to be in the direction of gaining ever increasing amounts of control over our thinking and therefore our lives. For example, if adults can accept contradiction and not be forced by the need for stability to have ready answers to complex problems, they are in control. As adults' sense of identity or knowledge of themselves and others grows in depth and meaning, they become increasingly in control of how they think about themselves. Reflective minds and minds not crowded with detail but in search of concepts, ideas and principles mean that people are in control of their thinking and have greater control over their transactions within their social-historical contexts. This, therefore, became our organising concept of adult development, and we then focused our thinking on how educational experiences for adults could best enable the development of control.

We were reminded that our concept of control was similar to if not synonymous with Paulo Freire's (1972) concept of education moving man from being 'adapted', i.e. controlled by cultural myths and the thinking of others, to being 'integrated', i.e. in control. Therefore, we spent a great deal of time reflecting upon Freire's ideas and attempting to transfer them to the context of formal adult education. We made the assumption that if we could transfer the salient features of Freire's ideas to the formal context, then the approach devised should also apply within community and other forms of informal and/or non-formal education for adults. The following is a brief description of an andragogical theory or approach as we have defined it (Nottingham Andragogy Group, 1983).

Andragogy should be conceived as a philosophically and theoretically based approach to the education of adults which derives from the emerging theory of adult development and which rests upon an identifiable set of assumptions about the nature of adult beings, the nature of learning, education, knowledge and adult development. With reference to the nature of adult beings and adult development, our assumptions are the same as those which derive from the contextualist paradigm; namely, human beings are social beings and are socially and historically interactive. Therefore, whilst contributing toward their own development and developments in society and history, they are influenced by what they and others have created and this is a lifelong process. Adult learning involves thinking in the increasingly complex ways that adults have the potential to develop. In fostering learning, knowledge can be viewed as either an open or a closed system. When viewed as open it is something to which learners can add or which they can alter through critical and creative thought. Even when perceived as a closed system it is viewed as something which the learner can use to solve problems or even to create new systems. As a consequence, education is not about transmission but rather it is about selection, synthesis and discovery through the process of dialogue. Dialogue is an essential process in Freire's educational method and involves, among other things, conscientisation through problem posing.

We have made the distinction that andragogy is an approach rather than a method. By this we mean that it embodies and expresses a philosophy of education for adults which rests on the assumptions and theory we've identified. In adult education there are two approaches which can be adopted, i.e. pedagogy or andragogy. Whether or not our assumptions differ fundamentally from those held by people who practise progressive pedagogy with children and adolescents must be decided by those whose expertise and experience derive from that base. However, we would argue that those who use a pedagogical approach with adults base their practice and their philosophy on a set of assumptions which differ fundamentally from those we have delineated.

We have viewed methods as part of the approach, be it andragogy or pedagogy and, as such, they mediate not only the intended content but also content or information about the assumptions underpinning the approach. Our andragogic approach would not exclude any category or type of method, but most methods would constitute fundamentally different learning experiences depending on whether they are used pedagogically or andragogically. Within an andragogic approach, a 'peer learning group', which includes the tutor, negotiates the curriculum, the objectives and the methods which will be used. They also negotiate decisions or questions regarding assessment and evaluation. Negotiation implies a sharing of power by all members of the group rather than an abrogation of power by the tutor; all members of the group contribute to decision making and the resourcing of learning. Method selection is based on decisions regarding the appropriateness for reaching a particular learning goal. The rationale for placing method selection as well as other decisions within the learning group rather than solely with the tutor is that to do so mediates the assumption that creative and critical thinking are important for all stages of the educational experience. It is therefore just as important to think creatively and critically about what to learn, how to learn and how to evaluate learning, as it is to do so in the process of learning. Also it is more likely to take place in learning if encouraged throughout the educational experience, because the approach is implying that adults have the potential to be in control of their learning and that it is therefore important for them to take and use this control.

Though we have couched our description of andragogy within the context of group learning, we feel that the assumptions hold equally well for individual learners. Our own experience has shown that it is a much more complex process to enable a group to become self-directed and in control than it is to enable individuals. But perhaps because of the complexity, the experience of learning and development is all the more valuable. It is hopefully clear that the andragogic approach involves a realignment of relationships within the learning group and a realignment of the learning group's relationship to learning and knowledge. These realignments are based on the recognition that in an adult educational or learning experience everyone is potentially a developing adult, and therefore the teacher cannot be assumed to be developmentally (as we have defined the term) superior to anyone else.

Other adult educationalists may well reject our theory of andragogy and choose to engage in their own analysis of current practice. We would welcome this debate and any critique which arises from others' evaluations especially if these derive from a consideration of our *adult* potential for development.

Note

1. The researchers who produced the plasticity model assumed that people developed through transactions or interactions with their contexts (contextualism), but continued to think in terms of predictable and unchanging cognitive competencies (organicism).

References

Allman, P. (1982) 'Adult Development: Implications for Student Support', a paper presented at the Comparative International Seminar on Local Support of Distance Students in Continuing and Higher Education, The Open University, East Midlands Regional Office, 23-28 September

Arlin, P.K. (1975) 'Cognitive Development in Adulthood: A Fifth Stage?', *Developmental Psychology, 11*, 602-6

Coombs, C.H. and Smith, J.E.K. (1973) 'Detection of Structure in Attitudes and Development Processes', *Psychological Review, 80*, 337-51

Erikson, E. (1959) *Identity and the Life Cycle. Psychological Issues*, No. 1, Monograph 1 with an introduction by Rapport, D.

Freire, P. (1972) *Pedagogy of the Oppressed*, Penguin, Harmondsworth

Gibbs, G. (1981) *Teaching Students to Learn: A Student-Centred Approach*, The Open University, Milton Keynes

Gilligan, C. and Murphy, J.M. (1979) 'Development from Adolescence to Adulthood: The Philosopher and the Dilemma of Fact' in Kuhn, D. (ed.), *Intellectual Development Beyond Childhood*, Jossey-Bass, London, pp. 85-99

Huppert, F. (1982) 'Does Mental Function Decline with Age?', *Geriatric Medicine*, January, pp. 32-7

Knowles, M.S. (1978) *The Adult Learner: A Neglected Species*, 2nd edn, Gulf Publishing Co., New York

Kohlberg, L. (1976) 'Moral Stages and Moralization: The Cognitive Developmental Approach' in Lickona, T. (ed.) *Moral Development and Behaviour*, Holt, Rinehart and Winston, New York

Kuhn, T.S. (1962) *The Structure of Scientific Revolutions*, University of Chicago Press, Chicago

Labouvie-Vief, G. (1980) 'Adaptive Dimensions of Adult Cognition' in Datan, N. and Lohman, N. (eds.), *Transitions of Aging*, Academic Press, London

Loevinger, J. (1976) *Ego Development: Conceptions and Theories*, Jossey-Bass, San Francisco

Marcia, J.E. (1966) 'Development and Validation of Ego-Identity Status', *Journal of Personality and Social Psychology, 3*, 551-8

Maslow, A.H. (1970) *Motivation and Personality*, 2nd edn, Harper and Row, New York

Mezirow, J. (1981) 'A Critical Theory of Adult Learning and Education', *Adult Education, 32 (1)*, 3-24

Moshman, D. (1979) 'To Really Get Ahead, Get a Metatheory' in Kuhn, D. (ed.), *Intellectual Development Beyond Childhood*, Jossey-Bass, London, pp. 59-68

Neisser, U. (1982) *Memory Observed: Remembering in Natural Context*, W.H. Freeman, Oxford

Neugarten, B. (1977) 'Adult Personality: Towards a Psychology of the Life-Cycle' in Allman, L.R. and Jaffe, D.T. (eds.), *Readings in Adult Psychology: Contemporary Perspectives*, Harper and Row, New York

Nottingham Andragogy Group (1983) *Towards a Developmental Theory of Andragogy*, Monograph No. 9 in Adults: Psychological and Educational Perspectives. Series edited by Allman, P. and Mackie, K., Nottingham University Department of Adult Education

Perry, W.I. (1970) *Forms of Intellectual and Ethical Development in the College Years: A Scheme*, Holt, Rinehart and Winston, New York

Piaget, J. (1967) *Six Psychological Studies*, Random House, New York

_____ (1971) *Biology and Knowledge*, University of Chicago Press, Chicago

_____ (1972) 'Intellectual Evolution from Adolescence to Adulthood',

Human Development, 15, 1-12
Riegel, K. (1973) 'Dialectic Operations: The Final Period of Cognitive
Development', *Human Development, 16,* 346-70
Rogers, C.R. (1961) *On Becoming a Person: A Therapist's View of Psychotherapy,*
Houghton Mifflin, Boston
Schaie, K.W. (1975) 'Age Changes in Adult Intelligence' in Woodruff, D.S. and
Birren, J.E. (eds.), *Ageing: Scientific Perspectives and Social Issues,* D. Van
Nostrand, New York, pp. 111-27
Sinnot, J.D. (1975) 'Everyday Thinking and Piagetian Operativity in Adults',
Developmental Psychology, 18(6), 430-43

A CRITICAL THEORY OF ADULT LEARNING AND EDUCATION

Jack Mezirow

Source: *Adult Education* (Adult Education Association of the USA, Washington, 1981) 32 (1), pp. 3-24.

[In the first part of his paper, which is not reproduced here, Jack Mezirow discusses the application of Jurgen Habermas's theory of knowledge to adult learning and education. Habermas has differentiated three generic areas in which human interest generates knowledge:

(1) the area of 'work', involving instrumental action to control or manipulate the environment, exemplified by the empirical-analytical sciences (e.g. physics, geology);
(2) the 'practical' area, involving interaction to clarify the conditions for communication and intersubjectivity, exemplified by the historical-interpretative sciences (e.g. history, theology, descriptive social sciences);
(3) the 'emancipatory' area, involving an interest in self-knowledge and self-reflection, exemplified by the critical social sciences (e.g. psychoanalysis, the critique of ideology).

Each of these three areas has its own techniques of interpretation, assessment and inquiry, and its own needs.[1]

Mezirow argues that the least familiar of the three areas or domains, the emancipatory, is of particular interest to adult educators.] [...]

Perspective Transformation

It is curious that the most distinctively adult domain of learning, that involving emancipatory action, is probably least familiar to adult educators. However, some readers will recognize the concept of

124

emancipatory action as synonymous with 'perspective transformation.' This mode of learning was inductively derived from a national study of women participating in college re-entry programs (Mezirow, 1975). Through extensive interviews, it became apparent that movement through the existential challenges of adulthood involves a process of negotiating an irregular succession of transformations in 'meaning perspective.' This term refers to *the structure of psychocultural assumptions within which new experience is assimilated and transformed by one's past experience.* For many women studied, such psychocultural assumptions involved the traditional stereotypic view of the 'proper' roles of women and the often strong feelings internalized in defense of these role expectations by women themselves.

Perspective transformation is the emancipatory process *of becoming critically aware of how and why the structure of psychocultural assumptions has come to constrain the way we see ourselves and our relationships, reconstituting this structure to permit a more inclusive and discriminating integration of experience and acting upon these new understandings.* It is the learning process by which adults come to recognize their culturally induced dependency roles and relationships and the reasons for them and take action to overcome them.

There are certain anomalies or disorienting dilemmas common to normal development in adulthood which may be best resolved only by becoming critically conscious of how and why our habits of perception, thought and action have distorted the way we have defined the problem and ourselves in relationship to it. The process involves what Freire (1970) calls 'problem posing,' making problematic our taken-for-granted social roles and expectations and the habitual ways we act and feel in carrying them out. The resulting transformation in perspective or personal paradigm is what Freire refers to as 'conscientization' and Habermas as emancipatory action. In asserting its claim as a major domain of adult learning, perspective transformation at the same time asserts its claim as a central function for adult education.

Our natural tendency to move toward new perspectives which appear to us more inclusive, discriminating and integrative of experience in attempting to resolve our disorienting dilemmas may be explained as a quest for meaning by which to better understand ourselves and to anticipate events. Carl Rogers has hypothesized '... a formative directional tendency in the universe which can be traced and observed in stellar space, in crystals, in microorganisms, in organic life, in human beings. This is an evolutionary tendency toward greater order, greater interrelatedness, greater complexity' (Rogers, 1978). As we will see, there are both cultural and psychological contingencies which can restrain our natural movement to learn through perspective transformation.

From our research on re-entry women, the dynamics of perspective transformation appeared to include the following elements: (1) a disorienting dilemma; (2) self examination; (3) a critical assessment of personally internalized role assumptions and a sense of alienation from traditional social expectations; (4) relating one's discontent to similar experiences of others or to public issues — recognizing that one's problem is shared and not exclusively a private matter; (5) exploring options for new ways of acting; (6) building competence and self-confidence in new roles; (7) planning a course of action; (8) acquiring knowledge and skills for implementing one's plans; (9) provisional efforts to try new roles and to assess feedback; and (10) a reintegration into society on the basis of conditions dictated by the new perspective.

The traumatic severity of the disorienting dilemma is clearly a factor in establishing the probability of a transformation. Under pressing external circumstances, such as death of a mate, a divorce or a family breadwinner becoming incapacitated, a perspective transformation is more likely to occur.

There appear to be two paths to perspective transformation: one is a sudden insight into the very structure of cultural and psychological assumptions which has limited or distorted one's understanding of self and one's relationships. The other is movement in the same direction that occurs by a series of transitions which permit one to revise specific assumptions about oneself and others until the very structure of assumptions becomes transformed. This is perhaps a more common pattern of development. The role transitions themselves are only opportunities for the kind of self-reflection essential for a transformation. In such cases the anomalous situation creating a disorienting dilemma may be the result of a more evolutionary personal history in which circumstances make a woman increasingly receptive to changing social norms regarding women's roles or internalized rigidities constraining her from becoming autonomous. There may be more women — and men too — familiar with Betty Friedan's 'problem without a name' than they are with many more easily labelled existential dilemmas of adulthood.

Paulo Freire has introduced adult educators to 'conscientization' as the process by which false consciousness becomes transcended in traditional societies through adult education.[2] The learning process in conscientization is seen in a different social context in women's consciousness raising groups and in college re-entry programs. From our study of this same process in re-entry women, it became apparent that Freire does not give sufficient cognizance to or make explicit the stumbling blocks which intervene to make this transformation in perspective itself highly problematic.

Although one does not return to an old perspective once a transformation occurs this passage involves a difficult negotiation and compromise, stalling, backsliding, self-deception and failure are exceedingly common. Habermas has clearly recognized this fact:

> We are never in a position to know with absolute certainty that critical enlightenment has been effective — that it has liberated us from the ideological frozen constraints of the past, and initiated genuine self-reflection. The complexity, strength and deviousness of the forms of resistance; the inadequacy of mere 'intellectual understanding' to effect a radical transformation; the fact that any claim of enlightened understanding may itself be a deeper and subtler form of self-deception — these obstacles can never be completely discounted in our evaluation of the success or failure of critique. (Bernstein, 1978, pp. 218-19)

In our study, we encountered women who simply transferred their identification from one reference group to another with the same absence of critical self-consciousness which characterized their traditional roles and relationships. However, our experience does not support the contention of Berger and Luckmann (1966) that perspective transformations, which they refer to as 'alternations,' involve a replay of the childhood process of primary socialization with its uncritical identification with and emotional dependency upon a new group of significant others. While these writers correctly emphasize the importance of significant others who represent the new and more attractive perspective, and a degree of identification is probably inevitable in the process of taking their perspective, the crucial difference between this process and that of a primary socialization is that adults are capable of being consciously critical or *critically reflective* in effecting these relationships. Children are critically unselfconscious and usually unaware of how circumstances have contrived to dictate their relationships and commitments to parents or mentors charged with their socialization.

In many cases of perspective transformation new commitments become mediated by a new critical sense of 'agency' and personal responsibility. Rather than a simple transfer of identification to a new reference group, a new set of criteria come to govern one's relationships and to represent conditions governing commitments as well. Rather than simple identification, the process may be more accurately described as one of *contractual solidarity*. Commitments are made with implicit mutual agreement among equals (in the sense of agency) concerning conditions of the relationship, including periodic review and renegotiation with the option of terminating the relationship. Such insistence upon reciprocity and equality often represents positive movement toward greater autonomy and self-determination. A superior perspective is not only one that is a more inclusive or discriminating experience of integrating but also one that is sufficiently permeable to allow one access to other perspectives. This makes possible movement to still more inclusive and discriminating perspectives. [...]

Critical Reflectivity

Perspective transformation fills an important gap in adult learning theory by acknowledging the central role played by the function of critical reflectivity. Awareness of *why* we attach the meanings we do to reality, especially to our roles and relationships — meanings often misconstrued out of the uncritically assimilated half-truths of conventional wisdom and power relationships assumed as fixed — may be the most significant distinguishing characteristic of adult learning. It is only in late adolescence and in adulthood that a person can come to recognize being caught in his/her own history and reliving it. 'A mind that watches itself' may be Albert Camus' definition of an intellectual, but it also describes an essential function of learning in adulthood. [...] Only in late adolescence or adulthood does one find theorizing about alternative paradigms of thought as sets of assumptions which significantly influence our selection of data and our interpretation of evidence.

The concept of critical reflectivity which plays so crucial a role in the adult learning process and in perspective transformation needs phenomenological study. We can simply become aware of a specific perception, meaning or behaviour of our own or of habits we have of seeing, thinking or acting. This is an act of *reflectivity*. *Affective reflectivity* refers to our becoming aware of how we feel about the way we are perceiving, thinking or acting or about our habits of doing so. Through *discriminant reflectivity* we assess the efficacy of our perceptions, thoughts, actions and habits of doing things; identify immediate causes; recognize reality contexts (a play, game, dream, or religious, musical or drug experience, etc.) in which we are functioning and identify our relationships in the situation. *Judgmental reflectivity* involves making and becoming aware of our value judgments about our perceptions, thoughts, actions and habits in terms of their being liked or disliked, beautiful or ugly, positive or negative.

Political, economic, sexual, technological and other cultural ideologies which we have assimilated become manifest in a set of rules, roles and social expectations which govern the way we see, think, feel and act. These ways of perception, thought and behaviour become habituated. Donald Maudsley (1979) has adapted the term 'meta-learning' to describe 'the process by which learners become aware of and increasingly in control of habits of perception, inquiry, learning and growth that they have internalized.' He sees these habits as important elements in understanding meaning perspectives. Meta-learning is a common element in almost every kind of learning from learning manual skills to learning in psychotherapy. Perspective transformation involves not only becoming critically aware of habits of perception, thought and action but of the cultural assumptions governing the rules, roles, conventions and social expectations which dictate the way we see, think, feel and act.

Critical awareness or critical consciousness is 'becoming aware of our awareness' and critiquing it. Some of the ways this is done may be discerned by reflecting upon the assertion 'John is bad.' The act of self-reflection which might lead one to question whether good or bad are adequate concepts for understanding or judging John may be understood as *conceptual reflectivity*. This is obviously different from the *psychic reflectivity* which leads one to recognize in oneself the habit of making precipitant judgments about people on the basis of limited information about them (as well as recognizing the interests and anticipations which influence the way we perceive, think or act). These two forms of critical consciousness may be differentiated from what may be called *theoretical reflectivity* by which one becomes aware that the reason for this habit of precipitant judgment or for conceptual inadequacy is a set of taken-for-granted cultural or psychological assumptions which explain personal experience less satisfactorily than another perspective with more functional criteria for seeing, thinking and acting. Theoretical reflectivity is thus the process central to perspective transformation.

There is an implicit ordering in the modes of reflectivity previously described, with most levels of reflectivity incorporating those preceding them. The degree to which they are age-related is unknown. However, critical consciousness — and particularly theoretical reflectivity — represents a uniquely adult capacity and, as such, becomes realized through perspective transformation. Perspective transformation becomes a major learning domain and the uniquely adult learning function. If adult education is to be understood as an organized effort to facilitate learning in the adult years, it has no alternative but to address the distinctive learning needs of adults pertaining to perspective transformation. [...]

A Critical Theory of Adult Education

We have examined in some detail the nature and development of perspective transformation as the third — and the uniquely adult — of Habermas' three domains of learning. By clearly differentiating these three interrelated but distinct 'knowledge constitutive' areas of cognitive interest, Habermas has provided the foundation for formulating a comprehensive theory of adult education. As each domain has its own learning goal (namely, learning for task-related competence, learning for interpersonal understanding and learning for perspective transformation), learning needs, approaches for facilitating learning, methods of research and program evaluation are implied or explicit.

This extension of Habermas' theory of areas of cognitive interest is reinforced by the experience of adult educators. We have understood through conventional wisdom that educational design and methodology must be a function of the learning needs of adults and that formula or package programs which do not fully address the differences in goal and nature of the learning task are of questionable value. Perhaps it is because we have been marginal to the mainstream of education for so long that we have been able to sustain our own rather distinctive perspective on learner centeredness in conceptualizing our role. At any rate, we have tacitly recognized the vast differences in helping adults learn how to do something or to perform a task from helping them develop sensitivity and understanding in social relations and from helping them effect perspective transformation.

As educators, we need not concern ourselves with the philosophical question of whether Habermas has succeeded in establishing the epistemological status of the primary knowledge-constitutive interests with categorically distinct object domains, types of experience and corresponding forms of inquiry. There is sufficient force in his analysis to warrant serious examination of this contention as a hypothesis for investigation of and design of appropriate approaches for facilitating learning relevant to these three domains of learning. Despite their obvious interrelatedness in everyday life, a compelling argument has been made for recognizing that each involves its own different way of knowing and each is different enough to require its own appropriate mode of inquiry and educational strategy and tactics.

Educators have not only failed to recognize the crucial distinction among the three domains, but have assumed that the mode of inquiry derived from the empirical-analytic sciences is equally appropriate to all three learning domains. The behavioral change model of adult education — derived from this approach and therefore appropriate to facilitating learning concerned with controlling and manipulating the environment — has been undiscriminatingly applied as appropriate to the other domains as well. This misconception has become so pervasive that the very definition of education itself is almost universally understood in terms of an organized effort to facilitate behavioral change. Behaviorism has become a strongly institutionalized ideology in both psychology and education. Habermas' analysis of primary cognitive interests helps us demythify the learning process as well as our way of thinking about facilitating learning.

If you were to ask most professionals in adult education to outline how they would conceptualize program development, the model would probably be one which sets educational objectives in terms of specific behaviors to be acquired as dictated by a task to be accomplished. The task or role to be played is analyzed to establish its requisite skills, behaviors or 'competencies.' This is often referred to as a 'task analysis.' The difference would constitute a 'needs assessment.' An educational program is composed of a sequence of educational exercises reduced to their component elements with immediate feedback on each learning effort. Education is evaluated by subtracting measured learning gains in skills or competencies from behavioral objectives.

There is nothing wrong with this rather mechanistic approach to education as long as it is confined to task-oriented learning common to the 'technical' domain of learning to control and manipulate the environment. It is here such familiar concepts as education for behavior change, behavioral objectives, needs assessment, competency-based education, task analysis, skill training, accountability and criteria-referenced evaluation are appropriate and useful. In this domain research and program evaluation based upon the empirical-analytic model of inquiry have relevance and power.

It is only when educators address the other two domains of learning, social interaction — including educational process — and perspective transformation, using the same model that they have been wrong and generally ineffectual. The most common form this has taken is to attempt to broaden behavioral skills necessary to perform the task for which education is required. The assumption is that these are learned much like any other behavioral skill except that practice occasionally requires the use of hypothetical reality contexts, such as role playing, which are unnecessary in learning to operate a lathe or to perform other manual tasks.

Inherently different modes of systematic inquiry and educational design are implicit in the processes involved in the other two primary domains of learning. The second, social interaction, calls for an educational approach which focuses on helping learners interpret the ways they and others with whom they are involved construct meanings, ways they typify and label others and what they do and say as we interact with them. Our task is to help learners enhance their understanding of and sensitivity to the way others anticipate, perceive, think and feel while involved with the learner in common endeavors. Educators can assist adults to learn to take the role of others, to develop empathy and to develop confidence and competence in such aspects of human relations as resolving conflict, participating in discussion and dialogue, participating and leading in learning groups, listening, expressing oneself, asking questions, philosophizing, differentiating 'in order to' motives from 'because' motives and theorizing about symbolic interaction. Studies of symbolic interaction, 'grounded theory' strategies of comparative analysis and phenomenological analyses seem especially appropriate for both educational research — especially that relating to educational process — and evaluation.[3] Our work through the Center for Adult Education would be included in these efforts (Mezirow, 1975; Mezirow and Rose, 1978; Mezirow *et al.*, 1975).

Perspective transformation, the process central to the third learning domain, involves other educational approaches. Here the emphasis is on helping the learner identify real problems involving reified power relationships rooted in institutionalized ideologies which one has internalized in one's psychological history. Learners must consequently be led to an understanding of the reasons imbedded in these internalized cultural myths and concomitant feelings which account for their felt needs and wants as well as the way they see themselves and their relations. Having gained this understanding, learners must be given access to alternative meaning perspectives for interpreting this reality so that critique of these psycho-cultural assumptions is possible.

Freire has demonstrated how adult educators can precipitate as well as facilitate and reinforce perspective transformation. Beginning with the problems and perspectives of the learner, the educator develops a series of projective instructional materials — contrasting pictures, comic strips or stories posing hypothetical dilemmas with contradicting rules and assumptions rooted in areas of crucial concern to learners. Included will be representations of cultural discrepancies perceived by the educator which are taken for granted by the learners. Socratic dialogue is used in small group settings involving learners who are facing a common dilemma to elicit and challenge psycho-cultural assumptions behind habituated ways of perceiving, thinking, feeling and behaving. Emphasis is given equality and reciprocity in building a support group through which learners can share experiences with a common problem and come to share a new perspective. An ethos of support, encouragement, non-judgmental acceptance, mutual help and individual responsibility is created. Alternative perspectives are presented with different value systems and ways of seeing.

Where adults come together in response to the same existential dilemma for the purpose of finding direction and meaning, projective instructional materials may be unnecessary. In a support group situation in which conditions for Habermas' 'ideal speech' are approximated, all alternative perspectives relevant to the situation are presented. Critical reflectivity is fostered with a premium placed on personalizing what is learned by applying insights to one's own life and works as opposed to mere intellectualization. Conceptual learning needs to be integrated with emotional and aesthetic experience.

The research technique used by ethnomethodologists called

'breaching' for studying meaning perspectives might also be used as an effective instructional method to foster perspective transformation. This would involve educational experiences which challenge the taken-for-granted assumptions about relationships in order to call them into critical consciousness. For example, learners used to traditional teacher-student relationships can be helped to examine implicit assumptions by being placed in a learning situation in which the educator refuses to play the traditional authority role of information giver or activities director but rather limits his or her response to that of a resource person. This typically generates strong negative feelings in learners who are unable to cope with the unexpected lack of structure. By subsequently helping learners see the reasons for their feelings rooted in the assumptions of an institutionalized ideology, real progress can be made toward perspective transformation. Through similar modified T group[4] experiences with provision for a continuing support structure, individuals can be helped to recognize the way psycho-cultural assumptions about authority relationships have generated their habits of perception, thought and behavior and be assisted to plan and take action.

While Habermas is correct in suggesting that psychoanalysis and critique of ideology are appropriate methods for inquiry in this domain of learning, they are also appropriate educational methods. The process of perspective transformation may also be studied using interviews; comparing movement in problem awareness, expectations and goals; or through comparative analysis to inductively ascertain commonalities.

Perspective transformation, following the cycle delineated earlier, also involves learning needs attendant upon systematically examining existing options, building confidence through competence in new roles, acquiring knowledge and skills to implement one's plans and provisionally trying out new roles and relationships. These learning needs involve all three learning domains. In everyday life few situations (e.g., self-instruction in a manual skill) will involve only one learning domain. They are intricately intertwined. To be able to facilitate learning adult educators must master the professional demands of all three and become adept at working with learners in ways that will be sensitive to both the interrelatedness and inherent differences among them.

I see no serious ethical issues involved in education for perspective transformation. Helping adults construe experience in a way in which they may more clearly understand the reasons for their problems and understand the options open to them so that they may assume responsibility for decision making is the essence of education. Bringing psycho-cultural assumptions into critical consciousness to help a person understand how he or she has come into possession of conceptual categories, rules, tactics and criteria for judging implicit habits of perception, thought and behavior involves perhaps the most significant kind of learning. It increases a crucial sense of agency over ourselves and our lives. To help a learner become aware of alternative meaning perspectives relevant to his situation, to become acquainted with them, to become open to them and to make use of them to more clearly understand does not prescribe the correct action to be taken. The meaning perspective does not tell the learner what to do; it presents a set of rules, tactics and criteria for judging. The decision to assume a new meaning perspective clearly implies action, but the behavior that results will depend upon situational factors, the knowledge and skills for taking effective action and personality variables discussed earlier.

Education becomes indoctrination only when the educator tries to influence a specific action as an extension of his will, or perhaps when he blindly helps a learner blindly follow the dictates of an unexamined set of cultural assumptions about who he is and the nature of his relationships. To show someone a new set of rules, tactics and criteria for judging which clarify the situation in which he or she must act is significantly different from trying to engineer learner consent to take the actions favored by the educator within the new perspective. This does not suggest that the educator is value free. His selection of alternative meaning perspectives will reflect his own cultural values, including his professional ideology — for adult educators one which commits us to the concept of learner self-directedness as both the means and the end of education.

Inasmuch as the overwhelming proportion of adult learning is self-directed (Tough, 1978) and uses the experience of others as resources in problem solving, those relatively few occasions when an adult requires the help of an adult educator must be understood in their broader context. Clearly, we must attempt to provide the specialized educational resource adult learners seek when they choose to use an adult educator, but our professional perspective needs to be unequivocal: we must respond to the learner's educational need in a way which will improve the quality of his or her self-directedness as a learner. To do less is to perpetuate a dysfunctional dependency relationship between learner and educator, a reification of an institutionalized ideology rooted in the socialization process.

Although the diversity of experience labeled adult education includes any organized and sustained effort to facilitate learning and, as such, tends to mean many things to many people, a set of standards derived from the generic characteristics of adult development has emerged from research and professional practice in our collective definition of the function of an adult educator. It is almost universally recognized, at least in theory, that central to the adult educator's function is *a goal and method of self-directed learning.* Enhancing the learner's ability for self direction in learning as a foundation for a distinctive philosophy of adult education has breadth and power. It represents the mode of learning characteristic of adulthood.

Each of three distinct but interrelated domains — controlling and manipulating the environment, social interaction and perspective transformation — involves different ways of knowing and hence different learning needs, different educational strategies and methods and different techniques of research and evaluation. A self-directed learner must be understood as one who is aware of the constraints on his efforts to learn, including the psycho-cultural assumptions involving reified power relationships embedded in institutionalized ideologies which influence one's habits of perception, thought and behavior as one attempts to learn. A self-directed learner has access to alternative perspectives for understanding his or her situation and for giving meaning and direction to his or her life, has acquired sensitivity and competence in social interaction and has the skills and competencies required to master the productive tasks associated with controlling and manipulating the environment.

A Charter for Andragogy

Andragogy, as a professional perspective of adult educators, must be defined as an organized and sustained effort to assist adults to learn *in a way that enhances their capability to function as self-directed learners.* To do this it must:

(1) progressively decrease the learner's dependency on the educator;
(2) help the learner understand how to use learning resources — especially the experience of others, including the educator, and how to engage others in reciprocal learning relationships;

(3) assist the learner to define his/her learning needs — both in terms of immediate awareness and of understanding the cultural and psychological assumptions influencing his/her perceptions of needs;

(4) assist learners to assume increasing responsibility for defining their learning objectives, planning their own learning program and evaluating their progress;

(5) organize what is to be learned in relationship to his/her current personal problems, concerns and levels of understanding;

(6) foster learner decision making — select learner-relevant learning experiences which require choosing, expand the learner's range of options, facilitate taking the perspectives of others who have alternative ways of understanding;

(7) encourage the use of criteria for judging which are increasingly inclusive and differentiating in awareness, self-reflexive and integrative of experience;

(8) foster a self-corrective reflexive approach to learning — to typifying and labeling, to perspective taking and choosing, and to habits of learning and learning relationships;

(9) facilitate problem posing and problem solving, including problems associated with the implementation of individual and collective action; recognition of relationships between personal problems and public issues;

(10) reinforce the self-concept of the learner as a learner and doer by providing for progressive mastery; a supportive climate with feedback to encourage provisional efforts to change and to take risks; avoidance of competitive judgment of performance; appropriate use of mutual support groups;

(11) emphasize experiential, participative and projective instructional methods; appropriate use of modeling and learning contracts;

(12) make the moral distinction between helping the learner understand his/her full range of choices and how to improve the quality of choosing vs encouraging the learner to make a specific choice.

I believe the recognition of the function of perspective transformation within the context of learning domains, as suggested by Habermas' theory, contributes to a clearer understanding of the learning needs of adults and hence the function of education. When combined with the concept of self-directedness as the goal and the means of adult education, the essential elements of a comprehensive theory of adult learning and education have been identified. The formulation of such a theory for guiding professional practice is perhaps our single greatest challenge in this period of unprecedented expansion of adult education programs and activities. It is a task to command our best collective effort.

Notes

1. See Trent Schroyer's *The Critique of Domination: the Origins and Development of Critical Theory* (Beacon Press, Boston, 1973) and Thomas McCarthy's *The Critical Theory of Jurgen Habermas* (MIT Press, Cambridge, 1979), the most complete synthesis of Habermas' work in English.

2. See Joseph Gabel, *False Consciousness; An Essay on Reification* (Harper Torchbooks, New York, 1975).

3. For a review of related research see A. Jon Magoon, 'Constructivist Approaches in Educational Research', *Review of Educational Research, 47* (1977), 651-93.

4. Conventional T group experience fosters psychic rather than theoretical reflexivity.

References

Berger, Peter L. and Thomas Luckmann (1966), *The Social Construction of Reality*, Doubleday, Garden City, New York

Bernstein, Richard J. (1978) *The Restructuring of Social and Political Theory*, University of Pennsylvania Press, Philadelphia

Freire, Paulo (1970) *Pedagogy of the Oppressed*, Herter and Herter, New York

Maudsley, Donald B. (1979) 'A Theory of Meta-Learning and Principles of Facilitation: An Organismic Perspective', Doctoral dissertation, University of Toronto, Toronto

Mezirow, Jack (1975) *Education for Perspective Transformation: Women's Re-entry Programs in Community Colleges*, Center for Adult Education, Teachers' College, Columbia University, New York

_____ (1975) *Evaluating Statewide Programs of Adult Basic Education: A Design with Instrumentation*, Center for Adult Education, Teachers' College, Columbia University, New York

Mezirow, Jack and Amy Rose (1978) *An Evaluation Guide for College Women's Re-entry Programs*, Center for Adult Education, Teachers' College, Columbia University, New York

Mezirow, Jack, Gordon Darkenwald and Alan Knox (1975) *Last Gamble on Education: Dynamics of Adult Basic Education*, Adult Education Association of USA, Washington, DC

Rogers, Carl (1978) 'The Formative Tendency', *Journal of Humanistic Psychology, 18*, 23-6

Tough, Allen (1978) 'Major Learning Efforts: Recent Research and Future Directions', *The Adult Learner, Current Issues in Higher Education*, National Conference Series, American Association for Higher Education, Washington DC

Part 3

INDIVIDUAL LEARNING

The four chapters in this section deal with a mode of adult
learning which has been largely disregarded until comparatively
recently. Allen Tough gives a résumé of his research, which
has effectively highlighted the enormous significance of self-
planned and self-directed learning programmes amongst the adult
populations of a range of countries. He focuses, in the latter part,
on learning directed towards major personal change, a concern
also shown by Mezirow and Freire in this Reader. The chapter by
Michael Moore, which takes its inspiration in part from the work
of Tough, seeks to develop a theoretical framework and typology
for understanding the range of individual learning. Noting the past
and continuing importance of correspondence tuition and other
forms of distance education, Moore stresses the variation of
individual learning programmes in terms of the distance between
learner and teacher and the degree of learner autonomy.

The chapters by John Stephenson and Luis Espina Cepeda
provide two contrasted case studies of individual learning programmes, although in each case an element of learning in the
group or in the community is also involved. Stephenson describes
a programme offered by an English institution of higher education, which involves face-to-face tuition, but allocates the major
responsibility for devising and implementing the programme of
study to the individual student. Cepeda describes a distance
teaching programme provided in the Canary Islands, the major
focus of which is on basic education, and which is delivered in a
directive fashion.

SELF-PLANNED LEARNING AND MAJOR PERSONAL CHANGE

Allen Tough

Source: R.M. Smith (ed.), *Adult Learning: Issues and Innovations* (ERIC Clearing House in Career Education, Northern Illinois University, 1976), pp. 58-73.

The first item on Chart 1 outlines the focus or phenomenon that has fascinated me for the last ten years or so. I have called it a learning project, but what I suggest in parentheses would be an even more accurate title — a major learning effort. The focus is on people trying to learn, trying to change. People of course learn without trying, but that is not what I'm looking at. What I suggest that we look at is highly deliberate effort; we define that as effort where more than half of the person's total motivation had to be learning and retaining certain definite knowledge or skill — so that less than half of the person's motivation can be pleasure or enjoyment.

And I've suggested that there has to be a clear focus. The person has to know what he or she is trying to learn. Someone who walks into a museum for an hour knowing that he will learn something but not knowing what, simply does not qualify by our criteria. We have a minimum time period, seven hours — that is, over a period of several months a person has to spend at least seven hours trying to gain this particular knowledge and skill. Now in fact the average learning project is around 90 or 100 hours, so we do not have to use that seven hour cut-off all that often. My reason for choosing the seven hours was partly as a magic number, and partly it's about one working day; and my feeling has been that if someone devotes the equivalent of a working day to trying to learn something, it is worthwhile looking at it.

Number two on Chart 1 gives the various populations of the study interviewed by our group in Toronto and by graduate students and others all across the USA, Canada, Ghana and New Zealand. Combining the results of all these studies we find that the differences are not great. In fact, the data found in each study are roughly the same as data found in the other studies. And that is what number

Chart 1: Learning Projects

---

1. A learning project (major learning effort):
   — highly deliberate effort
   — to gain and retain certain definite knowledge and skill
   — clear focus
   — at least 7 hours

2. Populations surveyed:
   — Toronto: pre-school mothers; elementary school teachers;
     lower white-collar women and men; factory workers;
     municipal politicians; social science professors;
     unemployed men; IBM salesmen; professional men;
     16-year-olds and 10-year-olds
   — Vancouver: members of public employees' union
   — Syracuse: suburban housewives
   — Tennessee: large rural and urban populations
   — Nebraska: adults over 55
   — Fort Lauderdale: adults who recently completed high school
   — Atlanta: pharmacists
   — Kentucky: parish ministers
   — West Africa (Accra, Ghana): secondary school teachers;
     bank officers; department store executives
   — New Zealand: several North Island populations

3. A middle or median person:
   — conducts 8 different learning projects in one year
   — spends a total of 700 hours altogether at them

4. Who plans the learning efforts from one session to the next?
   — the learner: 68%
   — a group or its leader/instructor: 12%
   — a pro or friend in a one-to-one situation: 8%
   — a nonhuman resource (records, TV, etc.): 3%
   — mixed (no dominant planner): 9%

5. Out of 100 learning projects, 19 are planned by a professional educator and 81 by an amateur.

6. Most common motivation: some anticipated *use* or application of the knowledge and skill.
   Less common: curiosity or puzzlement, or wanting to possess the knowledge for its own sake.
   Rare (less than 1% of all learning efforts): credit.

---

three on Chart 1 deals with — how common this phenomenon is, and how much time it takes. Those figures pertain to the middle or median person (that is, half of the people in these populations have learned more and spent more time learning and half the people have spent less). And you will notice that this person conducts eight different learning projects, eight major learning efforts each year — in eight quite different areas of knowledge and skill.

People spend a total of 700 hours at this activity — highly deliberate efforts to learn. The figure is probably low — at least for a great many populations — for two reasons. First, many of our interviewers have failed to get the full number of hours. Almost every interviewer reports missing some learning projects. Then some of the later studies have actually had much higher figures than that seven hundred. That works out to almost two hours a day — an incredible figure when you think about it.

Number four on the Chart describes who planned the learning effort from one session to the next — not who did the initial planning — the day-to-day deciding about what to learn and how to go about it. And, of course, the majority is self-planned. The learner himself or herself decides which step to take next in the learning effort — the learner plans the path. It is often a zigzag path which seems helter-skelter, but the learner does decide from one session to the next what and how to learn.

Now what has happened I think, looking at the research for the last 15 years (or even longer), is that until fairly recently people looked only at the tip of the iceberg. Only a small part of the iceberg shows above the water's surface. In adult learning or adult education that small highly visible tip of the iceberg is groups of people learning — in auditoriums, classrooms, workshops, or conferences. That is what adult educators have noticed and paid attention to over the years. Rightly so. That's an important phenomenon. [...]

We came along, in a simple-minded way, and interviewed people about all of their learning efforts. We found they couldn't remember them. So we developed probe-sheets that suggested some things that people learn about. And we also took an hour and a half (at least an hour) in most of the interviews to study just this phenomenon.

We really pushed, poked, probed, and helped the person recall. We found it took people about 20 to 25 minutes to really start getting on our wavelength and start to recall their projects, at least beyond three or four of them. [...] Nearly everyone recalls quite a few — and it is a rare person who remembers only one or two or three. In the Toronto group we found only one 'zero,' and in most of the other studies there were either no zeros or very few.

We've looked at this total iceberg then and most of it is in the invisible part, the self-planned part. It is invisible to the learners; it is invisible to other people around them. It is a phenomenon that we are just not in touch with; it is not very common at a dinner party to say, 'And what are you trying to learn lately?' It is not something that you talk about. We talk about courses and conferences, but not the other kinds of learning. At least we do not put it all together in a single phenomenon — an effort to learn.

You will notice on the chart that 12 per cent of all major learning efforts are conducted in groups, planned by the group or the leader, or instructor. Less than 10 per cent are conducted in a one-to-one situation — the way we all, or most of us, learn to drive a car, play the piano or tennis. The figure that surprises me most is the 3 per cent for non-human resources. It was thought that programmed instruction and television series, language records, and so on would be much more popular than they turned out to be. Then there is the 9 per cent that is mixed. Of course, almost all of those are self-planned plus something else, so the self-planned figure of 68 per cent should be raised to something like three-quarters or 77 per cent.

In number five I have tried to capture all the figures in one very simple statistic, that is, if you look at one hundred learning projects, about 20 are planned by professionals and about 80 by the learner himself or herself or some other amateur planner.

Turning now to what people learn about or learn to do, we find that there is incredible diversity. If you ask a room full of people to make lists of their recent personal learning projects you will find a mind-boggling variety of topics. An implication of this is a very very old one in adult education — that no one institution could possibly meet the needs of all learning projects for all adults. In fact I do not think any institution can even comprehend all of the items you get on such lists. So adult education must be pluralistic; it could not possibly be monopolistic as youth education primarily is. Anyone who has studied adult education knows that this is one of the basic characteristics of the field; there is tremendous diversity of institutions. We begin to see why, because of the incredible diversity of learning needs.

It will perhaps be useful to try to answer some questions frequently put to us about our research.

Question: 'How do you distinguish between activities and learning projects, or are they one and the same?' What we are really looking at is the intention of the activity. So that regardless of what the person is doing, if he is trying to learn, trying to change through that activity, then we call it a learning project. People do learn in other ways. There are lots of activities that lead to learning. But if that is not the person's primary intention then we do not include it in our definition of a learning project.

Question: 'Do you define learning as change?' Yes, it can be internal change — within one's head — understanding, information, or whatever. I define a learning project as an effort to change.

Question: 'Is some sort of stress a prerequisite for a learning project to begin?' No, perhaps approximately one-third of all learning projects begin because of this, but a lot begin for other reasons — curiosity, for example. The desire to build a porch around my house may not come out of stress; it may simply be something I want to do. Growing vegetables might be initiated because you don't have money to buy them, or it might just be for fun.

Another important factor is that these learning projects can continue over many years. In West Africa we found a great many projects that went back ten or fifteen years. Students at my institution now are trying to trace some of the projects back to see what the origins are, and they are often going back to childhood — so that you can't understand the present learning project without knowing what the learner's previous interests were. There really is a long-term aspect. Some are seasonal, like tennis. Some come and go, like raising kids, in the sense that a different kind of crisis will arise at different times. The kids seem to go through periods of plateau when everything is rather sunny; then things seem to fall apart. He or she won't sleep or eat, or hits people. Then you turn to Dr Spock or your neighbors or pediatrician about how to deal with it. Then you go through another period of several months when you are not learning anything or putting in the effort.

There are other learning projects (I think this is a typical American pattern) that are very brief. I have to make a decision by Wednesday, so I will read everything I can now and ask people about it, and then I'll make the decision. Or with child-rearing, you may have a crash program for five days. This seems to be the American style. I say that because we were not picking this up in West Africa even among business executives, who did not seem to have so many of these short-term projects.

Question: 'What about variations in the learning as the result of work or other activities that are taken on primarily for reasons other than learning?' It is not always true that people learn from their work. The trend that I see is that people are choosing jobs that seem to be educative, and corporations or employers that will be educative. They are asking a little less now of pension plans and that sort of thing and a little more about the kind of organization it is. General Electric did a survey on the future of business values and they clearly found this shift toward looking at how educative a job or task is. I enjoyed interviewing one fourth-grade teacher who chose things to teach that he wanted to learn about. He knew that was an effective way to motivate himself. I have heard Sunday School teachers say the same thing. So we do choose some of our tasks partly in order to learn. It is a fascinating phenomenon.

Major Personal Change

In the last few years I have begun to focus my own energy on one specific area of learning projects. Not that I think that the others are unimportant, but my own interest is to study major personal change. Major means that the learning effort is designed to produce major changes, significant changes, in the person. Personal change suggests that it is somehow a personal thing. It is a change in life-style, attitudes, emotional reactions, male-female relationships, or whatever it happens to be. All of these seem more personal than learning about what is happening over in the Middle East or something like that. I'm not putting down the importance of that, but just trying to explain my own focus on the major or immediate types of changes.

There follow two charts that deal with this area. Chart 2 lists the content or curriculum of this area, i.e. what it is that people can try to change in themselves. Chart 3 lists the how, the paths, the ways, the steps, the techniques and methods. I would like the reader to look over those two charts — try to be aware of your reactions as you do so — your mental, emotional, and intellectual reactions. What do these charts do to you? What do they do to your thinking and what do they do to your feelings?

Here are some common reactions of persons encountering the items listed, followed by my own comments.

Reaction: 'You get down to some very basic things, and I find myself involved in quite a few of them.' This is a very common reaction — to recognize yourself in some of the items.

Reaction: 'Seems to be something you do from childhood through adulthood.' Some of these things go all through your lifetime — not like those short-term projects we mentioned earlier.

Reaction: 'Many seem to be types of experiences that many people have not begun to consider.' No one person is going to be involved in all of these things. Probably most of them never will be involved in them. Some of them may 'bother' you. Perhaps some of you would like to change in a lot of these ways, but find you are not using many methods to do so. That is a fairly common reaction.

Reaction: 'Looking at the list, I feel that the majority of them could or would occur outside formal institutions.' Yes, there is change in formal institutions, but many of them tend not to provide these kinds of experiences.

Reaction: 'It seems to me that a lot of these are motivated out of prevailing discontent with materialistic society.' Right, these aren't very materialistic lists. They are also lists that assume that the person

Chart 2: What Personal Changes Can Someone Strive For?

a. self-understanding
b. express genuine feelings and interests
c. close, authentic relationships with others
d. broad understanding of history, geography, cultures, universe, future
e. better performance on the job; reshape the job or its meaning; new job
f. quit drinking; stop beating children; quit heroin
g. cope better with the tasks necessary for survival
h. body free from excessive tenseness and wasted energy; physical fitness
i. new priorities among goals (desired benefits); a fresh balance of activities or expenditures
j. reshape relationship with mate; new mate or partner (or an alternative living arrangement); new circle of friends
k. capacity for finding a calm center of peace and inner strength amidst the turmoil
l. adequate self-esteem
m. reduction of psychological and emotional problems and blocks that inhibit full human functioning
n. improved awareness and consciousness; more open-minded and inquiring; seeking an accurate picture of reality
o. greater sensitivity to psychic phenomena and to alternate realities
p. freedom, liberation, looseness, flexibility
q. competence at psychological processing, at handling own feelings and personal problems
r. zest for life; joy; happiness
s. liberation from female-male stereotyping, or from other role-playing
t. emotional maturity, positive mental health; higher level of psychological functioning
u. spiritual insights; cosmic consciousness
v. less selfish and more altruistic; a greater effort to contribute to the lives of others
w. acceptance and love of self and others; accept the world as it is
x. come to terms with own death

Chart 3. Some Methods For Personal Growth

1. books
2. conversations with a close friend or an informal helper; relationship with mate or love partner
3. jogging; diet; bioenergetics; massage; acupuncture; biofeedback; sports; movement and da, e therapy
4. yoga exercises; martial arts (t'ai chi; aikido; judo; karate)
5. individual counseling; individual psychotherapy; group therapy
6. behavior modification
7. encounter groups; sensory awareness; psychosynthesis; Gestalt therapy groups; Transactional Analysis; psychodrama; art therapy
8. individual use (whenever appropriate) of personal exercises and psychological processing such as thinking, listing wishes and fears, interpreting dreams, keeping a journal, moving to music, contemplation and reflection, listening to one's unconscious
9. consciousness-raising groups and literature for women and men
10. out-of-body experience or other psychic experiences; astronauts' experience of seeing the earth from outer space
11. guided fantasies; directed daydreams; Transcendental Meditation; Mind Games; hypnotic trance
12. re-living one's birth or infancy; primal therapy
13. religious, spiritual, cosmic-unity, symbolic, or consciousness-altering experiences — via religious services, spiritual practices, mysticism, psychedelic drugs, Mind Games, prayer, wilderness solitude, music, meditation, sex, chanting, spinning, baptism in the Holy Spirit, Zen, Buddhism, Christianity, Judaism, Islam, Taoism
14. Tarot; I Ching
15. alert childbirth; living with children; Parent Effectiveness Training
16. films; television; audiovisual environment; self-improvement tapes and kits
17. tackling a challenging task or an educative job; working in a growth-facilitating organization
18. course; conference; discussion group; management training ;organizational development
19. self-help groups and other peer-groups
20. music; arts; crafts
21. deliberate change in life-style; new circle of friends; new neighborhood; expressive clothes
22. travel or live abroad; live within a commune or some other subculture or culture

isn't scrambling to get enough money to eat, not severely crippled in some emotional way, that some of his basic needs are taken care of. People who do not have enough money would not even know what these lists are all about.

Reaction: 'It seems to me that many of the methods are for the person who is aware that they are available and not necessarily for the guy who is just sitting at home. I can't see him dealing with a lot of these methods.' Many of these methods have been developed in the last ten or fifteen years; so they are not generally known to the public. My own project is to try to develop a bridge between this array of available techniques and people who should know about them. It is partly their recency, and partly that they seem strange to people. Half the methods on the list probably bothered you when you first heard about them — even one like jogging. So there are a lot of reasons that people do not know about these kinds of things. [...]

Reaction: 'It is interesting that almost everything on the personal changes list is a type of assessment or judgment about progress that is very "individual". I have to decide for myself whether or not that change has occurred. I might get some feedback from other people, but it is my decision and no one else can tell me whether or not I've pulled it off.' True, most of these items are very hard to measure. We have found that people who are learning on their own are pre-occupied with evaluation of how well they are doing and what level they are at. They develop all kinds of ways of dealing with that. One of them is to have a conversation with someone who is an acknowledged expert. There are other ways. Certainly some items on this list are very hard to evaluate. How do I know when my self-esteem has reached an adequate level? These are all subtle matters. The thing that amazes me is that we now have some technologies that produce some of these changes, and that is a big step. Another big step would be to help people know where they are and how far they have moved.

Reaction: 'Though this is geared toward middle-class individuals, I think that for adult basic learners, one of the things that's missing here is learning from one's children.' That's a fascinating notion — learning from one's children.

Reaction: 'There seems to be willingness to risk. You might find out something that you do not like about yourself.' That is right. These are risky patterns, not safe patterns. That is the choice of the learner.

Reaction: 'I have the feeling that educators are pretty much staying away from teaching and talking about values, and our schools are not making these things known as they should.' That is right. Now somebody suggested that adult educators are not experiencing many of these things themselves. That could be one reason. In fact the way that these often get into the curriculum is that a teacher goes to a workshop or something similar and gets turned on to new technologies — rather than through a curriculum guide or something similar.

Reaction: 'I find it very hard to believe a couple of comments, that people don't grow or don't want to grow. I just don't believe that.' I don't know. I do know that there are a lot of risks involved, and we don't always want to take risks. [...]

Perhaps I should add that I do not want to be a salesman for any of these methods. I do not recommend them wholeheartedly to all people. I am simply trying to list methods that some people use for growth — that is, methods that a particular person might use in an attempt to grow.

Implications

We can consider now some implications for action — for educators and educational institutions — looking at some better kinds of help that could be provided. What do we do to facilitate, to help people learn more or better things for themselves? Or, how can we help people with major personal change?

I have five answers to that question that I will state fairly quickly. The first one is rather strange. It is to look not at the program the institution provides for people but to look at the staff of the institution. The concept here is to look at educators or teachers as learners instead of looking at them just as teachers, or people who are facilitating the learning of other people. I think probably the largest change in our institutions will come from learning how to facilitate the learning of the staffs of those institutions.

I don't mean that educators don't learn. We've found that elementary teachers, for example, spend an average of two hours a day learning to be better teachers. But at the same time institutions tend to do very little to facilitate the learning of their own staff members. To me this is just an incredible situation. If any institutions in society should be facilitating learning and change among their own staffs, they should be schools, colleges, and adult education programs. But in fact they don't. One of our doctoral students who had interviewed the elementary school teachers decided to try to put into practice the recommendations at the end of his dissertation. He put himself on the line and became the principal of our campus lab school. He has just transformed that place in three years. He's done it by focusing his efforts on helping these teachers to become better teachers. [...] He is helping the teachers individually, or in groups of two or three, to set their learning goals and go ahead to become better teachers, however they want to do it. One of the first things he did was to give them Wednesday afternoon off — for learning. He brought parents in to handle the kids. It sounds so obvious and so superior to having one day a year for 'teacher development day.'

The second suggestion, or implication, is to add 'major personal change' to the curriculum — at whatever level. And as I suggested earlier, this is in fact being done — mostly in an underground or back-door way. That is, an individual teacher gets turned on to the notion and introduces it to his or her class. [...]

Now a third implication is suggested by Ivan Illich and Everett Reimer, who have received publicity for saying that the monopoly of the school system should be broken, that education should be more pluralistic. Illich and Reimer make some specific suggestions. They mention three mechanisms; one of these is the skill exchange. The idea of a skill exchange is very simple. If I want to learn how to play the guitar I dial a telephone number and say that I want to play the guitar. Then they give me the names and telephone numbers of two or three people who have phoned in earlier and said that they would enjoy teaching someone to play the guitar. I then meet with one or two or three of these people and decide which one I want to learn from. I might volunteer later to teach someone else. Usually the meeting takes place in a public building or a coffee shop, so that if people don't hit if off there is no great harm done. The system is very cheap and the idea has spread to at least twenty cities in Canada and the USA.

Another suggestion is a 'peer matching service.' This occurs when you are not looking for a teacher — somebody who is bettter than you — but for someone who is at your level. If I want to improve my chess playing or my tennis playing, I might want to find a partner who plays at about my level. Or, I might want to find somebody to talk to about inflation. The idea is to match people who can learn together as peers, not as one teaching the other.

Then there is a 'directory of freelancers' — people who will want to be paid to facilitate learning. [...]

A couple of other suggestions: these apply specifically to educational institutions. One of them is to increase the amount of choice and increase the amount of help for students. It has to be a two-sided thing. Our first step usually is increasing the amount of choice in *how* people learn. That is not so scary to instructors — saying to the student, 'Here's what you have to learn but there are two or three paths to get there.' The other kind of choice would be to give people freedom in *what* they learn; that is a little scarier unless limited to procedures like giving out a range of assignment possibilities or a list of topics for essays. One way to increase that a little is to make the last item something like, 'Or any other topic chosen by the student and approved by the teacher.' The way I do it in my graduate course in

Toronto is to set boundaries about the subject matter. But that is about the only restriction I have on what people learn or how they learn. I simply say that they have to learn about this phenomenon, major personal change, for 130 hours, and then they pass the course. It's deceptively simple, and it seems to be fairly effective for me in that course with that subject matter. I'm not urging all instructors to do it.

The students are creative in the ways in which they go about learning in that course. They read, of course. They also analyze their own learning and changes. Some will deliberately put themselves into the thing that they least desire to learn — or something very threatening (during which they often keep a diary). They also interview each other. My impression is that the range of methods is actually greater when I give them freedom than if I were to try to make up the methods for them. And, of course, what they learn is also incredibly varied. It's a pass-fail course, so I haven't had much problem with grading. One or two persons probably cheat, but I am not planning to drop the system just because of that.

A final suggestion is to decrease the emphasis on credit. Our research found less than 1 per cent of adult learning projects are conducted for credit. So, it is quite clearly demonstrated that people will learn for reasons other than credit. [...] Reducing the emphasis on credit could reduce the monopolistic aspect of adult education.

THE INDIVIDUAL ADULT LEARNER

Michael Moore

Source: Copyright © The Open University 1983 (specially written for this volume).

The Individual Mode

The individual mode consists of all educational relationships in which the learner is separate from other learners, and in which there is a one-to-one relationship with an educator — even though communication might be conducted across time and space, through print and other media.

The most simple examples of the individual mode of adult education include the coaching a golfer receives from the 'pro', instruction in a driving school, apprenticeship to a craftsman, and tutorials of every kind. However, the overwhelming majority of individual learners do *not* learn in face-to-face situations like these, but, when engaged in deliberate and planned learning, do so in situations where they are not only separate from other learners, but are separated from their educators also. It is very common for teaching in the individual mode to be 'at a distance', with adults learning by using correspondence courses, programmed learning packages, computers, audio and video tapes, radio and television.

Individual adult learners very often plan their own learning programmes. Tough (1971) has shown that as much as 70 per cent of systematic adult learning is planned by the learners themselves. They may use distance teaching programmes, or only parts of such programmes, to meet their own, personal objectives, often without direct contact with the institution which prepared the teaching materials, or indeed with any other educational institution or educator. The extent to which adults plan, carry out, and evaluate their learning is a measure of their learning 'autonomy'.

Independent Study

In the tutorial system adopted at Oxford and Cambridge Universities, the student reads assigned materials and reports to a tutor, who responds to the student's submission, gives guidance, and monitors progress. When introduced to American universities after the First World War, the system was called 'independent study', a term now widely used on both sides of the Atlantic. The superiority of independent study over class teaching was believed to be the opportunity it gave for the development of the particular interests of the student — within the narrow boundaries set by the tutor — and the personal relationship which it permitted between teacher and student (Wedemeyer, 1971).

Independent study would have remained an educational idea of only limited interest if it had remained confined to the university campus. As long as a century ago, however, it became apparent to some educators, both within and outside the universities, that it ought to be possible to give tutorials to students who could not attend in person, by sending instructions and giving responses, in writing, through the post. The first correspondence colleges to provide tutorials 'at a distance' were established in the 1880s. In the USA, the universities themselves established correspondence departments. In Britain, the University of London was established in 1836 as an 'examining' university, awarding degrees to persons who demonstrated their knowledge in examinations, regardless of where and how they learned. By the beginning of the twentieth century, correspondence instruction and 'schemes of study' in certain subjects were also provided. Generally, however, British universities were never to take independent students or distance teaching as seriously as their counterparts in other countries, especially in the 'new countries' like Canada, Australia, South Africa and the USA.

In Britain, it was left to private enterprise, in colleges like Wolsey Hall and the University Correspondence College, to offer tuition for independent study, but the method could never develop as it did in publicly funded universities overseas. By the year 1940 in the USA, for example, 48 universities provided tutorials by correspondence. By the mid-1960s, when Britain first considered an Open University, there were 3 million American students on 15,000 different correspondence courses, and half of these were taught by the universities and colleges. In Sweden, one person in eight was taking a correspondence course, and half the 3.5 million students in higher education in the USSR were using the correspondence form of independent study (Sivatko, 1969; MacKenzie *et al.*, 1968). In just over half a century, the idea of the individual learner, guided in his study by an individual teacher, had spread from the exclusive cloisters of the old universities into the public domain.

The term 'independent study' retained its original meaning — the individual tutorial free of restrictions of class teaching — but it acquired a new meaning too. This was the idea of physical, or geographic, independence — the learner being independent in space and time from the teacher, linked only by a man-made medium of communication. In recent years, of course, the methods of communication available have changed and been added to; as well as written correspondence instruction, we now have programmed packages of many kinds, self-directed reading guides, teaching on audio- and video-tapes, by computer, telephone, radio and television. Teachers who use these media have usually been motivated by a desire to reach the widest possible population of learners. For the individual learner there is now a greater richness of resources than ever before, though in using some of them the learner may have little of the personal relationship with a tutor, little of the close guidance, which previously characterised independent study by tutorial, whether face-to-face or by correspondence. The learner may be required to make educational decisions which were, in earlier forms of independent study, made by the tutor. There is now a distance between learner and teacher which is not merely geographic, but educational and psychological as well. It is a distance in the *relationship* of the two partners in the educational enterprise. It is a 'transactional distance' (Boyd, Apps *et al.*, 1980).

Transactional Distance

The concept of transactional distance was first recognized and used as a basis for a theory of individual learning about ten years ago. Until then, although there was a great deal of learning and teaching in the individual mode, it had been almost entirely ignored by researchers in the field of adult education. Individual learning in general, and independent study in particular, had not been systematically described, no attempt had been made to identify its essential characteristics, there was no way of discriminating among its various forms. In short, there was no theory. And as a result this mode of study was overlooked by researchers. In one book on adult education research written in the 1950s, for example, some 20 pages were given to group research, 32 to the community, 14 to discussion methods, and none to correspondence study! On the contrary, it was said, 'Clearly, adult education will take place in groups almost exclusively' (Brunner *et al.*, 1959, p. 197).

In the past ten years the situation has changed dramatically. The field of independent study is now very well established, and the idea of distance as one of its distinguishing characteristics is generally accepted (see for example Holmberg, 1982; Keegan, 1980; Wedemeyer, 1982).

Distance teaching may be defined as:

> The family of instructional methods in which the teaching behaviours are executed apart from the learning behaviours, including those which in a contiguous situation would be performed in the learner's presence, so that communication between the teacher and the learner must be facilitated by print, electronic, mechanical or other devices. (Moore, 1972)

Obviously, there is separation between learner and teacher in all educational situations. One educator of children in face-to-face settings has distinguished between what happens before he meets a class and what happens in the class. Such activities as deciding on objectives and planning the lesson he calls the 'pre-active' stage of teaching, whilst asking questions, responding to students' ideas and giving guidance he calls 'inter-active' (Jackson, 1971). In distance teaching, however, even the interactive stage of teaching is conducted away from the physical presence of the learner.

Educators who prepare a 'lesson' for a correspondence course must decide not only on objectives and teaching strategies, but must also anticipate students' responses and reactions, and prepare their own replies to them. They must give directions and advice, explanations and interpretations. This teaching, both interactive and pre-active, begins in a different place and time from the learning, and is eventually communicated to the learner. The same can be said of educators who plan and present a teaching programme on radio or television, or on video tape, in a programmed text or on computer. Even the correspondence *tutor*, who is able to give guidance and instruction of a very individual nature, does so at a different time and place than that in which the student is engaged in learning. While separation, or distance, distinguishes independent study, therefore, there are degrees of separation.

Transactional distance is a function of two variables called 'dialogue' and 'structure'. Dialogue describes the extent to which, in any educational programme, learner and educator are able to respond to each other. This is determined by the content or subject matter which is studied, by the educational philosophy of the educator, by the personalities of educator and learner, and by environmental factors, the most important of which is the medium of communication. For example, an educational programme in which communication between educator and the independent learner is by radio or television permits no dialogue. A programme by correspondence is more dialogic, yet not to the same extent as one in which correspondence — or radio or television — is supplemented by telephone communication.

Structure is a measure of an educational programme's responsiveness to learners' individual needs. It expresses the extent to which educational objectives, teaching strategies and evaluation methods are prepared for, or can be adapted to, the objectives, strategies and evaluation methods of the learner. In a highly structured educational programme, the objectives and the methods to be used are determined for the learner, and are inflexible. In a linear, non-branching programmed text, for example, there is less opportunity for variation, according to the needs of a particular individual, than there is in those correspondence courses which permit a wide range of alternative responses by the tutor to individual students' questions and assignment submissions.

Figure 1: Types of Distance Teaching Programmes

	Type	Programme Types	Examples
Most Distance	—D—S	1. Programmes with no dialogue and no structure	Independent reading study programmes of the 'self directed' kind
	—D+S	2. Programmes with no dialogue but with structure	Programmes such as those in which the communication method is radio or television
	+D+S	3. Programmes with dialogue and structure	Typically programmes using the correspondence method
Least Distance	+D—S	4. Programmes with dialogue and no structure	E.g., a tutorial programme

In a programme in which there is little structure, and dialogue is easy, interaction between learner and teacher permits very personal and individual learning and teaching. Close guidance, direction and explanation are possible, even praise and admonition. Distance is low. Using the variables dialogue and structure, it is possible to classify individual learning programmes into four sets as in Figure 1. In Figure 1, +D represents dialogue, +S structure, —D no dialogue, and —S no structure. The most distant programmes are those of the —D—S type, and the least distant are the +D—S type. These are theoretical poles, and all programmes fall between them. The variables by which we are defining distance are qualitative, and programmes may be regarded as 'more' or 'less' distant. A correspondence programme is likely to be less distant than a programmed text, since it is likely to be less structured and more dialogic. However, among correspondence programmes great variability in distance will be found, with some being more dialogic than others, and others being no more dialogic or unstructured than programmed instruction. Thus, it is not intended to classify communications methods in this model, but only the uses to which methods are applied in educational programmes. Other variables, which it is not possible to discuss here, such as the learner's and the teacher's personality and characteristics, and the course subject matter, are also significant.

Where distance is low, a close relationship between learner and teacher is possible, whereas where distance is high it is less possible. Some programmed texts, for example, attempt to establish dialogue by use of the branching technique, but an admonitory statement like, 'Oops! you didn't follow instructions' (Mager, 1962, p. 5), will have less effect on the learner's emotion than a similar statement from a known correspondence tutor delivered by telephone, or face to face.

This relationship between distance and the learner's emotion is important when we consider the other dimension of independent study, learner autonomy. The success of any particular learner in a very distant independent study programme will depend on the extent to which he can work without emotional support from a tutor, as well as on the extent to which he can make decisions for himself about learning needs, objectives, study procedures and evaluation. In other words, it is necessary for success when distance is high to be a competent, autonomous learner.

The Importance of Individual Learning

In recent years, there has been a major shift in thinking about education, a change described by Henri Dieuzeide (1970) as being no less than a 'Copernican Revolution' in educational thought. This change involved, at first, a transfer of attention on the part of educational researchers from teaching to learning, and later, as a consequence, from a traditional concern with group learning and 'classes' to a greater interest in learning by individuals and 'individualised instruction'. Finally, there has also been a move among some educators away from teacher-controlled learning to the promotion of 'autonomous learning'.

Three developments have led to these changes. The first was the discovery by educational researchers that the key to improving learning lay in the study of the relationship between teaching methods and learner characteristics, not in the study of teaching alone. For many years the behaviour of the teacher received most attention from researchers and, in adult and higher education especially, there was a long search to find the 'best method' of teaching. The lecture was compared with discussion methods, programmed instruction with televised instruction, one form of each of these methods with another. But the results were disappointing, though they pointed in the same direction. When different methods are used on different groups of learners and the achievements of the groups are compared, *no* particular method appears to be measurably better than any other (Dubin and Taveggia, 1968). However, this conclusion is only true when the subject under study is a *group* of learners and when it is based on a comparison of the *mean* performance of groups exposed to different teaching methods.

When such groups are compared, differences within each group cancel each other out, so that in general no method appears superior to any other. But *within* each group some learners can be seen to respond more favourably to each particular method. One method may be superior, therefore, *for each particular student*, but this method will differ from person to person. One important new area of research which this discovery has opened up is to identify the particular abilities and personality characteristics which favour the application of given teaching methods; a search for 'aptitude-treatment interactions' (Cronbach and Snow, 1977). One of the most fruitful lines of inquiry has been into the learner characteristics known as cognitive styles. It is now believed that the key to successful education is the identification of the dynamics of individual learners, and the provision of appropriate methods of instruction for each individual. This would appear to be extremely demanding of teachers' skills in analysis, and perhaps impossible. However, between this ideal, and the 'shotgun' approach of placing all learners in a class and giving them all the same treatment, a practical approach is to provide learners with access to a wide variety of teaching methods and resources, and to give them freedom to explore, to discover and to use those which the learners themselves find most effective.

This approach has been very successful in primary education — and also in independent study by adults. The most successful institutions of independent study are 'multi-media' institutions, presenting subject matters in a *variety* of ways, generally through distance teaching, and allowing sufficient learner autonomy for each student to select the medium and the teaching techniques which are suited to his cognitive style, ability and personality.

Where educational institutions have been unable, or unwilling, to provide facilities and support for such independent study, many adults have planned and carried out learning programmes of their own, using such distance teaching materials as they have been able to locate, in public libraries and in the broadcast media, for example. This has been the second development which has contributed to the recent growth of interest in independent study, that is, the discovery of the extent of such autonomous learning by adults.

Millions of adults, it now appears, have been deliberately and systematically learning, using educational resources of all kinds outside the educational system, and have been overlooked by it. It has been shown that the typical adult undertakes about five learning projects every year, to each of which he devotes on average 100 hours. About three-quarters of these projects are completely self-directed, whereas only about 20 per cent are planned by a professional educator (Tough, 1971). Adults use a wide variety of resources, including all kinds of books, monographs and journals, programmed instruction, computer assisted instruction, radio, television, audio and video tapes — in short they use distance teaching materials in pursuit of their own, self-directed, learning objectives. Their learning projects are not usually academic, but are concerned with family, work, hobbies, politics, religion and other adult concerns. Some educational institutions have recently started to prepare materials to support this kind of learning.

The third factor which has contributed to the new interest in individual learning is the application to adult education of the insights of developmental psychologists, especially their discoveries about stages of development in adulthood, about psychological individuality and about adult self-concepts.

Psychologically speaking, the years of adulthood are years of ever increasing individuation. In other words, as one gets older one becomes more peculiarly oneself, and more unlike other people in one's perceptions, interests, attitudes, ways of thinking, perhaps even one's appearance. Every person is a unique being, growing in his or her own way, and in a continuous state of change. As we all experience birth, adolescence and death, we also experience other, though less dramatic, transitions throughout adulthood. The research evidence is by no means complete, but there is considerable agreement about the general nature of the main stages of adult development (Cross, 1981).

The findings of researchers have two extremely important implications for adult educators. First, we are becoming aware of the learning needs which accompany such developmental tasks as becoming a parent, or facing the difficulties and opportunities of mid-life change (Knox, 1979). 'Readiness', says Cross, 'appears to be largely a function of the socio-cultural continuum of life phases. The implication is that educators should capitalize on the "teachable moments" presented by the developmental tasks of the life-cycle' (Cross, 1981, p. 238).

Secondly, it is apparent that the process of individuation means that the psychological context in which any person encounters any of these transitions *will be different from that of anyone else.* Paradoxically, *life's transitions are common to all, yet experienced differently by each individual* and, in turn, contribute further to the uniqueness of each individual. Therefore, learning must be different for each individual, and educational programmes to aid adult learning must be structured to allow each individual to meet his particular needs.

Autonomous Learning

In certain educational theories it is assumed that systematic learning is not possible without teaching, that learning only occurs in response to teaching, and that it is the teacher's responsibility to see that learning occurs. It was this belief in the dependence of learners which led educators to herd learners into classes, to teach each group as if the individual differences of interest, motivation, cognitive style and developmental stage could be ignored, and as if learning could be effected only if the teacher practised the right tricks. For many people such teacher-led education does not work after leaving school, so they go ahead with planning and pursuing their own learning, using whatever resources they can obtain. It is quite natural for healthy adults to avoid the kind of teaching which assumes dependence and passivity. By definition the adult is a person who has a self-concept of being self-directing and self-controlled. Passivity and dependence must occur in the self-concept of the child, but with maturity one expects to make one's own decisions. Unfortunately, as Knowles has explained, when children mature and become self-directing in every other way, the wish to be responsible and self-directing in learning is often frustrated by professional teachers. It is possible to leave school adult in every other way but still dependent, or at least retarded in independence, as a learner (Knowles, 1970). Adult educators have a responsibility to help such learners to develop their independence, and also to act in their own teaching in ways which respect and advance the independence of their learners.

There are two kinds of psychological independence, emotional and instrumental (Heathers, 1955). Instrumental independence involves the ability to undertake an activity, including learning, without seeking help; emotional independence is the capacity to pursue the activity without seeking reassurance, affection or approval in order to complete it. The drive to achievement is derived from a need for *self-approval.*

This brings us to the heart of the difference between learning by the adult and by the child, and demonstrates the specially adult nature of independent study. The child is normally, and quite properly, dependent both instrumentally and emotionally on his teacher. The teacher deliberately uses the child's need for affection as a device for achieving learning, rewarding learning with signs of his approval. The adult learner might on occasions be instrumentally dependent, but should never be emotionally dependent. If his motivation in learning is to win approval from the educator, or if he uses the educational relationship to win affection, he has reverted to the dependency of childhood. The teacher who tries to induce learning by playing on the emotional vulnerability of the learner is teaching — or attempting to teach — as a teacher of children. The adult should not be treated in this way. The adult is entitled to:

> approach subject matter directly without having an adult in a set of intervening roles between the learner and the subject matter. The adult knows his own standards and expectations. He no longer needs to be told, nor does he require the approval and rewards from persons in authority. (Boyd, 1966, p. 180)

This is what is meant by autonomous learning. Autonomous learners — and this means most adults, most of the time — are able to identify learning needs, when faced with problems to be solved, as well as skills they don't have and information they are lacking. Sometimes formally, often unconsciously, they set objectives and define criteria for their achievement. Autonomous learners know, or find, where and how and from what human and other resources they may gather the information they require, collect ideas, practise skills and achieve their goals. They then judge the appropriateness of their new skills, information and ideas, eventually deciding whether their goals have been achieved or can be abandoned.

If, as we are suggesting, this is the normal behaviour of the adult, how does it affect teaching? First, it means giving up all pretence at 'motivating' learners. Adults have a natural desire to learn, especially to solve problems in their everyday lives, but also to enlarge their knowledge and experience. The educator's business is to help the adult to decide on the objective for learning at any particular time, and to help locate the resources and best strategies for achieving the objective. It should be an instrumental relationship, with the attitude of the educator non-directive and responsive.

It should be apparent that the autonomous learner is rarely self-sufficient, nor need be. He is not an intellectual Robinson Crusoe. He has recourse to teachers, and uses them for his own purposes, but the medium through which he communicates with teaching depends on the extent to which he is autonomous. The adult who is emotionally dependent is likely to seek a face-to-face relationship with a teacher; one who is emotionally independent but instrumentally dependent might look for help to a distance teaching programme in which distance is low. The most autonomous learner is only on occasions instrumentally dependent, so need not rely on only one teacher. He can draw on a wide range of resource persons, through writings, broadcasts, and recordings, as well as in person.

A Typology of Individual Learning Programmes

Just as we classified individual learning programmes according to the transactional distance, so we can also classify them by the degree of autonomy which is exercised by the learner.

A learning programme is a purposeful, deliberate and planned activity, or series of activities, by a learner intended to result in a change in knowledge, behaviour, or attitude. A teaching programme is a purposeful, deliberate, and planned activity, or series of activities, by a teacher intended to change the knowledge, behaviour, or attitude of a learner. An educational programme is a mixture of both learning and teaching programmes. In examining educational programmes we may ask:

1. About goal setting. To what extent are the goals determined by the learner or by the teacher? Are they the goals of the learner's programme, or of the teacher's?
2. About programme implementation. To what extent is the selection of resource persons, and books and other media, and the sequence and pace of learning experiences, the decision of the teacher or of the learner?
3. About evaluation. To what extent are decisions about the method and criteria to be used in evaluation made by the learner or the teacher?

By applying these questions the typology of individual learning programmes summarised in Figure 2 has been generated.

Figure 2: Types of Individual Learning Programmes by Variable Learner Autonomy

	Goal setting	Implementation	Evaluation
A — Learner determined	A	A	A
('Autonomous')	A	A	N
	A	N	A
	A	N	N
N — Teacher determined	N	A	A
('Non-autonomous')	N	N	A
	N	A	N
	N	N	N

In Figure 2, programmes range from those in which the learner exercises maximum control over the educational processes (AAA) — the most 'adult' of programmes — to those permitting very little autonomy (NNN). These extremes are theoretical only, and an infinite range of variations lies between them. The following examples illustrate the typology.

Type AAA: Someone who feels a need to be a better cook, who sets the objective of being able to cook three varieties of fruit pies with a success rate of 90 per cent, where success is determined by his family eating the pies, who chooses to learn by using a 'teach yourself' book and following a televised cookery course, has made all decisions about learning. Teaching in this case is highly distant, and the programme may be described as highly autonomous.

Type AAN: This is a class of programmes of lower autonomy, in which the learner's achievement is judged by an external agent. The area of learning which is offered for testing is chosen by the learner, as is the means for achieving competence. The student in the University of London external degree system may select areas of study, may study as he will, and may present himself for the evaluation of the University examiners. At a different level, a musician might offer himself for adjudication at a festival, having studied items of his own choosing.

Type ANA: Having identified certain learning objectives, learners sometimes surrender the direction of their learning to a teacher. Perhaps this can be illustrated by sports' players who seek a professional's instruction, with each player having different techniques needing correction, and each with different criteria for achievement in mind.

Type ANN: A programme type in which the learner, once having defined learning objectives, enters a controlled series of learning activities, and is evaluated by a teacher or other external agency. A person who chooses to learn the skills of driving an automobile, and enrolls with a professional instructor, has little control over the instruction, and none over the evaluation.

Types NAA and NNA: These are the least common programme types, in which the learner accepts all objectives (and, in NNA, the teacher's implementation procedures as well), but makes the evaluation decisions himself. The person who takes a correspondence course, with its set objectives, but having followed every stage of the course then decides not to take the final examination has completed a programme of the NNA type. Many people may manipulate the instruction process also, for example, by doing some assignments and not others. They therefore control the implementation process, and their programmes are of the NAA type.

Type NAN: A common type of programme where the student has some control over the implementation procedures, but where the goals are prescribed by an authority and evaluation is by an external agency. The majority of school and college independent study programmes fall into this category.

Type NNN: Another common type of programme, especially where professional certification is at stake. The objectives for learning, the means, and the evaluation of achievement, are in the control of the teaching authority.

The Field of Independent Study in Two Dimensions

By superimposing the typology of distance teaching programmes upon the typology of autonomous learning, the total field of individual learning may be displayed diagrammatically, as in Figure 3. In Figure 3, programmes range from 1-D-S, a programme of high learner autonomy using a very distant teaching programme, through programmes of diminishing independence to type 8+D-S, in which the learner has minimal control of the educational processes, there is dialogue between teacher and learner, and little structure in the programme.

Figure 3: Typology of Educational Programmes in Individual Mode

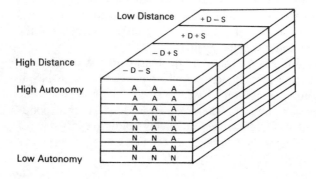

Conclusion

In this brief review of what is a vast field of educational activity there
has been no place for considering *why* individual learning is
important. Yet it is important, because we believe that the individual
is important. The theory and the practice of individual learning are
founded on a set of values and assumptions which many of us will
share, and which are vital to the health of our society. They are the
values of western, democratic, Judaeo-Christian society. They
include a belief in the intrinsic and fundamental worth of every
individual soul. They include the liberal view that the individual
should be free to exercise choice, and to grow in an individual way,
unimpeded by state control and direction. They include the democratic ideal that each person has a right and duty to be consulted and
to consult on the future. Because individual learning asserts the
potential and the importance of self-development, it has not always
enjoyed the same support from the state which is given to more social
forms of education.

But individual learning is a mode of education which reflects, and
also promotes, the very values which give our society its meaning, for
ultimately it is the well-being and growth of each individual which is
the purpose of, and justification for, the democratic state. The relationship of an individual and State was quite clear to Erich Fromm,
who, on escaping from Germany as the Nazis came to power, wrote:

> There is one way to define the real meaning of the difference
> between democracy and Fascism. Democracy is a system that
> creates the economic, political and cultural conditions for the full
> development of the individual. Fascism is a system that, regardless
> under which name, makes the individual subordinate to extran-
> eous purposes and weakens the development of true individuality.
> (Fromm, 1941, p. 301)

Adult educators are privileged to be able to contribute to the cultural
conditions which enhance the full development of the individual in
our society.

References

Boyd, R. (1966) 'A Psychological Definition of Adult Education', *Adult Leadership, 13*, 160-2, 180-1

Boyd, R.J., Apps, J.W. *et al.* (1980) *Redefining the Discipline of Adult Education*, Jossey-Bass Inc., San Francisco

Brunner, E., Wilde, D., Kirchner, C. and Newbury, J. (1959) *An Overview of Adult Education Research*, Adult Education Association of the USA, Washington, DC

Cronbach, L.J. and Snow, R.E. (1977) *Aptitudes and Instructional Methods*, John Wiley, New York

Cross P. (1981) *Adults as Learners*, Jossey-Bass Inc., San Francisco

Dieuzeide, H. (1970) *Educational Technology and Development in Education*, UNESCO, IEY Special Unit, Paris

Dubin, R. and Taveggia, T. (1968) *The Teaching-Learning Paradox*, University of Oregon Center for the Advanced Study of Educational Administration, Eugene

Fromm, E. (1941) *Escape from Freedom*, republished by Avon Books, New York, 1965

Heathers, G. (1955) 'Acquiring Dependence and Independence: A Theoretical Orientation', Journal of Genetic Psychology, *87*, 277-91

Holmberg, B. (1982) *Recent Research into Distance Education*, Zentrales Institut für Fernstudienforschung, Hagen, West Germany

Jackson, P. (1971) 'The Way Teaching Is' in Hyman, R. (ed.), *Contemporary Thought on Teaching*, Prentice Hall, Englewood Cliffs

Keegan, D. (1980) 'On Defining Distance Education', *Distance Education*, 1(1), 13-36

Knowles, M. (1970) *The Modern Practice of Adult Education*, Association Press, New York

Knox, A. (1979) 'Programming for Adults Facing Mid-life Change', *New Directions for Continuing Education*, 2 (1979)

Mackenzie, O., Christensen, E. and Rigby, P. (1968) *Correspondence Instruction in the United States*, McGraw-Hill, New York

Mager, R. (1962) *Preparing Instructional Objectives*, Fearon, Belmont, California

Moore, M. (1972) 'Learning Autonomy: the Second Dimension of Independent Learning', *Convergence, 5*, 76-87

Sivatko, J.R. (1969) 'Correspondence Instruction', *Encyclopedia of Educational Research*, 4th edn., Ebel, R. (ed.), Macmillan, New York

Tough, A. (1971) *The Adult's Learning Projects: A Fresh Approach to Theory and Practice in Adult Learning*, Ontario Institute for Studies in Education, Toronto
_____ (1971) 'Independent Study' in *The Encyclopedia of Education*, Deighton, L. (ed.), Free Press, New York, vol. 4, pp. 548-57.

Wedemeyer, C. (1982) *Learning at the Back Door: Reflections on Non-Traditional Learning in the Life Span*, University of Wisconsin Press, Madison

3.3

HIGHER EDUCATION:
SCHOOL FOR INDEPENDENT STUDY

John Stephenson

Source: T. Burgess and E. Adams (eds.), *Outcomes of Education* (Macmillan, London, 1980), pp. 132-49.

On the Diploma in Higher Education (DipHE) programme in the School for Independent Study at North East London Polytechnic, we have dispensed with pre-arranged syllabuses and externally imposed assessments and have made exclusive use of students' own Statements. These Statements cover students' own self-assessment of interests, abilities and achievements at the outset; their long-term aspirations and more immediate educational goals; their detailed plans for learning; and the details of their terminal assessment. [...]

Our purpose is to provide students with an educational experience which enables them to be generally competent and independent. By this we mean that they should be capable of coping with a wide variety of different situations, many of them unfamiliar, without being dependent upon the direction of others. We are convinced of the relevance of this by our observations of the nature of society and the needs of individuals within it. Many of the traditional props, such as the extended family, and the Church, are less important than in the past. The skills and aptitudes demanded by jobs are changing, with retraining and constant change of practice becoming the normal experience. There is considerable mobility, bringing young people into new and different social environments. Social practices, moral codes and personal relationships are much more flexible, with more onus being placed on the individual to determine his own code of practice. In short, change is becoming normal, and the capacity to cope with and participate in change is increasingly at a premium.

We are encouraged by our view of the nature of knowledge itself. It is clear that what is known is constantly being extended, refuted or disregarded. What it was essential to know in a given situation ten years ago is very often not essential now. New or different knowledge is constantly being applied to the same situation in response to

169

people's greater understanding of that situation, their changing perception of it, and the greater volume of possible relevant knowledge from which to choose. What were previously held to be fundamental truths are often no longer assumed to be so. Current fundamental truths will themselves in turn be discarded, replaced or refined. In other words, the identification of a given body of knowledge as essential for any educated person to have is increasingly becoming a difficult and even futile task. In its place, the ability to learn, challenge and extend knowledge is much more useful.

Thirdly, we have been influenced by our view of the nature of learning and the ways in which knowledge is extended. At its simplest level we believe in learning by doing, which in this case means directly involving the student in his own learning process. We believe that trial and error is a natural and effective method of learning, involving, as it does, an original tentative shot at setting out the nature of a problem and a possible solution; having a go to see if it works; and, in the light of its failure, producing a more sophisticated statement of the nature of the problem. People who are competent at learning in this way are most likely to be capable of coping with changing circumstances, without dependence upon others to show the way.

Fourthly, we were conscious of a feeling that many students pursuing courses of higher education were doing so largely because of the social and economic pressure on them to gain the highest level of qualification of which they were capable. In many cases this meant shopping around to find the course or college most likely to take them. Even when a happy marriage is arranged whereby the student gets into a generally relevant field or subject there are problems. For instance, course planners' assumptions about the general level at which all freshers must begin inevitably frustrate all but the predictable student. Syllabuses include items which relate more to the interests of staff or the range of expertise available in the department than to the actual needs or interests of the student. Little if any effort is made to diagnose which skills and knowledge the student brings with him. Neither are the specific requirements implied by the student's own aspirations for his life after he's finished formal education taken into account. In short, there is often a severe mismatch between what is provided and what is needed. [...]

Finally, we wished to give more recognition to the importance of the affective domain in education. The ability to cope with the unfamiliar is as much dependent upon self-confidence as it is on the problem solving and other related skills. Our own observations, matched by those of the employers who were consulted, were that many school leavers lacked purpose and confidence. We believed that a process of self-analysis supported by tutorial and peer group guidance would help to stimulate purposeful personal development, and that the achievement of personally set goals would lead to the development of self-confidence. If such achievement is further applauded by the real world and the educational establishment, then self-confidence is substantial and assured.

For all these reasons, argued at greater length in the documents setting out the DipHE programme, we deliberately confront each student with his new, unfamiliar situation, namely his own education for the next two years. We require him to formulate his own educational problem, devise his own solution to that problem, implement that solution, and, at the end, test and demonstrate the extent to which it is successful. We have rejected the opposite and traditional practice of learned and external bodies arrogantly determining the educational problem of others (usually in large bundles), imposing their own mass solutions (called syllabuses), and applying a common test of achievement. This is nearly always done on a knowledge rather than skill basis. Such approaches as these deny students their own valuable learning experience.

We recognise the advantages of the existing system of externally imposed syllabuses and assessments in establishing public confidence. Not only do the public in general and employers in particular need to be satisfied that the end product of education has a warranty of quality backed by the collective authority of the educational establishment, but also the student himself needs some external criticism and recognition of the value of what he proposes to do and what he achieves. Where inexperienced non-expert students are trusted with tasks normally assigned only to established academics, public recognition is not only desirable, it is absolutely essential. The importance of the Statement to our work is that it is the main vehicle for requiring students to make public and explicit the rationale for, and details of, their proposed programmes, thus exposing them to rigorous public criticism. If they survive this process then recognition can follow quite readily.

What the Statement consists of

The Statement consists of an agreement between the student, the Polytechnic, and his tutor, that a particular programme of study is both valid and feasible and if completed would be worthy of the

award of a CNAA DipHE. [...] Attached to the formal agreement
are six Appendices A to F prepared by the student himself. What
follows is an example of one such Statement produced in 1978 by a
full-time student after one term's experience.

APPENDIX A
Educational Experience

1959-64:
   Attended six years of primary schooling and graduated with
   Grade 1 Primary School Certificate
1965-9:
   Attended five years of Secondary Schooling and securing two O
   levels in English Literature and Needlework
1970-71:
   Attended Secretarial School and obtaining Pitman's Certificate in
   Typewriting and Shorthand

Other Relevant Experience
1972:
   Worked as a secretary to the directoress of a modeling agency
1973:
   Worked as a clerk in a large textile factory
1974-5:
   Attended State Enrolled Nurses' training securing a State
   Enrolled Nurses' Diploma
1976-7:
   Worked as a State Enrolled Nurse at Plaistow Maternity Hospital

A very varied background beginning with an involved experience
in school. Was associated with a variety of clubs and societies, both
academic and recreational. I was an active member of the Red Cross
Society and the School Literary, Debating and Dramatic Society.
Participated in a number of inter-school debates and school plays.
Through this experience I gained a lot of confidence in public speaking and working with other members of the club.

After leaving school I went into Secretarial School because that's
what my parents wanted me to do. After a year's training I worked as
a secretary for a year and had to leave because the agency was closing
down. Then I worked as a clerk for about a year in a large textile
factory. My experience in both jobs have made me familiar with office
routine and internal politics of large, private and public enterprises.

I went into nursing to get away from the daily office routine.

Having worked as a nurse for more than four years, I have come in contact with people at all levels from patients to staff. A nurse, besides performing nursing duties has to reckon with the emotions, attitudes and problems of her patients. During emergencies and daily nursing routine we work as a team with colleagues, the medical, administrative and other hospital staff.

My reason for leaving nursing is because for a long time I have had a desire to pursue a course of higher education. This desire is the course of a few reasons. First being that it would enable me both to improve my standing in society and at the same time make a more worthy contribution to the community that I live in. Another reason being that I would like to improve myself and I feel that the challenge of a course in higher education would be a very appropriate way to go about doing it. This way, I feel that I am not just self-indulging in a particular fashion but also having a tangible and beneficial effect in society and myself.

I feel that I am a credible person now at twenty-five years of age, for pursuing a high education course specially my specialist subject which is Information Processing. I feel that studying this subject would stretch my capabilities which until today have not been done so to the fullest.

I have also travelled quite widely in and around South East Asia and Europe. This experience has made me a more self-confident and independent person.

APPENDIX B
Present Position

Looking at the résumé outlined in Appendix A, I feel that I do possess certain skills and capacities which I acquired more as an accidental by-product of my past education and job experience.

I can, however, identify certain skills that I now possess. They are:
(i) Typewriting
     Intermediate Stage Gross speed — 40 words per min. Accuracy: 100 per cent
(ii) Report Writing
     Only as far as my past education and jobs have required and allowed to exercise this skill.
(iii) Oral Capabilities
     I can in most instances make myself be understood and I don't have any difficulties understanding anyone.
(iv) Languages

Can speak five languages — English, Malay, Punjabi, Hindi and Hokkien (a Chinese dialect). Written knowledge of English, Malay and Punjabi.

(v) Organising

I am fairly competent in this skill as I was responsible for the running of a ward in a hospital.

The one weakness that stands out like a sore thumb, is a tendency to put things off to the last minute in particular working on a given assignment, but I'm always capable of meeting deadlines.

APPENDIX C
Outline Future Planning

After gaining the Diploma, I hope to go on to attain a Degree and then do postgraduate work in Information Studies, especially in the use of computers for Information Processing as applied to libraries.

Hopefully I would like to get a BA by Independent Studies at North East London Polytechnic or a place at any of the colleges which offer degree courses for Information Studies.

I do not have definite vocational plans as this will depend on the work I do in the next few years but I can envisage working in one of the following fields of employment.

Government Departments: Many departments have information services for the use of their staff and public usage e.g. Foreign and Commonwealth Office, Ministry of Agriculture, Fisheries and Food, Department of Industry, Department of Health and Social Security and The Public Records Office

Academic: Universities, Polytechnics and Technical Colleges, National and Scientific Libraries

Industry: Manufacturing, Technical, Commercial, Financial establishment

APPENDIX D
Skills, Knowledge and Qualities Needed

Individual Work

1. The ability to demonstrate a knowledge of program skills and program techniques relevant to my area of studies
2. The ability to demonstrate documentation skills
3. Acquire File Handling Techniques
4. A fluency in Cobol programming language

Group Work
Acquire Diagnostic Skills
The ability to
1. Locate and collect data and information
2. Assimilate data selectively, modify and adapt data to new problem areas
3. Identify real life problems and operations and make keen observational analysis of these situations
4. To collaborate with others in the group in organising, researching and developing projects and putting them into operation, within constraints of time and resource

APPENDIX E
Proposed Programme of Study

Individual Work
Methods of Study
1. Tutorial
   Through weekly tutorials with my Individual Work Tutor in which I will discuss my project work
2. Lectures
   Through attending lectures in Faculty of Business Studies every Monday and Friday
3. Projects
   Through project work in the use of Computer Systems

1st Year
Terms 2 and 3
   1. *OBJECTIVES*
a. To be able to identify problems solveable by a computer and those that are not
b. To become aware of computer peripherals e.g. Line Printer, Card-Reader, Teletype
   2. *AREAS OF STUDY*
a. To use data and program operation equipments
b. To become familiar with the COBOL programming
c. A knowledge of program techniques
d. A knowledge of file structure
e. Attend lectures on Advanced Programming. Syllabus: Linear Lists, Arrays, Trees Structures, File Organisation, Data Structure Handling, Languages and Grammars, Compilers.
   3. *ASSIGNMENTS TO BE COMPLETED*
a. To run a number of elementary programs using COBOL — by

the end of term 2

b.   To complete a basic Retrieval project on the implement of a system based upon the journals holding of NELP — by the end of term 3

2nd Year

A system for the 2nd year cannot at this stage be specified in detail as it is not yet known what systems will be available within NELP.

   The program will however be moulded in the following format.

Terms 1 and 2

   1. *AREAS OF STUDY*

a.   A detailed study of one or two particular Retrieval systems, possibly the MARC (Machine Readable Catalogue) and BLAISE (British Library Automation Information System).

b.   Attend lectures on Information Storage and Retrieval.

Syllabus: File Organisation, Sorting and Searching Database Techniques, Virtual Storage Techniques.

   2. *ASSIGNMENTS TO BE COMPLETED*

a.   Essay on Information Storage and Retrieval. Length: Approx. 2000 words — by end of term 1

b.   Exercises in the use of one or both of the MARC or BLAISE Systems and if possible assist in a live situation, e.g. write or implement some software relevant to the system — by the end of term 2

Term 3

Document and consolidate studies, i.e. write dissertation and present documentation of program systems produced.

   I append a booklist as an indication of the basic reading I will be pursuing, although I will expand the booklist in the course of my study.

Group Work

I will follow the project program of the school and will contribute Individual Reports on the projects which will describe and analyse:

a.   Individual contribution to the group project

b.   How specific skills were used during the project

[…]

APPENDIX F

Methods of Assessment

I will submit as evidence of my work achieved throughout the program, my final individual product which will be

a.   Dissertation on the nature and size of the program of Informa-

tion Retrieval. General review of modern methods and techniques.
Length: approx. 7,000 words
b. *Projects*
1st Year: Journal listing system of NELP
2nd Year: Software enhancement for MARC system and exercises in
    Information Retrieval using BLAISE. Subject to these being the
    systems available at NELP
These will demonstrate the skills listed in relation to Individual Work
in Appendix D.

My work will be assessed by my tutor and assessors who are
competent in this field.

Group Work
This will be assessed by my ability to use basic diagnostic skills listed
in Appendix D and I will use the opportunity to discuss my knowledge and employment of these skills with my individual report in the
set situation.

The Statement has three main components. First, Appendices A,
B, and C represent the formulation of the student's educational
problem as perceived by himself; secondly D and E represent the
proposed detailed educational solution to the problem; and finally
Appendix F represents the basis on which the appropriateness of the
solution is tested. These three components roughly correspond with
the various phases of the DipHE programme and what follows is a
brief description of how they are produced.

The Formulation of the Educational Problem (A, B, C)

This takes place in the first three or four weeks of the programme.
During this period the student is with a group of fifteen peers with a
personal tutor. Each appendix is written in sequence and preparation
for each lasts about a week. For Appendix A the problem is to encourage the student to open up about himself and for him to feel
sufficiently secure to be able to do so. Much use is made of team
building exercises to boost the support from peers in which the tutor is
expected to join. Students are encouraged not only to write down
their personal histories, focusing on what seems to them to be most
important, but also to exchange their writings with their colleagues
and tutors who do not reject or denigrate anything which is written or
said but give their reactions to it. As often as not, this process of
mutual exchange of experiences and reactions leads to a more

thoughtful and penetrating personal history by the end of the week. Students are able to compare their own lot with that of others and very quickly find themselves talking at great length about themselves and in return asking searching questions of their fellows. The group of fifteen frequently breaks down to sets of four to six for this activity so that a variety of experiences and reactions is encountered. At intervals during this week the School provides specific inputs such as seminars on the aims of education, the wider context of the DipHE in Higher Education, and the factors which contribute to success or failure in school. There is discussion, in particular, on the value of planning educational experiences and the importance of starting with the student rather than the subject. Wherever possible the activities are made enjoyable and everyone is made conscious of the need to support each other. There is no rigid timetable of activities, except on the few occasions when an input is required for the whole year group (e.g. an introduction to the staff of the Polytechnic's counselling services), which means that groups operate rather like an infant class where the class teacher has the freedom to switch activities to suit the moods and changing needs of the group.

Appendix B is a more analytical version of A, where the student is encouraged to set out his strengths and weaknesses. This is particularly difficult and students find themselves constantly adding to their personal inventories. The pattern of provision is as before, with the addition of self-evaluation exercises. Tests of specific skills, such as literacy and numeracy, are available but for other less obvious skills group exercises leading to mutual evaluation are used. Access to the Polytechnic's counselling tutors and other specialists is arranged as required. Inevitably there is constant reference back to Appendix A which continues to develop during this phase.

For Appendix C, access to careers advisers and ideally to specialists in the chosen field is very important. Students are encouraged not only to indicate likely destinations but also to explore the implications of getting there. For instance, a student wishing to become a teacher would need to know the requirements for gaining recognition, the different ways in which it can be achieved, some indication of his preferred route, and to show some understanding of the place his DipHE would have in it. Again, discussions in sets are very useful in helping students to come to terms with what they want to do. For many of them it is the first time they have ever been required to think seriously about the future. It is quite legitimate for students to remain doubtful about their preferences, provided they are clear about their doubt and that it is expressed in such a way as to form a useful basis for educational planning. An example would be 'I wish to work with adolescents but I wish to keep open the options of probation work, teaching, or youth and community work. The implication of keeping these options open are that my Diploma programme should contain...' Students are then required to indicate a first tentative solution to the problem they are setting for themselves. In one brief paragraph they set out the general lines of their proposed programme of study and then submit their total Interim Statement, as it is called, to external criticism and validation.

Preparing the Solution (D and E)

Once the Interim Statement is approved the student can proceed to plan his programme, knowing that he is generally on the right lines. Clearly, detailed planning can only take place on the basis of experience in the chosen areas, so this phase of the course, lasting four months, consists of various placements and workshop activities. For instance, the potential teacher of deaf children would be introduced to those Polytechnic staff who share the same interest and who have appropriate experience and expertise. Preliminary background work is begun, schools for the deaf are visited, practising teachers in the field are interviewed, and arising from all those discussions, observations, self-assessments of specific abilities, and negotiations, the student is able to state with confidence those learning outcomes it would be most helpful for him to achieve (Appendix D) and the most appropriate ways of achieving them (Appendix E). The student's own specialist tutor is crucial in this activity, acting as adviser, critic, assessor and source of information and contacts. The contract between them not only spells out the content of the programme, but also indicates the learning methods, frequency of tutorial contacts, types and amount of assignments to be completed, and location and duration of field placements.

Completion of the Programme (F)

When the Final Statement is validated, and the programme implemented as planned, the student is required to present for assessment precisely what he set out to present. He is kept to what he set for himself in Appendix D and the means of assessment stated in F. Aimless wandering from his own purpose-built syllabus is therefore not encouraged and is unlikely to lead to success. The questions asked by the Assessment Board are, 'Has this student achieved what is set out in Appendix D in the manner indicated in Appendix F?' and secondly, 'Has he done so at a level comparable to that which would be expected of an undergraduate completing his second year of his Honours Degree course?' If 'yes', then a Diploma is awarded. If 'no', then it is not. This is extremely important because the fact that what is put into Appendices D and F is for real means that students take that part of the planning process extremely seriously. It also ensures that the Statement actually does represent an accurate profile of the work done.

Validation of Final Statements

Initially, all Statements are scrutinised within the School, with a number of tutors, including those not familiar with the student, considering the total package in terms of its cohesion, demand on resources and whether it is likely to lead to the award of the Diploma. In particular the following questions are asked:

Do Appendices A and B provide sufficient evidence of critical self-appraisal?
Is a sense of direction indicated in Appendix C? Is there an awareness in the implications (vocational and academic) of stated intentions?

In Appendix D is there:
— a clear statement of learning objectives which relate to both Individual and Group Work?
— a consistency between these objectives and the goals indicated in Appendix C?
— sufficient emphasis on content (skills/knowledge) especially in terms of Individual Work?
— a clear reference to transferable skills in terms of Group and Individual Work?
— evidence that objectives are sufficiently refined as to be manageable within the context of the programme?
— sufficient regard to coherence and presentation?

In Appendix E is there:
— an overall awareness of the reality of implementing objectives outlined in Appendix D?
— an outline of the substantive elements of Individual Work?
— a clear statement of commitment to a specified output of work within the Individual Work context?

- sufficient indication of the phasing of work in terms of time and emphasis?
- some indication of the nature and frequency of contacts with Special Interest Tutors?

In Appendix F is there:
- a reference to the skills and knowledge (outlined in D) to be demonstrated via Individual Work?
- an indication of the Individual Work product showing sufficient relationship to the above?

When the School's judgement is clear, a sample of the Statements is sent to a panel of people external to the Polytechnic, who meet together and decide whether the School's judgement is appropriate. As a Board they interrogate the School on its judgement and interview all students whose Statements are in some way in doubt, and a range of the rest. Once validated, the Statement represents a commitment by the Polytechnic to resource the programme and, under arrangements agreed with the CNAA, becomes the basis for assessment for the award of DipHE.

Whilst the validated programme is being implemented, students are encouraged by their personal tutors to monitor continually their own progress and the relevance of their programme. It is obvious that throughout the two years of work the student will learn more about his long-term intentions, the detailed implications of his originally stated intentions, the degree of ease or difficulty of different parts of his programme, the relative appropriateness of its various components, and detailed criteria of assessment. To achieve this fine-tuning the student must become accustomed to asking for feedback on his performance and criticism of his programme from both his personal tutor and his specialist tutor. Tutors in their turn must see their role as essentially one of supplying such feedback and criticism in a manner which fosters confidence. Eventually, students learn to exercise their own judgements and to use tutorial and other comments as a means of testing their own judgement of performance rather than the performance itself. To facilitate this process of development, the Validating Board meets each term and can therefore consider proposals for changes more or less as required by the student. It is important to state, however, that the same demands for explicit rationale are made as in the original validation so that changes are deliberate and conscious and not whimsical or uncontrolled drift.

Membership of the Board is made up of individuals who, by their status or achievement, represent success in the outside world. They are not, in the main, the conventional external examiners and this is deliberate policy. At present they consist of an ex Senior Civil Servant, a retired Inspector of Education, a Business Consultant, an Architect, a former Senior Local Government Official, and a Business Executive. We see validation as essentially different from assessment in that a) it represents an important learning experience; b) it provides the opportunity for students to find solutions outside the normal academic solutions; c) it allows students to justify proposals on grounds other than the extent to which they are assessable by conventional means; and d) we are operating a programme designed to help people cope with life outside college and not just with academic work. This last reason is crucial.

Preparation for validation is a formidable task for the student. A good deal of effort is put into making as explicit as possible the precise nature of the student's educational problem, and the proposed solution, and into communicating the proposal as clearly as possible. The effect of this is that the student is made to be explicit to himself, and to be as clear in his own mind, as he can be about what he wants to do, why he wants to do it, and how he proposes to do it. His commitment to completion of the programme is very high as a consequence. Further, once this revered and august body has validated his statement, the student has the confidence of knowing that what he, as a humble student, is proposing is thought by the establishment to be well worth doing, particularly in terms appropriate to the student himself.

There are also external payoffs of validation. Public confidence in the quality of the proposed programme is guaranteed by this disinterested group of personalities. The Statement itself, suitably endorsed by the Validating Board, and eventually by the DipHE Assessment Board, forms a very useful and informative profile of the student and his work. Potential employers of the student, for instance, will learn more about him from his Statement than by any conventional public certification.

The preparation of Statements has the considerable bonus of being a valuable educational process in itself. Students learn quickly how to communicate effectively both orally and in writing, how to analyse complex situations, how to give and receive critical advice, how to support others in group situations, how to set out a problem, and above all how to negotiate their way around a vast and bureaucratic institution. At the end of this process they understand the difference between long-term educational aims and short-term objectives, and have knowledge of a variety of methods of learning and assessment.

For Assessment, we use the normal established bodies for external assessment of Polytechnic/CNAA sponsored awards. It is very important that we do this in order to establish comparability of standards with other students, to preserve public confidence in the student's achievement, and to give the student marketable credit for his work. To help us do this, there is an Assessment Board constituted on exactly the same basis as Boards for CNAA Degrees, i.e. including external examiners approved by the Council itself. In order to cope with the wide variety of programmes we try to include as full members of the Board an examiner from each of the main activity areas (e.g. the Arts, Natural Sciences etc.). The procedures depend initially, as with CNAA Degrees, on internal assessment by specialist tutors in the appropriate field. In most cases this is the student's own special interest tutor. We also receive a further report from a 'disinterested person', who has not been personally involved with the student but who is competent to judge work at this level in the relevant field. In some cases, particularly where the work is in an obscure or unusual area, written testimonials are solicited, often by the student himself, from established figures in other institutions. External examiners have full access to all disinterested persons, and can personally interview each student. In practice, all students about whom there is even the slightest doubt are seen, together with a sample of the rest. External examiners read a selection of students' work sent to them in advance (work of their choice), spend about three days in the School meeting with tutors, students and inspecting the total range of work, and attend a final formal meeting to approve the agreed pass list. Afterwards they submit their criticisms and comments to the Polytechnic and the CNAA.

Problems of Running such a Scheme

[...] Work of the kind described in this chapter requires a tutor to behave in ways different from normal. He starts by listening to students and proceeds by responding to needs as they become apparent. He has three main roles to play. First, he must build up the student's confidence in himself by recognising that he, the student, has something positive to contribute and by establishing a client/

consultant relationship. Secondly, the tutor must continually challenge the student's logic and self-assertions as an aid to increasing his self-awareness, and at the same time give constant feedback on the student's performance. Thirdly, the tutor must be able to respond quickly with appropriate information or learning activities as the needs become apparent. This can be done by the tutor himself or by contracting the student out to colleagues more expert in a particular field. In brief it calls for a considerable shift in the tutor's perception of his role, almost a total reversal. Yet our experience so far has suggested that staff themselves respond very favourably when they are offered the opportunity of moving outside their traditional constraints, and that the most effective agents for staff development are the students themselves.

Another problem is to match specific student needs with specific tutor expertise. So far we have placed over four hundred students without more than a handful being totally unable to find a specialist tutor. It means that instead of producing a fixed timetable in advance, the School must provide agencies for the exchange of information and market places for the arrangement of meetings of students and potential tutors.

There are also implications for the availability of resources. Specialist facilities, provided mainly for other groups of students, need to be available by negotiation to DipHE students. Learning resources should be arranged in resource centres and loaned out on a library basis. These principles are very difficult to establish, particularly when they are currently managed by self-contained discipline-based Departments. Part of the solution depends on the ways in which the institutions can compensate the host Department for their use.

It must also be recognised that there are problems for students too. Initially there is a period of disorientation, when previous assumptions about themselves and education are being exposed and questioned. Secondly, there can be frustration if making the right choices proves difficult or the tutors and resources are not readily available. Thirdly, there is a potential for isolation, since there is not a whole group of peers doing exactly the same things and with whom it is possible to exchange information and views and to get some feel of how much relative success is being achieved.

There are also considerable technical difficulties over things like assessment. Normal assessments generally operate on a ranking basis with cut-offs between success and failure rather arbitrarily determined. For rankings to take place a number of students doing comparable work is necessary and this we haven't got. We are therefore forced to assess the actual level of each achievement in isolation and this is extremely difficult particularly with affective skills. Our current solution is to demand from the student explicit Statements of precisely what is to be assessed and to ask academics experienced in examining other undergraduate courses in similar fields to state whether in their opinion what is presented is the sort of thing which a student completing his second undergraduate year might reasonably be expected to do.

We will not, of course, know how successful our use of Statements is for some time yet. We will need to follow up the progress of our Diplomats to see how they fare and of course this we are doing. Our preliminary judgement, based on our own observations of their personal development over the two year period, is that the student benefit is considerable. We have no plans to revert to more traditional methods.

The question that inevitably arises is whether our work is generally applicable to other areas of education. We are convinced that the educational problems to which our work is a tentative solution are general problems, and are present in all institutions of education from primary school to university, and that the educational value of independent study is not constrained by age, level or institutional context. It is also worth noting that those students who appear to have most difficulty with coping with the problem of their own education are those who have transferred directly either from secondary school or from other courses of higher education. Those who come from 'real life' fare much better. We take this to be an indication that educational institutions are not themselves very successful at helping their pupils/students to become more competent.

A further consideration is whether established institutions are capable of adapting themselves in this way. It is important to appreciate in this respect the extent to which North East London Polytechnic is like nearly every other school or college. It has subject departments and faculties, has staff largely with conventional school and college backgrounds, and is constrained educationally by the demands of a publicly established validating body. All that is needed is a small group of committed and energic staff, supported by the Director or Head, who can work out the detailed solutions to the local problems of inertia and tradition. Their solutions, of course, are likely to differ from ours in some respects according to their circumstances and creativity.

3.4

RADIO ECCA: A DISTANCE LEARNING SYSTEM IN THE CANARY ISLANDS

Luis Espina Cepeda

Source: A. Kaye and K. Harry (eds.), *Using the Media for Adult Basic Education* (Croom Helm, London, 1982). pp. 208-28.

Introduction

The Canary Islands, part of Spain, lie off the north-western coast of Africa. They have a total area of 7,300 square kilometres (2,800 square miles), and a population of over 1,500,000 people. The main settlement, Las Palmas, with some 400,000 inhabitants, is the eighth largest town in Spain. In spite of their location, the islands receive the radio and television broadcasts of the national station, Radio-television Espanola, and are also served by a number of local commercial radio stations.

Radio ECCA is an independent, non-commercial station with a primarily educational function. 'ECCA' stands for 'Emisora Cultural de Canarias' (Cultural Station of the Canaries), and is now also the trademark for the educational system created by the radio station, which has spread from the Canaries to the Spanish mainland and Latin America. It was founded in 1963 by Francisco Villen Lucena of the Society of Jesus (Jesuits), and they retain ultimate control over the administration and management of the station. Its operation, however, has been handed over to the Ministry of Education for 'adult education and experiments in distance education'. Resources for running the station, which had a total income of 127 million pesetas in 1979, come from student fees (53.5 per cent of income in 1979) and from subsidies from the state and other sources. There are at present nearly 50 teachers, appointed and paid for by the Ministry, based at the station.

Radio ECCA's first priority was to teach basic reading and writing skills, and its principal focus of attention was, and still is, the poorest classes of society. Since its inception, Radio ECCA has diversified its provision to provide some educational opportunities at a more

186

advanced level, with the aim of continuing to reflect the needs of the population. Its fundamental purpose is seen as being to raise the cultural level of the population with a view to bringing about greater individual freedom and a progressively increasing awareness of, and involvement in, community life.

Between 1965, when the first lessons were broadcast, and 1981 Radio ECCA enrolled 175,000 students, some 11.5 per cent of the total population of the Canary Islands. It would not have been possible, because of their location, work, family responsibilities and other circumstances, for many of these students to have regularly attended conventional courses at established educational centres. Even if they could have attended such courses the educational budget for the region would have been insufficient to meet a demand for adult education on this scale.

Three quarters of Radio ECCA's students have been aged between 20 and 45 years. A survey carried out in 1972 indicated that 41 per cent of its students lived in small towns, villages and the surrounding countryside, 27 per cent in larger towns and 32 per cent in Las Palmas itself. 'Housewives' accounted for 31 per cent of the enrolment, students of other educational institutions for 27 per cent, and unskilled and semi-skilled workers for 40 per cent.

Areas of Provision

Radio ECCA's activities are centred on three areas:

(1) The broadcasting of courses leading to an academic qualification. When Radio ECCA was established, over 10 per cent of the Canary Islands' adult population were total illiterates, and it was natural that its initial focus was on literacy education. In a series of six courses, the total illiterate was given the opportunity to progress towards the 'Certificade de Estudios Primarios', which was at that time an essential prerequisite for employment. When, in 1973, this requirement was relaxed and other alterations were made in the Spanish education system, Radio ECCA modified and extended its academic curriculum. At present a series of five 'Popular culture' courses, including the first stage towards literacy, are offered, followed by three courses which prepare students for the 'Titulo de Graduado Escolar', which represents the final stage of primary education in Spain. In these courses it is intended that students should

'not only strive to obtain a qualification but should also broaden their horizons, working progressively towards full personal development. In 1980-1, as part of its programme of offering a second opportunity to the adult population, Radio ECCA also introduced courses leading to the 'Bachillerato', the secondary qualification which can lead to university entrance.

(2) Since its foundation Radio ECCA has also provided non-academic courses (not leading to a qualification) aimed at improving both quality of life and job performance. Courses have been provided for some years in English, and in Accountancy and Commercial Mathematics. There is a 'Parents' School' ('Escuela de Padres') which aims to help parents in the task of educating their children. Courses currently in preparation include a course for the training of group leaders, courses on techniques of evaluation (for teachers), on preventive medicine (for a wide popular audience), on techniques of management at an elementary level for small traders, and even on photography. Through the ECCA system it is possible to teach virtually any subject by radio.

(3) The third area of activity is less clearly defined but no less im-portant. During those times when its education programmes are not being transmitted (i.e. three hours per day on working days and all day on holidays), ECCA's broadcasts are devoted to entertainment. The station has a considerable listening audience, one of the largest of any station in the Canary Islands, due to its expertise in presenting entertainment programmes and to the fact that it does not use commercial advertising. Educational elements are sometimes slotted into the entertainment programming; campaigns have been mounted to encourage a positive attitude towards self-help or towards study, and towards wider objectives such as community development, the necessity of being well-informed on election issues, and promoting awareness of consumer pressures at Christmas time. Through its frequent use of the telephone and the recorded interview, Radio ECCA attempts to become the voice of the people, especially of those whose views are not usually heard. ECCA treats its audience with great respect; it does not base campaigns on controversial issues but promotes programmes of clear positive value to the community. However, this third area of cultural activity is much less precisely defined than the other two, a factor which makes it difficult to evaluate.

Media and Methods

ECCA describes its teaching system as 'un sistema tridimensional'; it is based on three elements frequently found in combination in distance education: print materials, radio, and face-to-face tuition.

Every ECCA lesson is centred upon a 'lesson master sheet' ('esquema' — see Figure 1). The teacher has a copy of the lesson master sheet in front of him while he broadcasts over the radio, and the student follows his own copy simultaneously. This specially produced printed material, prepared by ECCA's education staff and printed in its own workshop, fulfils the function of worksheet, blackboard or slate.

The student is required to respond to the radio teacher by writing on the lesson master sheet during the course of the broadcast. The master sheet is therefore the means of maintaining both the continuous attention of the student and the necessary communication between teacher and student. In addition, a full set of master sheets comprises a student's text book. Exercises are included on the back of each master sheet; these are designed to be completed after the student has listened to the radio broadcast. The student will receive assistance from the exercises in consolidating his learning, and ECCA uses the exercises as part of its student evaluation process. Full comprehension of an ECCA radio lesson cannot be achieved without a lesson master sheet. In addition, the master sheets for different courses are complemented by various other types of printed material produced by ECCA for its students; notes or technical memoranda ('notas o apuntes tecnicos') on difficult topics, synoptic tables, special exercise sheets, complementary texts, etc.

The second element of the ECCA system is the 'radio lesson' ('clase'), which resembles neither a lecture nor any other traditional type of radio programme. It might perhaps best be described as a detailed explication of the content of the lesson master sheet. The student listens to the radio lesson not seated in his armchair as he would normally listen to the radio or watch television, but seated at a work table, pencil in hand, carrying out the teacher's instructions. ECCA's radio lessons are above all student-active, since the student is constantly at the 'blackboard'. In addition, radio lessons are highly personalised. The objectives of ECCA's specially designed radio lessons are to stimulate interest in the theme covered in the master sheet, to explain the content fully and clearly, and to encourage the student's involvement in private study.

Figure 1: A Lesson Master Sheet

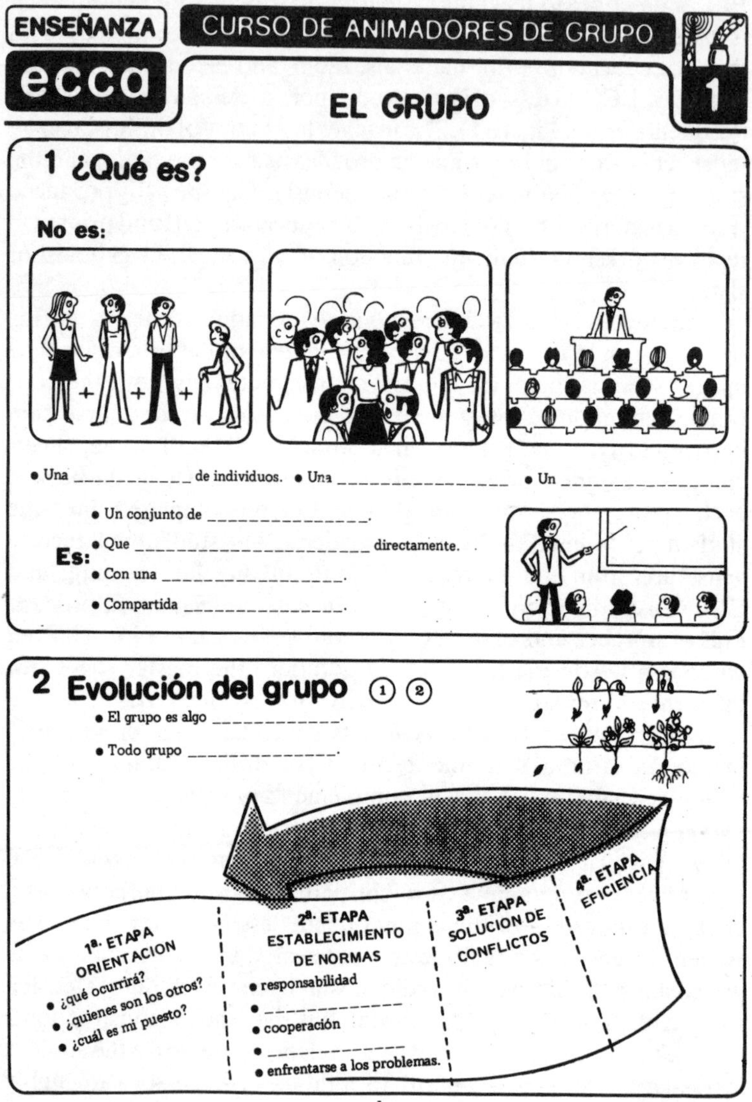

ENSEÑANZA ecca | CURSO DE ANIMADORES DE GRUPO | 1

EL GRUPO

1 ¿Qué es?

No es:

- Una _____ de individuos.
- Una _____
- Un _____

Es:
- Un conjunto de _____.
- Que _____ directamente.
- Con una _____.
- Compartida _____.

2 Evolución del grupo ① ②

- El grupo es algo _____.
- Todo grupo _____.

1ª. ETAPA ORIENTACION
- ¿qué ocurrirá?
- ¿quienes son los otros?
- ¿cuál es mi puesto?

2ª. ETAPA ESTABLECIMIENTO DE NORMAS
- responsabilidad
- _____
- cooperación
- _____
- enfrentarse a los problemas.

3ª. ETAPA SOLUCION DE CONFLICTOS

4ª. ETAPA EFICIENCIA

-1-

3 Características del grupo

PERSONAS

- Son _____
- Necesitan conocerse

OBJETIVOS ③

- Deben ser _____ y explicados
- Deben ser compartidos por todos

PERTENENCIA ④

- Es una vivencia _____
- Si no se da no se forma el grupo

INTERACCION ⑤

- Las personas dialogan entre sí. Se comunican
- Entre las personas surgen relacoones y _____

ROLES ⑥ ⑦

- Cada persona desempeña un _____
  y una _____ en el grupo
- Los hay que favorecen la buena marcha o
  que la obstaculizan

NORMAS ⑧

- En todo grupo hay unas normas explicitadas
  e implicitadas
- Para que funcionen bien deben acordarse por
  _____

-2-

ECCA's radio lessons are not scripted; the teachers who present the lesson are well prepared to improvise within the guidelines of the lesson master sheet before the microphone, just as a teacher would improvise when talking face-to-face with a group of students.

The third element of the ECCA system is the 'tutor' ('profesor orientador'). If the learning process ended with the radio lesson, the ECCA system would be relatively easy to organise. The complexity and the particular quality of the system arise from the personal contact which all students must maintain each week with a tutor. ECCA students are attached to a tutorial centre ('centro de orientacion') as near to home as possible; this is the venue for the weekly meeting between student and tutor. The tutor's duties are as follows: he hands out the booklet of lesson master sheets for the following week, collects work completed in the previous week, guides the student and tries to resolve difficulties which have arisen. He also explains the most difficult points covered in the previous week's work, makes on-the-spot evaluations, and most important of all, seeks to motivate and encourage the student. In addition, the tutor collects the student's weekly fee payment, and reports back to ECCA on the progress of students. A great number of activities are carried out on a one-to-one basis, but groups also meet together for one or two hours at a time, so that there is the possibility of considerable flexibility within the system. The nature of the different courses dictate whether the one-to-one or the group alternative is chosen.

The interrelationship of the three elements of the ECCA system provides enormous educational potential. The carefully planned integration and synchronisation which characterise this system underpin its effectiveness in teaching and motivating adult students. The system could not function if any one element was absent, and no one element could function separately from the other two. But success is not cheaply bought; the success of the system is ensured only by great expenditure of personal and organisational effort.

Course Creation

The major technical difficulty presented by the creation of an ECCA course lies in the fact that the creative act of teaching is divided between different persons. At ECCA, teaching is performed by:

(a) a teacher, or a team of teachers, who devise the course, create the printed material and plan the integration and synchronisation of its various elements;

(b) a team of two teachers, a man and a woman, who record the radio lesson, always synchronising it with the previously prepared lesson master sheet; and

(c) the tutor, who meets the students in person every week.

All these teachers have to work with the knowledge that the whole operation encompasses a single teaching act, albeit that the individual parts are separately created and performed. It is essential that a common plan of action should always be followed so that the student is not distracted by an awareness that the different elements of the course are not properly integrated.

The first stage of the teaching process is the formulation of the course, which is carried out by Radio ECCA's Pedagogical Department. This has two sections, one responsible for academic courses and the other for non-academic courses. In each of these sections the teachers work in their own specialist area or discipline. This work involves a broad study of the subject material which is to be taught; the determination of the objectives of the course and an account of its outline; and detailed planning of the content to be included and the activities to be devised.

Only when this work is completed can the work of creating the printed materials be undertaken; materials to be employed by students, tutors, and the teachers who are involved in recording radio lessons. Course creation in distance education is a slow process which must be carried out systematically. At Radio ECCA, courses are usually prepared a year in advance.

The creation of a course requires knowledge of the students for whom it is intended. Before presenting its first radio lessons, Radio ECCA piloted lessons for more than a year with a group of students whose immediate reactions were taped so as to enable amendments and improvements to be made. Recently, before launching the first stage of the 'Bachillerato' course, ECCA spent a year testing it with a group of students. Courses are continually being reshaped by information fed back from students.

Course Production

Radio ECCA possesses its own workshop which handles all its

printed materials. A special department, organised and run by teachers, is responsible for page preparation. The drawing of illustrations and the layout of printed text are regarded as tasks for teachers, because the educational effectiveness of the lesson master sheet depends to a great extent on how well or how badly the information it contains is presented. The fact that the print workshop belongs to ECCA is particularly important in view of the considerable number of courses which are produced and the many students requiring materials. More than 20 million sheets are printed every year in the workshop.

Course creation and printing of materials are carried out at the ECCA headquarters in Las Palmas, not only for the Canary Islands but for all the Spanish provinces. Significant savings are made by centralising the printing of course materials, but all the other processes and activities which characterise the ECCA system are undertaken separately by each mainland province.

Radio ECCA has facilities at Las Palmas for the production and recording of radio lessons. The lessons are always pre-recorded to avoid inaccuracies and to ensure precise timings. Recording is carried out one or two days before transmission. Radio lessons are newly recorded every year so as to effect maximum communication with the student. The lessons are recorded by one man and one woman teacher, not merely by radio presenters. Well-prepared teachers find room for improvisation in the radio lesson so that the best possible use can be made of available time and the greatest possible assistance given to students.

Whereas printed materials are produced centrally and then distributed throughout the whole of Spain, ECCA encourages the recording of radio lessons locally. In this way, local language variations can be incorporated and the educational effectiveness of the lessons can be increased by their adaptation to local needs and environments. The total system is considered less effective in provinces where there are relatively few students and where local recording is therefore not considered feasible.

Course Distribution

Part of the ECCA distribution system involves the establishment of a weekly communication channel which follows the pattern

ECCA→ Tutor → Students → Tutor → ECCA

The setting up of this two-way communication is straightforward in theory, but can in certain cases prove to be the most problematic aspect of the whole system. The fact that communication is weekly makes the task more difficult, but it also offers so many advantages, assisting the students in following courses and facilitating the feed-back process, that ECCA does not wish to reduce its frequency.

Each week ECCA sends to its tutors the printed material to be distributed to students on its various courses. The delivery cycle is important in motivating students; it helps to maintain continuous interest and to reduce the tendency to drop out, which commonly occurs in systems where all the materials for a course are delivered at once.

In order that the distribution mechanism should function as smoothly as possible, the tutor sends to ECCA a brief report containing details of student enrolments and dropouts. In return ECCA sends the tutor a detailed list of all the materials to be distributed to students. Additional information is sent when tutors report on students' progress and assessment.

The student usually follows the course in his own home, tuning in to ECCA's transmission at certain set times. The frequency of radio lessons varies according to the course, ranging from one per week to one per day. In certain Spanish provinces where ECCA's courses are broadcast on local commercial radio stations, their transmitters are not always sufficiently powerful for the student to tune in. Successful experiments have, however, been carried out using audio cassettes. The delivery and distribution of cassettes has been arranged weekly through the radio station-tutor link.

Student Enrolment

A perennial problem in adult education is how to persuade the potential student to enrol on a course. There is little point in creating a good course if adults are not motivated to study it. The enrolment campaign therefore plays a vital part, and Radio ECCA has the invaluable advantage of being able to exploit its own broadcasting facilities. Since it does not transmit commercial advertising, the full strength of this powerful medium can be focused on cultural themes.

During the time when radio lessons are not being transmitted, ECCA's output is very much orientated towards publicising its educational activities. Using different techniques such as repeated

slogans, surveys, interviews, short features and even complete programmes, ECCA mounts its publicity campaign to persuade adults
that they should study. Variations on the basic message, 'You should
study', 'It is never too late to study', 'Don't say "I don't know"', are
frequently repeated.

Various other means of persuasion are employed, such as posters,
leaflets, letters to potential students and to persons or institutions
capable of motivating people to study, press announcements, broadcast announcements on other radio stations and on television, and
personal contacts with cultural organisations and associations.

A few months before the beginning of the courses, the station
intensifies its campaign. It tries to motivate the people to study, very
often using the voices of those who are studying or have studied; it
also broadcasts details of how, when and where it is possible to
become a student. The insistence with which the message is presented
has earned ECCA the affectionate nickname 'Radio Jaqueca', a play
on the Spanish words for 'migraine' and 'prattle'. Once the courses
are under way, the station turns its attention to retaining its students
by encouraging them to persevere in the task which they have
undertaken.

Radio ECCA's strongest message is its own continuing existence;
it motivates through what it does ('por lo que hace') rather than by
what it says ('lo que dice'). The persuasive powers of a radio station
devoted exclusively to educating people are somewhat difficult to
quantify, but are nevertheless of vital importance. The public image
which a station of this kind creates is its principal means of motivating
the people.

The effectiveness of ECCA's campaign is clearly demonstrated by
comparison with the results of the publicity mounted by commercial
radio stations in other Spanish provinces using ECCA courses. These
stations lack the sharp educational focus which ECCA can achieve,
and as a result their student numbers are much lower.

The recruitment and enrolment of students in the Islands necessitates an extensive infrastructure. The tutorial centres, where the
weekly meetings between students and tutors take place, are also
used as enrolment centres. ECCA has sited more than 600 centres
throughout the Islands (mostly in schools) wherever their transmissions reach. The multiplicity of centres enables the student to
enrol without having to travel far from his home.

Student Support

The tutorial centre has a clear educational function which is defined by the methodology of each course. In general it is the place where students can clear up doubts, receive additional information on difficult points covered in the course, and complete practical exercises. The second, separate, function of the centre is to maintain and if possible increase the student's motivation.

It is vital that the adult student should realise that a person exists who knows him personally and who is familiar in depth with his work. By this means the impersonality which is often a characteristic of distance learning systems is eliminated. The influence of the tutor on the student is of paramount importance, in fostering the commitment to study, providing encouragement in moments of despondency, inspiring confidence, and generally bringing a human touch to the educational process. This boosting of morale is also assisted by regular contact with the other adults at the tutorial centre.

Radio ECCA employs a network of more than three hundred teachers (many of whom work full-time as school teachers) as tutors. For so many teachers to work in so many places with one common methodology is not easy, and indeed it is a task not always successfully carried out. Induction courses are held for new tutors, a particularly important factor in mainland provinces where ECCA courses are being introduced for the first time. Adequate preparation is essential in such a complex integrated system.

Assessment and Evaluation

In the ECCA system of education by radio it is possible to apply an assessment procedure for individual students which is very similar to that used in conventional full-time study centres. This is made possible by students' weekly attendance at their tutorial centres. A description follows of the assessment procedure used by ECCA in courses leading to an academic qualification. The remaining courses use all or some of these elements according to circumstances.

One of the most important moments in the assessment process is when the student comes along to enrol and is placed on a course. As each course has specified objectives and pre-determined content, it is possible to assess which course is appropriate for the new student. For this purpose the tutor administers an entry test to each student who wishes to enrol. Once the student is placed on the most appropriate course his further progress is conditional upon his performance within the system. The daily exercises on the reverse side of each lesson sheet provide a broad base for the student assessment purposes.

On the 'Popular culture' courses, the tutor collects the master sheet exercises from the students each week, and returns the corrected exercises at the following week's meeting with whatever written comments he feels are appropriate. On more advanced courses the daily exercises are corrected by the student himself with the help of a self-correction master sheet supplied for the purpose. The tutor nevertheless oversees the student's work and his self-corrected exercises. Students who correct their own work are required in addition to complete a two-part weekly assessment sheet, one part on Arts and one on Sciences, the answers to which do not appear on the self-correction master sheet. The sheet is collected by the tutor for his assessment and is returned to the student the following week. These completed assessments provide the tutor with an additional guide to the work of the student.

Students also take part in three assessment sessions during each course, held either at the tutorial centre or at another place where all the students on the course can conveniently meet. During these sessions, each student has to complete a number of written tests, the contents of which are not made known to him beforehand. The results of these written tests provide the main basis for the student's marks. The mark obtained in the final and most difficult test of the course is set against the average mark of the assessment tests completed during the year, to produce the student's final mark. This final assessment is not worked out with mathematical rigidity, but takes into account the tutor's direct personal knowledge of the student. ECCA headquarters staff may also be involved in the calculation of the final assessment. The three partial assessments and the final assessment are all recorded in ECCA's student files, which are created at the beginning of each course.

The ECCA system offers much the same opportunity for assessment as a conventional institution and the entire procedure is organised with great care. Any arbitrary assessment made during the course will come to light when the partial assessment marks are compared with the mark for the final assessment test. The normal outcome of this comparison is a mark somewhere between the partial and final assessment marks, which seems to indicate that the procedure works well.

ECCA students' academic results are similar to those of students in conventional institutions. In the final general basic education examination in 1979, leading to the 'Titulo de Graduado Escolar', ECCA students throughout Spain achieved a 58 per cent pass rate. The question paper for these examinations is approved by the Ministry of Education and the grades are awarded by a tribunal supervised by an inspector from the Ministry.

Another piece of data relevant to the evaluation of ECCA's teaching is the permanent nature of the student's interest. In distance education, it is notoriously difficult to maintain student interest, and the dropout rate is often high. In ECCA, over 50 per cent of students, and in some courses 70 per cent or 80 per cent, complete their courses. However, the trust and affection which the people of the Islands display towards ECCA is its most valued testimonial and the most important factor in an evaluation of its overall effectiveness.

Part 4

GROUP LEARNING

The first two chapters in this part of the Reader are by
Americans, and both adopt a humanistic or personal growth
approach to the facilitation of learning in groups, the mode which,
as is indicated in the chapters by Allen Tough and Michael Moore
in this Reader, has traditionally been seen as the major focus for
adult educational activity.

Carl Rogers' concern is with a particular kind of group, the
encounter group, where the emphasis is on the use of a close
group environment to encourage self-revelation and bring about
greater understanding and acceptance. Despite this fairly narrow
focus, the stages in the development of a typical encounter group
which Rogers identifies — milling around, resistance to personal
expression or exploration, description of past feelings, expression
of negative feelings, exploration of personally meaningful
material, expression of interpersonal feelings within the group,
self-acceptance and the beginning of change, the cracking of
façades, the individual receives feedback, confrontation, the
helping relationship outside the group, the basic encounter, the
expression of positive feelings and closeness, behaviour change —
are applicable to other kinds of groups.

Thomas Gordon focuses on the role of the group leader, which
is seen as being to release the creative power of a group to realise
its purposes and goals. He pays particular attention to the leader's
role as listener.

The final chapter in this section, by Tom Douglas, does not
confine itself to any one kind of group, but indicates a number of
different ways in which the behaviour, performance and
development of any adult educational group may be monitored
and evaluated.

THE PROCESS OF THE ENCOUNTER GROUP

Carl Rogers

Source: *Encounter Groups* (Allen Lane, The Penguin Press, London, 1970), pp. 14-42.

What really goes on in an encounter group? This is a question often asked by persons who are contemplating joining one, or who are puzzled by the statements of people who have had the experience. The question has been of great interest to me also. [...]

As I consider the terribly complex interactions that arise in 20, 40, or 60 or more hours of intensive sessions, I believe I see certain threads which weave in and out of the pattern. Some of these trends or tendencies are likely to appear early, some later in the group sessions, but there is no clear-cut sequence in which one ends and another begins. The interaction is best thought of, I believe, as a rich and varied tapestry, differing from group to group, yet with certain kinds of trends evident in most of these intensive encounters and with certain patterns tending to precede and others to follow. Here are some of the process patterns I see developing, briefly described in simple terms and presented in roughly sequential order.

1. *Milling around.* As the leader or facilitator makes clear at the outset that this is a group with unusual freedom and not one for which he will take directional responsibility, there tends to develop a period of initial confusion, awkward silence, polite surface interaction, 'cocktail-party talk', frustration, and great lack of continuity. The individuals come face to face with the fact that 'there is no structure here except what we provide. We do not know our purposes, we do not even know each other, and we are committed to remain together over a considerable period of time.' In this situation, confusion and frustration are natural. Particularly striking to the observer is the lack of continuity between personal expressions. Individual A will present some proposal or concern, clearly looking for a response from the group. Individual B has obviously been waiting for his turn and starts off on some completely different tangent as though he had never heard A. One member makes a simple suggestion such as, 'I think we

should introduce ourselves', and this may lead to several hours of highly involved discussion in which the underlying issues appear to be: Who will tell us what to do? Who is responsible for us? What is the purpose of the group?

2. *Resistance to personal expression or exploration.* During the milling-around period some individuals are likely to reveal rather personal attitudes. This tends to provoke a very ambivalent reaction among other members of the group. One member, writing of his experience afterward, says, 'There is a self which I present to the world and another one which I know intimately. With others I try to appear able, knowing, unruffled, problem-free. To substantiate this image I will act in a way which at the time or later seems false or artificial or "not the real me". Or I will keep to myself thoughts which if expressed would reveal an imperfect me.'

It is the public self that members tend to show each other, and only gradually, fearfully, and ambivalently do they take steps to reveal something of the private self. [...]

3. *Description of past feelings.* In spite of ambivalence about the trustworthiness of the group, and the risk of exposing oneself, expression of feelings does begin to assume a larger proportion of the discussion. The executive tells how frustrated he feels by certain situations in his industry; the housewife relates problems she has with her children. [...]

4. *Expression of negative feelings.* Curiously enough, the first expression of genuinely significant 'here and now' feeling is apt to come out in negative attitudes toward other group members or the group leader. In one group in which members introduced themselves at some length, one woman refused, saying that she preferred to be known for what she was in the group and not in terms of her status outside. Very shortly after this, a man in the group attacked her vigorously and angrily for this stand, accusing her of failing to cooperate, of keeping herself aloof from the group, of being un-reasonable. It was the first *current personal feeling* brought into the open in that group.

Frequently the leader is attacked for his failure to give proper guidance. [...]

Why are negatively toned expressions the first current feelings to be expressed? Some speculative answers might be the following. This is one of the best ways to test the freedom and trustworthiness of the group. Is it *really* a place where I can be and express myself, positively and negatively? Is this *really* a safe place, or will I be punished?

Another quite different reason is that deeply positive feelings are much more difficult and dangerous to express than negative ones. If I say I love you, I am vulnerable and open to the most awful rejection. If I say I hate you, I am at best liable to attack, against which I can defend. Whatever the reasons, such negatively toned feelings tend to be the first 'here and now' material to appear.

5. *Expression and exploration of personally meaningful material.* It may seem puzzling that, following such negative experiences as the initial confusion, the resistance to personal expression, the focus on outside events, and the voicing of critical or angry feelings, the event most likely to occur next is for some individual to reveal himself to the group in a significant way. The reason for this no doubt is that the individual member has come to realize that this is in part *his group.* He can help to make of it what he wishes. He has also experienced the fact that negative feelings have been expressed and accepted or assimilated without catastrophic results. He realizes there is a freedom here, albeit a risky freedom. A climate of trust is beginning to develop. So he begins to take the chance and the gamble of letting the group know some deeper facet of himself. One man tells of the trap in which he finds himself, feeling that communication between himself and his wife is hopeless. A priest tells of the anger he has bottled up because of unreasonable treatment by one of his superiors. What should he have done? What might he do now? A scientist at the head of a large research department finds the courage to speak of his painful isolation, to tell the group that he has never had a single *friend* in his life. By the time he finishes, he is letting loose some of the tears of sorrow for himself which I am sure he has held in for many years. A psychiatrist tells of the guilt he feels because of the suicide of one of his patients. A man of 40 tells of his absolute inability to free himself from the grip of his controlling mother. A process which one workshop member has called 'a journey to the center of self,' often a very painful process, has begun. [...]

6. *The expression of immediate interpersonal feelings in the group.* Entering into the process, sometimes earlier, sometimes later, is the explicit bringing into the open of feelings experienced in the immediate moment by one member towards another. These are sometimes positive, sometimes negative. Examples would be: 'I feel threatened by your silence.' 'You remind me of my mother, with whom I had a tough time.' 'I took an instant dislike to you the first moment I saw you.' 'To me you're like a breath of fresh air in the group.' 'I like your warmth and your smile.' 'I dislike you more every

time you speak up.' Each of these attitudes can be, and usually is, explored in the increasing climate of trust.

7. *The development of a healing capacity in the group.* One of the most fascinating aspects of any intensive group experience is to observe the manner in which a number of the group members show a natural and spontaneous capacity for dealing in a helpful, facilitating, and therapeutic fashion with the pain and suffering of others. As one rather extreme example of this I think of a man in charge of maintenance in a large plant who was one of the low-status members of an industrial executive group. As he informed us, he had 'not been contaminated by education.' In the initial phases the group tended to look down on him. As members delved more deeply into themselves and began to express their own attitudes more fully, this man came forth as without doubt the most sensitive member of the group. He knew intuitively how to be understanding and accepting. He was alert to things which had not yet been expressed but were just below the surface. While the rest of us were paying attention to a member who was speaking, he would frequently spot another individual who was suffering silently and in need of help. He had a deeply perceptive and facilitating attitude. This kind of ability shows up so commonly in groups that it has led me to feel that the ability to be healing or therapeutic is far more common in human life than we suppose. Often it needs only the permission granted — or freedom made possible — by the climate of a free-flowing group experience to become evident. [...]

8. *Self-acceptance and the beginning of change.* Many people feel that self-acceptance must stand in the way of change. Actually, in these group experiences as in psychotherapy, it is the *beginning* of change.

Some examples of the kinds of attitude expressed would be these: 'I *am* a dominating person who likes to control others. I do want to mold these individuals into the proper shape.' 'I really have a hurt and overburdened little boy inside of me who feels very sorry for himself. I *am* that little boy, in addition to being a competent and responsible manager.' [...]

This feeling of greater realness and authenticity is a very common experience. It would appear that the individual is learning to accept and to *be* himself and is thus laying the foundation for change. He is closer to his own feelings, hence they are no longer so rigidly organized and are more open to change. [...]

9. *The cracking of façades.* As the sessions continue, so many

things tend to occur together that it is hard to know which to describe first. It should again be stressed that these different threads and stages interweave and overlap. One of the threads is the increasing impatience with defenses. As time goes on the group finds it unbearable that any member should live behind a mask or front. The polite words, the intellectual understanding of each other and of relationships, the smooth coin of tact and cover-up — amply satisfactory for interactions outside — are just not good enough. The expression of self by some members of the group has made it clear that a deeper and more basic encounter is *possible*, and the group appears to strive intuitively and unconsciously toward this goal. Gently at times, almost savagely at others, the group *demands* that the individual be himself, that his current feelings not be hidden, that he remove the mask of ordinary social intercourse. In one group there was a highly intelligent and quite academic man who had been rather perceptive in his understanding of others but revealed himself not at all. The attitude of the group was finally expressed sharply by one member when he said, 'Come out from behind that lectern, Doc. Stop giving us speeches. Take off your dark glasses. We want to know *you*.' [. . .]

If I am indicating that the group is quite violent at times in tearing down a façade or defense, this is accurate. On the other hand, it can also be sensitive and gentle. The man who was accused of hiding behind a lectern was deeply hurt by this attack, and over the lunch hour looked very troubled, as though he might break into tears at any moment. When the group reconvened, the members sensed this and treated him very gently, enabling him to tell us his own tragic personal story, which accounted for his aloofness and his intellectual and academic approach to life.

10. *The individual receives feedback.* In the process of this freely expressive interaction, the individual rapidly acquires a great deal of data as to how he appears to others. The hail-fellow-well-met finds that others resent his exaggerated friendliness. The executive who weighs his words carefully and speaks with heavy precision may discover for the first time that others regard him as stuffy. A woman who shows a somewhat excessive desire to be of help to others is told in no uncertain terms that some group members do not want her for a mother. All this can be decidedly upsetting, but so long as these various bits of information are fed back in the context of caring which is developing in the group, they seem highly constructive. [. . .]

11. *Confrontation.* There are times when the term feedback is far too mild to describe the interactions that take place — when it is better

said that one individual *confronts* another, directly 'levelling' with him. Such confrontations can be positive, but frequently they are decidedly negative. [...]

12. *The helping relationship outside the group sessions.* No account of the group process would be adequate, in my opinion, if it did not mention many ways in which group members assist each other. One of the exciting aspects of any group experience is the way in which, when an individual is struggling to express himself, or wrestling with a personal problem, or hurting because of some painful new discovery about himself, other members give him help. This may be within the group, as mentioned earlier, but occurs even more frequently in contacts outside the group. When I see two individuals going for a walk together, or conversing in a quiet corner, or hear that they stayed up talking until 3.00 a.m. I feel it is quite probable that at some later time in the group we will hear that one was gaining strength and help from the other, that the second person was making available his understanding, his support, his experience, his caring — making himself *available* to the other. An incredible gift of healing is possessed by many persons, if only they feel freed to give it, and experience in an encounter group seems to make this possible. [...]

13. *The basic encounter.* Running through some of the trends I have just been describing is the fact that individuals come into much closer and more direct contact with each other than is customary in ordinary life. This appears to be one of the most central, intense, and change-producing aspects of group experience. To illustrate, I should like to draw an example from a recent workshop group. A man tells, through his tears, of the tragic loss of his child, a grief which he is experiencing *fully* for the first time, not holding back his feelings in any way. Another says to him, also with tears in his eyes, 'I've never before felt a real physical hurt in me from the pain of another. I feel completely with you.' This is a basic encounter. [...]

One member, trying to sort out his experiences immediately after a workshop, speaks of the 'commitment to relationship' which often developed on the part of two individuals — not necessarily individuals who have liked each other initially. He goes on to say, '... the incredible fact experienced over and over by members of the group was that when a negative feeling was fully expressed to another, the relationship grew and the negative feeling was replaced by a deep acceptance for the other ... Thus real change seemed to occur when feelings were experienced and expressed in the context of the relationship. "I can't *stand* the way you talk!" turned into a real understanding and affection for you the *way* you talk.' This statement seems to capture some of the more complex meanings of the term basic encounter.

14. *The expression of positive feelings and closeness.* As indicated in the last section, an inevitable part of the group process seems to be that when feelings are expressed and can be accepted in a relationship, then a great deal of closeness and positive feeling results. Thus as the sessions proceed, an increasing feeling of warmth and group spirit and trust is built up, not out of positive attitudes only but out of a realness which includes both positive and negative feeling. One member tried to capture this in writing shortly after a workshop by saying that if he were trying to sum it up, '. . . it would have to do with what I call confirmation — a kind of confirmation of myself, of the uniqueness and universal qualities of men, a confirmation that when we can be human together something positive can emerge.' [. . .]

15. *Behavior changes in the group.* It would seem from observation that many changes in behavior occur in the group itself. Gestures change. The tone of voice changes, becoming sometimes stronger, sometimes softer, usually more spontaneous, less artificial, with more feeling. Individuals show an astonishing amount of thoughtfulness and helpfulness toward each other.

Our major concern, however, is with the behavior changes that occur following the group experience. This constitutes the most significant question, on which we need much more study and research. One person gives a catalog which may seem too pat, but which is echoed in many other statements, of the changes he sees in himself. 'I am more open, spontaneous. I express myself more freely. I am more sympathetic, empathic, and tolerant. I am more confident. I am more religious in my own way. My relations with my family, friends, and co-workers are more honest and I express my likes and dislikes and true feelings more openly. I admit ignorance more readily. I am more cheerful. I want to help others more.'

Another says, '. . . Since the workshop there has been found a new relationship with my parents. It has been trying and hard. However, I have found a greater freedom in talking with them, especially my father. Steps have been made toward being closer to my mother than I have ever been in the last five years.' Another says, 'It helped clarify my feelings about my work, gave me more enthusiasm for it, made me more honest and cheerful with my co-workers and also more open when I was hostile. It made my relationship with my wife more open, deeper. We felt freer to talk about anything and we felt confident that anything we talked about we could work through.'

Sometimes the changes described are very subtle. 'The primary change is the more positive view of my ability to allow myself to *hear*, and to become involved with someone else's "silent scream".' [...]

Failures, Disadvantages, Risks

Thus far one might think that every aspect of the group process is positive. As far as the evidence at hand indicates, it appears that it is nearly always a positive process for a majority of the participants. Failures nevertheless result. Let me try to describe briefly some negative aspects of the group process as they sometimes occur.

The most obvious deficiency of the intensive group experience is that frequently the behavior changes that occur, if any, are not lasting. This is often recognized by the participants. One says, 'I wish I had the ability to hold permanently the "openness" I left the conference with.' Another says, 'I experienced a lot of acceptance, warmth, and love at the workshop. I find it hard to carry the ability to share this in the same way with people outside the workshop. I find it easier to slip back into my old unemotional role than to do the work necessary to open relationships.' [...]

A second potential risk involved in the intensive group experience, and one often mentioned in public discussion, is that the individual may become deeply involved in revealing himself and then be left with problems which are not worked through. There have been a number of reports of people who have felt, following an intensive group experience, that they must go to a therapist to work through the feelings which were opened up in the intensive experience of the workshop and were left unresolved. It is obvious that without knowing more about each individual situation it is difficult to say whether this is a negative outcome or a partially or entirely positive one. There are also very occasional accounts of an individual having a psychotic episode during or immediately following an intensive group experience. On the other side of the picture is the fact that individuals have also lived through what were clearly psychotic episodes, and lived through them very constructively, in the context of a basic encounter group. My own tentative clinical judgement would be that the more positively the group process proceeds the less likely it is that any individual would be psychologically damaged through membership in the group. It is obvious, however, that this is a serious issue and that much more needs to be known. [...]

There is another risk or deficiency in the basic encounter group. Until very recent years it has been unusual for a workshop to include both husband and wife. This can be a real problem if significant change has taken place in one spouse during or as a result of the workshop experience. One individual feels this risk clearly after attending a workshop. He says, 'I think there is a great danger to a marriage when only one spouse attends a group. It is too hard for the other spouse to compete with the group individually and collectively.' One of the frequent after-effects of the intensive group experience is that it brings out into the open for discussion marital tensions which have been kept under cover.

Another risk which has sometimes been a cause of real concern in mixed intensive workshops is that very positive and warm and loving feelings can develop between members of the encounter group (as is evident in some of the foregoing examples). Inevitably some of these feelings have a sexual component, and this can be a matter of great concern to the participants and a profound threat to their spouses if these are not worked through satisfactorily in the workshop. Also the close and loving feelings which develop may become a source of threat and marital difficulty when a wife, for example, has not been present, but projects many fears about the loss of her spouse — whether well founded or not — onto the workshop experience. [...]

One more negative potential growing out of encounter groups has become evident in recent years. Some individuals who have participated in previous encounter groups may exert a stultifying influence on new workshops they attend. They sometimes exhibit what I think of as the 'old pro' phenomenon. They feel they have learned the 'rules of the game', and subtly or openly try to impose these rules on newcomers. Thus, instead of promoting true expressiveness or spontaneity, they endeavor to substitute new rules for old — to make members feel guilty if they are not expressing feelings, or are reluctant to voice criticism or hostility, or are talking about situations outside the group relationship, or are fearful to reveal themselves. These 'old pros' seem to attempt to substitute a new tyranny in interpersonal relationships in the place of older conventional restrictions. To me this is a perversion of the true group process. We need to ask ourselves how this travesty on spontaneity comes about. Personally, I wonder about the quality of the facilitation in their previous group experiences.

4.2

THE GROUP-CENTERED LEADER

Thomas Gordon

Source: *Group-centered Leadership: A Way of Releasing the Creative Power of Groups* (Houghton Mifflin Company, Boston, USA, 1955), pp. 162-5 and 177-82.

[...] To the group-centered leader, a group exists for the realization of the purposes and goals of its members. These purposes and goals will vary from group to group and will vary from time to time within a single group, yet always the group is simply the means by which the members are enhanced through the achievement of *their* purposes. It is incompatible with the views and attitudes of the group-centered leader that a group should exist for the realization of the purposes and goals of the leader, apart from the group. It is also inconsistent with his philosophy that a group should exist for the accomplishment of the aims and objectives of someone outside the group. The group-centered leader, therefore, believes that responsibility should reside with the total group. It is the group, not the leader, who has the responsibility for setting its goals and defining its purposes; and consequently it is inconsistent with the values he holds to deny the group such responsibility. It is the group that should have the responsibility for making decisions on matters that will affect its members; and consequently the group-centered leader finds it incompatible with his values to make such decisions *for* the group. Finally, the group-centered leader believes that it should be the responsibility of the total group to set its own rules, its standards of member behavior, its laws and regulations, within the limits dictated by the external situation in which the group is operating.

Believing as he does that the group exists for the fulfillment of certain of the needs of its members, the group-centered leader sees the procedures, forms, structures, or rituals of the group as having no value in and of themselves. In so far as they contribute to the enhancement of the members of the group, however, they have definite value. The group-centered leader cannot accept the way some business or industrial executives worship 'policy' to the extent that human values are often made secondary to the value of rigidly

212

maintaining and sticking to 'the company's age-old policy.' Although the group-centered leader recognizes the need for a group to have policies, procedures, and rules of behavior, nevertheless it is his conviction that they should be merely the *products* of group functioning, the means by which the group may actualize itself, the instruments of the group. As such, they should serve the group rather than determine how the group always must function. For example, the writer has become increasingly aware of the extent to which strict adherence to the honored and universal 'parliamentary procedures' can strait-jacket a group so effectively that its functioning is no longer appropriate to the problems it must solve. One wonders how such a set of standard group procedures, which might have been very appropriate for a particular legislative body operating in a different century, could have become accepted as the required mode of operation for so many diversified groups varying all the way from a board of directors or a large corporation to a boys' club organized for fun and recreation.

Just as the group-centered leader prefers to operate on the basis of a philosophy characterized by faith in the individual, so he has chosen to adopt an attitude that the group can be trusted. [...] He has respect for the capacity of the group for self-direction, critical thinking, resistance to external influence, and appropriate problem-solving behavior.

The group-centered leader recognizes the existence of both positive and negative characteristics within every group. However, his clinical experience in dealing with individuals in the process of therapy has sensitized him to the fact that much of their negative behavior is a consequence of earlier experiences in which they have been subjected to the authoritarian control of parents, teachers, employers, and other leaders. In other words, individuals, and likewise groups, *can* become reactive, hostile, aggressive, destructive, submissive, dependent, suggestible — or they *may*, in Freud's words, 'want to be ruled and oppressed,' 'demand illusions,' 'submit instinctively to anyone who appoints himself as master.' They can and do exhibit these tendencies, but to the group-centered leader these are the tendencies of sick individuals, these are the characteristics of a group that has not been given the opportunity to develop and express its more constructive modes of behavior. [...] The conviction of the group-centered leader is that *groups develop these negative characteristics because they have already been controlled by powerful masters and authoritarian leaders.*

The group-centered leader has a respect for individual people. He tries to see each person as having a certain worth and significance quite unrelated to that person's social class, occupational status, personal traits, skills, abilities, appearance, race, religion, or other such characteristics. The significance of the person lies more in the fact that he is a complex, developing organism, a living demonstration of the miracle of life. Instead of respecting a group member because he happens to be very intelligent, comes from a prominent family, and occupies a high status position in his profession, the group-centered leader endeavors to respect this group member simply as a person — someone quite distinct from any other person. Even more important, the group-centered leader strives to develop an equal amount of respect for the person who possesses characteristics that in our culture are judged less desirable or who represents a class of people which has lower status and prestige in our cultural hierarchy. In short, the group-centered leader is constantly struggling to see the worth and significance of each person, divested of the traits, trappings, and symbols on which society ordinarily places some kind of value. He hopes to learn to respect the workers as much as the manager, the teacher as much as the principal, the dull and unattractive student as much as the bright and handsome one, the aggressive and defensive 'neurotic' as much as the more placid and secure 'normal,' the Jew as much as the Gentile, the child as much as the parent. The group-centered leader is attempting to break through the numerous cultural stereotypes by which we evaluate others, in order that he may learn to respect the person for being a person rather than merely a representative of a class of persons.

The group-centered leader prefers to adopt as his working hypothesis the belief that the individual has a vast store of untapped potential for positive, constructive, intelligent, and mature behavior. His is the positive, optimistic, and hopeful philosophy about the nature of man to which reference has already been made in an earlier chapter. The group-centered leader has grown to believe that the central core of man's personality, that which has been called his basic 'animal nature' or his 'organismic self,' is something that can be trusted and relied upon, not something that has to be checked, inhibited, controlled, and feared. Thus, if the group-centered leader is successful in facilitating the release of the person's potential, he is confident that what is released will be positive, social, forward-moving, and creative.

These two values of the group-centered leader, his respect for the uniqueness of the person and his faith in the positive quality of man's basic nature, are closely related and in fact inseparable. For if as a leader he had no faith in man's potential for positive and constructive behavior, it is unlikely that he would have much respect for the unique potential of each individual, or would put his energies into the task of releasing the individual's unique capacities. We will strive to release something only if we have faith in what comes out, and we will strive to control and bottle up that which we fear. This aspect of the group-centered leader's philosophy is difficult to communicate clearly. Perhaps because the opposite beliefs and attitudes have become so much a part of our thinking, it is not easy to find the words to express a belief in the positive nature of the human organism. [...]

The group-centered leader continuously performs certain distinctive functions throughout the life of the group, but especially during the initial stages of the group's development. These functions gradually are taken over by other members of the group as the members lose their initial dependence upon the leader; but during the early stages of the group's development, these functions are often performed predominantly by the leader.

When we analyze a role as complex as that of a group leader, we do some injustice to its dynamic and personal nature. We need to keep in mind at all times that picking apart the leader's role tends to depersonalize him, making him appear as a collection of discrete and mechanical techniques rather than as a real person with attitudes and feelings, functioning in an integrated and purposeful manner. Nevertheless, it can be extremely helpful to isolate and identify some of the distinctive behaviors of the group-centered leader, in this way making it easier for others to understand how the group-centered leader differs from other kinds of leaders. [...]

Listening

Probably the most important single function performed by the group-centered leader is that of listening to the contributions of others in the group. This would hardly seem worth mentioning were it not for the fact that the group-centered leader practices a very special and distinctive kind of listening.

What We Mean by Listening. Psychotherapists have introduced us to a new kind of listening. They have shown that it can be a powerful agent for helping persons with emotional problems. Its therapeutic effect can be understood when we consider that the emotionally disturbed individual himself suffers from faulty communication, both within himself and with others, and listening by the therapist seems to improve his communication dramatically. [...]

What the therapist has learned to do is to enter a relationship with another in which he consistently listens with understanding. He has discovered a way of getting into the thought processes of the other person or we might say that he has learned how to enter into the person's own unique 'frame of reference.' To do this requires an intent to understand how the other person is looking at the world, how he is perceiving things. The therapist puts on the spectacles of the other person so that he may view reality in the same way. This requires putting aside one's own spectacles, suspending one's own ideas, shutting out as completely as possible one's own way of looking at things.

This is precisely what the group-centered leader tries to do as he listens attentively to the expressions of his group members. Having no need to get his own idea across, having no secret intentions, having no particular goals which he expects the group to reach, he is thus more able to listen to the contributions of others without being concerned about their ultimate effect upon the group. In a sense, he 'permits' himself to listen with understanding because he has freed himself from the need to influence and direct the group's discussion.

This type of listening requires certain attitudes on the part of the leader. He must *want* to understand how the speaker is looking at the world. There must be an earnest intent to 'be with the other person,' with respect to *his* thoughts, feelings, and attitudes. Such an attitude is quite different from one that predisposes the listener to try to change the other person's way of looking at things. Instead of listening with the feeling, 'You should be seeing things differently,' the leader tries to maintain an attitude of, 'Let me try to understand how you *are* seeing things.' This attitude is different, too, from one which leads a listener to interpret or 'go beyond' what the speaker is perceiving at the moment. It is common practice, for example, for some group leaders to listen for the deeper meanings, for 'the unconscious aspects of communication,' for that which is not intended by the speaker. This is a different kind of listening attitude from the one we are describing. The group-centered leader tries to hear only what is present in the speaker's awareness and to read nothing additional into the communication.

The Test of Listening. Because we can never be sure that we have completely understood another person, it is important to test the accuracy of our listening. Unfortunately, in most situations involving an attempt to communicate with others, we rarely put our understanding to a test. Consequently, we often misunderstand others or distort their meanings. One of the best ways of minimizing this misunderstanding and distortion is for the listener to try to restate in his own language the expression of the speaker and then to check to see if the restatement is acceptable to the speaker. This is essentially what the group-centered leader is continuously doing throughout the initial stages of the group's development. He calls it 'reflection of feelings or meanings,' to convey that he is trying to mirror the speaker's expressions so accurately that the speaker himself is satisfied that he has been understood.

This is an extremely difficult thing to do, even momentarily. The reader who is interested enough to test out the accuracy of his own listening will find the following experiment both interesting and revealing:

> Choose a situation in which you have become involved in a controversial discussion or argument with another person. Suggest to the other that you both adopt a ground rule and follow this strictly throughout the discussion. The rule: Before either participant can make a point or express an opinion of his own he must first reflect aloud the statement of the previous speaker; he must make a restatement that is accurate enough to satisfy the speaker before he is allowed to speak for himself. [Suggested to the writer by S.I. Hayakawa, the semanticist]

This little experiment if it is seriously carried out, will demonstrate, first, that it is very difficult to adopt another's frame of reference. Second, it will give the participants a new kind of experience in which they will find that emotions tend to drop out and differences become minimized. Furthermore, each participant will discover that his own views are changing and will admit that he has learned something new from the other.

The Element of Risk in Listening. Not only does listening with understanding require a firm intent to understand another and a kind of rapt attention that we seldom give to speakers; it also requires a certain amount of courage and personal security. We run the risk of being changed ourselves, for when we really understand another we may be exposing our own ideas and attitudes to opposing ones. To understand completely an opposing point of view means that we have at least momentarily looked at the world through our adversary's spectacles — in a sense, we have tried to become *him* for the moment. In the process we have suspended judgement and withheld evaluation. Consequently, we run the risk of actually adopting the other's point of view or of having our view altered by his. To expose ourselves to such a change requires courage, because each of us is organized to resist change. It is upsetting to discover we are wrong. Therefore it takes a good measure of personal security to enter into a relationship knowing that the stage is being set for a possible alteration of ourselves.

Perhaps it is fortunate that there is some compensation for the risk assumed by one who is willing to listen with understanding. Strangely enough, listening to another also facilitates change in him. This has been proved by the clinical experience of psychotherapists and is supported by a growing body of research findings in this area. Clients who successfully complete a series of interviews with client-centered therapists show measurable changes in their attitudes toward themselves and toward others. There is also evidence that changes may occur in their basic values and in their personal philosophy.

Listening facilitates change in the speaker in a very indirect way. If a person knows someone is listening carefully and is trying to understand, he may make more effort to express his attitudes and ideas more clearly. By so doing, he may obtain new understandings simply because he is expressing his own ideas more clearly. In trying to understand another person, then, a listener may actually encourage that person to express himself more understandably. This is suggestive of the old saying that 'we never really know something unless we can explain it clearly to someone else.'

Why the Group-centered Leader Listens. We have mentioned several of the effects of listening with an intent to understand another. There are many by-products or expected results from this type of intensive listening. It may be useful at this point, however, to summarize some of the effects the group-centered leader has come to expect from his listening to the contributions of his group members.

First, group members will feel that their contributions are of sufficient worth to merit being listened to and understood by the leader. This should greatly facilitate participation by the members through reduction of the threat of devaluation.

Second, group members will make a greater effort to express their ideas and opinions more clearly, knowing that someone in the group is listening attentively and is going to reflect their ideas back to them for confirmation.

Third, group members will begin to drop their defensiveness, open their minds to new understandings, think more flexibly, reason more effectively. This should not only improve the quality of contributions but increase the problem-solving ability of the group as a whole.

Fourth, when conflicts or controversies arise in the group, each member is more likely to alter his own point of view rather than defend it vigorously and stubbornly.

Fifth, group members observing that the leader is listening with understanding will themselves begin to listen to each other more attentively and with more understanding.

Sixth, the leader himself will learn far more from listening to others in the group than he would through giving lectures, presentations, and other leader-centered activities.

These, then, are some of the important results the group-centered leader expects to achieve through listening with understanding and through testing his understanding by reflecting the meaning of members' verbal contributions. Each of these results will contribute significantly to the group-centered leader's long-range objectives and goals — (a) creating a nonthreatening group atmosphere conducive to creative participation by the members, and (b) facilitating communication so that the various members' contributions will be understood by the others and utilized by the group. [...]

OBSERVING, RECORDING AND EVALUATING

Tom Douglas

Source: *Groupwork Practice* (Tavistock Publications, London, 1976), pp. 96-116.

[...] Perhaps the easiest and most effective way to learn about group behaviour is to observe a group while a member of it. Groups are a common experience for all people, but few have ever taken time to watch what was going on, or even to wonder why people behave as they do. It is hard sometimes to go against the cultural conditioning of appearing not to be curious, but increases in the ability to observe are very rewarding for the group practitioner.

Firstly it is necessary to distinguish between 'content' and 'process'. Content is usually described as the subject-matter under discussion — what the group is talking about. Process is the way in which the group goes about the discussion. In most group discussions the members are inevitably drawn by the words, the meanings, and tend not to notice the process which is involved, i.e. who talks to whom, or how much. Focus on group process is looking at what the group is doing in the 'here and now', how it is working, its current procedures and organization. Focus on content is looking at the topics which may be largely abstract, oriented to the past, 'there and then', or the future, and not directly involving group members.

Obviously content serves often enough to give a clue to the process which is involved. For example when group members are talking about staff who are of little help, the process involved may be dissatisfaction with the leader's role. Or again talking about the poor performance of other groups they are involved in may indicate the process of dissatisfaction with their own group's performance. Process can only really be understood by observing what is going on in the group and attempting to understand it in terms of what has occurred in the group previously.

Patterns of communication are a fairly easily observed group process. It is simple to record facts like who talks and for how long and how frequently. It is also easy enough to note in what direction people look when they talk, e.g. at other possible supporters, the whole group, or off into infinity. The communication process can be illuminated by noting who follows each speaker, where interruptions occur, and what styles are used, e.g. questions, assertions, gesticulation and tone of voice. All of these factors may help to trace influence and power and the lack of them within a group.

Groups make decisions. As has been noted few people are able to assess clearly how a particular decision was reached unless forced to by being questioned, e.g. police interrogation after an accident. But the decision-making process, involving power, influence, knowledge, etc., is a very important group process and it is necessary that groups should know how decisions are made. There is no more effective way of maintaining interest in a group's activities than for its decision-making processes to be clearly understood and usable by *all* members of the group. These processes must therefore be examined and the influence used at each stage clearly illuminated.

Democratic procedures, voting, testing opinions, polling are often used. But other procedures stemming from the exercise of personal influence or anxiety are much less easily seen. Groups are fond of saying, 'Well, we decided to do so and so', when it is quite obvious that they did not do this at all. If the incident is recent enough, memories may still exist when questioned about what really took place before the 'apparent' unanimous decision was made.

So far the discussion has been concerned with the way in which a group attempts to work, to achieve its purpose. But within any group there are emotional factors which may disrupt or adversely affect the work of the group. These factors need to be recognized and understood for they tend to detract from the energy which is available for the group's purpose. Some of these factors are identifiable, some attach to some stages of a group's life rather than others. For instance in the early days of a group's existence or during the admission of a newcomer the problem of identity may occur. Members are concerned to know where they fit in the group, and what kind of behavior the group will accept and how they are coming across to the group. Later in the group's life they may be concerned with the problems related to power, control, and influence, in terms of knowing how much they have and whether holders of power are challengeable. Perhaps later still members will be concerned with intimacy, which is basically concerned with trust and personal involvement.

At most times a member will be concerned with the satisfaction of needs which he gets from the group. What he wants for the group and for himself may sometimes be in conflict, and keen observation is necessary in detecting the overt signs of this.

The behavioural patterns which emerge include resisting authority, attempting to satisfy individual needs at whatever cost to others, withdrawing from uncomfortable positions, and forming subgroups for support. Many other patterns occur and it is only with practice that the group worker can see them and become increasingly effective in his performance.

How to Diagnose Group Problems

[Extracts from an article of this name by L.P. Bradford, D. Stock and M. Morwitz (1970). In Robert T. Golembiewski and Arthur Blumberg, *Sensitivity Training and the Laboratory Approach.* Itasca, Ill.: F.E. Peacock.]

Three of the most common group problems are:
(1) *Conflict or fight*
(2) *Apathy and non-participation*
(3) *Inadequate decision-making*

1. *Fight.* Some ways in which fight can be expressed are:
(a) members are impatient with one another
(b) ideas are attacked before they are completely expressed
(c) members take sides and refuse to compromise
(d) members disagree on plans or suggestions
(e) comments and suggestions are made with a great deal of vehemence
(f) members attack one another on a personal level in subtle ways
(g) members insist that the group doesn't have the know-how or experience to get anywhere
(h) members feel that the group can't get ahead because it is too large or too small
(i) members disagree with the leader's suggestions
(j) members accuse one another of not understanding the real point
(k) members hear distorted fragments of other members' contributions

The following are several possible reasons for such behaviour:
(1) The group has been given an impossible job and members are frustrated because they feel unable to meet the demands made of them.
(2) The main concern of members is to find status in the group.

Although the group is ostensibly working on some task, the task is being used by the members as a means of jockeying for power.

(3) Members are loyal to outside groups of conflicting interests.

(4) Members feel involved and are working hard on a problem. Members may frequently express impatience, irritation, or disagreement because they have a real stake in the issue being discussed.

The obvious question arises: how can a member or leader tell which diagnosis is appropriate to a specific situation?

Let's re-examine our four reasons in terms of possible diagnoses:

If:

every suggestion made seems impossible for practical reasons; some members feel the committee is too small; everyone seems to feel pushed for time;

members are impatient with one another;

members insist the group doesn't have the know-how or experience to get anywhere;

each member has a different idea of what the committee is supposed to do; whenever a suggestion is made, at least one member feels it won't satisfy the large organisation;

Then:

the group may have been given an impossible job and members are frustrated because they feel unable to meet the demands made of them, or the task is not clear or is disturbing.

If:

ideas are attacked before they are completely expressed;

members take sides and refuse to compromise;

there is no movement towards a solution of the problem;

the group keeps getting stuck on inconsequential points;

members attack one another on a personal level in subtle ways; there are subtle attacks on the leadership; there is much clique formation;

Then:

the main concern of members may be in finding status in the group. The main interest is not in the problem. The problem is merely being used as a vehicle for expressing interpersonal concerns.

If:

the goal is stated in very general, non-operational terms;

members take sides and refuse to compromise;

each member is pushing his own plan;

suggestions don't build on previous suggestions, each member seeming to start again from the beginning;

members disagree on plans or suggestions;

members don't listen to one another, each waiting for a chance to say something;

Then:

each member is probably operating from a unique, unshared point of view, perhaps because the members are loyal to different outside groups with conflicting interests.

If:

there is a goal which members understand and agree on; most comments are relevant to the problem;

members frequently disagree with one another over suggestions;

comments and suggestions are made with a great deal of vehemence;

there are occasional expressions of warmth;

members are frequently impatient with one another;

there is general movement towards some solution of the problem;

Then:

probably, members feel involved and are working hard on a problem;

the fight being expressed is constructive rather than destructive in character and reflects real interest on the part of members.

2. *Apathy*

An apathetic membership is a frequent ailment of groups. Groups may suffer in different degrees from this disease. In some cases members may show complete indifference to the group task, and give evidence of marked boredom. In others, apathy may take the form of a lack of genuine enthusiasm for the job, a failure to mobilise much energy, lack of persistence, satisfaction with poor work.

Some ways in which apathy may be expressed:

(a) frequent yawns, people dozing off

(b) members lose the point of the discussion

(c) low level of participation

(d) conversation drags

(e) members come late; are frequently absent

(f) slouching and restlessness

(g) overquick decisions

(h) failure to follow through on decisions

(i) ready suggestions for adjournment

(j) failure to consider necessary arrangements for the next meeting

(k) reluctance to assume any further responsibility.

Here are some of the common reasons for apathy:

(1) The problem upon which the group is working does not seem important to the members, or it may seem less important than some other problem on which they would prefer to be working.

(2) The problem may seem important to members, but there are reasons which lead them to avoid attempting to solve the problem. If members both desire to achieve a goal and fear attempting to achieve it, they are placed in a situation of conflict which may lead to tension, fatigue, apathy, e.g. where subordinates feel they will be punished for mistakes, they will avoid taking action, hoping to shift responsibility to someone higher up the line of organisational authority.

(3) The group may have inadequate procedures for solving the problem. There may be lack of knowledge about the steps which are necessary to reach the goal. There may be poor communication among members within the group based on a failure to develop mutual understanding. There may be a poor co-ordination of effort so that contributions to the discussion are made in a disorganised, haphazard way.

(4) Members may feel powerless about influencing final decisions.

(5) A prolonged and deep fight among a few members has dominated the group. Frequently two or three dominant and talkative members of a group will compete with one another or with the leader so much that every activity in the group is overshadowed.

How to diagnose apathy:

If:

questions may be raised about what's really our job, what do they want us to do;

members fail to follow through on decisions;

there is no expectation that members will contribute responsibly, and confused, irrelevant statements are allowed to go by without question;

members wonder about the reason for working on this problem, suggestions are made that we work on something else;

the attitude is expressed that we should just decide on anything, the decision doesn't really matter;

members seem to be waiting for a respectable amount of time to pass before referring the decision to the leader, or to a committee;

members are inattentive, seem to get lost and not to have heard parts of the preceding discussion;

suggestions frequently 'plop', are not taken up and built on by others;

no-one will volunteer for additional work;
Then:
　the group goal may seem unimportant to the members.
If:
　there are long delays in getting started, much irrelevant preliminary conversation;
　the group shows embarrassment or reluctance in discussing the problem at hand;
　members emphasise the consequence of making wrong decisions, imagine dire consequences which have little reference to ascertainable facts, members make suggestions apologetically, are over-tentative, and hedge their contributions with many if's and but's, solutions proposed are frequently attacked as unrealistic, suggestions are made that someone else ought to make the decision — the leader, an outside expert, or some qualified person outside the group, members insist that we haven't enough information or ability to make a decision, and appear to demand an unrealistically high level of competence;
　the group has a standard of cautiousness in action, humorous alternative proposals are suggested, with the group completely unable to select among them;
Then:
　members probably fear working toward the group goal.
If:
　no-one is able to suggest the first step in getting started toward the goal;
　members seem to be unable to stay on a given point, and each person seems to start on a new track;
　members appear to talk past, to misunderstand one another, and the same points are made over and over;
　the group appears to be unable to develop adequate summaries, or restatements of points of agreement;
　there is little evaluation of the possible consequences of decisions reached, and little attention is given to fact-finding or use of special resources;
　members continually shift into related, but off-target tasks, complaints are made that the group's job is an impossible one, subgroups continually form around the table, with private discussions held off to the side, there is no follow-through on decisions or disagreement in the group on what the decisions really were;

complaints are made that you can't decide things in a group anyway, and the leader or somebody else should do the job;

Then:

the group may have inadequate problem-solving procedures.

If:

the view is expressed that someone else with more power in the organisation should be present in the meeting, that it is difficult to communicate with him at a distance, unrealistic decisions are made, and there is an absence of sense of responsibility for evaluation of the consequences of decisions, the position is taken that the decision doesn't really matter because the leader or someone else outside the group isn't really going to listen to what we say;

there is a tendency to ignore reaching consensus among members, the important thing being to get the leader to understand and listen, the discussion is oriented toward power relations, either within the group, jockeying to win over the leader, or outside the group, with interest directed toward questions about who really counts in the organisation;

doubts are voiced about whether we're just wasting our efforts in working on this program;

members leave the meeting feeling they had good ideas which they didn't seem able to get across;

Then:

members feel powerless about influencing final decisions.

If:

two or three members dominate all discussion, but never agree;

conflict between strong members comes out no matter what is discussed;

dominant members occasionally appeal to others for support, but otherwise control conversation;

decisions are made by only two or three members;

Then:

a conflict among a few members is creating apathy in the others.

3. *Inadequate Decision-making*

Getting satisfactory decisions made is often a major struggle in the group. Here is a list of common symptoms of inefficient decision-making.

If:

the group swings between making too rapid decisions and having

difficulty in deciding anything;
the group almost makes the decision but at the last minute retreats;
group members call for definition and redefinition of minute points;
the discussion wanders into abstraction;
Then:
there has been premature calling for a decision, or the decision is too difficult, or the group is low in cohesiveness and lacks faith in itself.
If:
the group has lack of clarity as to what the decision is, there is disagreement as to where consensus is;
a decision is apparently made but challenged at the end;
group members refuse responsibility;
there is continued effort to leave decision-making to leader, sub-group or outside source;
Then:
the decision area may be threatening to the group, either because of unclear consequences, fear of reaction of other groups, or fear of failure for the individuals.

Improving Group Efficiency — Diagnosis and Feedback

Human beings, and therefore groups, not only need continuous self-correction in direction, but also (and here they differ from machines) need to learn or grow or improve. Collecting adequate data and using this information to make decisions about doing things differently is one of the major ways of learning.

There are three basic parts to the process of changing group behaviour:
(1) collecting information
(2) reporting the information to the group
(3) making diagnoses and decisions for change.

Collecting Information

While analysis and evaluation of information and decision about what to do should be carried out by the total group, the collecting of information may be delegated. A number of patterns of delegation are possible:
(1) The leader, serving also as observer, can report to the group

certain pertinent observations he has made about problems and difficulties of group operation.

(2) The group may appoint one of its members, perhaps on a rotating basis, to serve as group observer, with the task of noting the manner in which the group works.

(3) A third method calls for all group members to be as sensitive as they can, while participating actively, to the particular problems the group faces.

What Information to Collect?

General questions such as these may help to get started:

(1) What is our goal? Are we 'on' or 'off the beam'?

(2) Where are we in our discussion? At the point of analysing the problem? Suggesting solutions? Testing ideas?

(3) How fast are we moving? Are we bogged down?

(4) Are we using the best methods of work?

(5) Are all of us working or just a few?

(6) Are we making any improvement in our ability to work together?

Methods of Observation

(1) Who talks to whom?

The number of lines made by the observer on this form (Figure 1) indicates the number of statements made in a fifteen minute period —

Figure 1

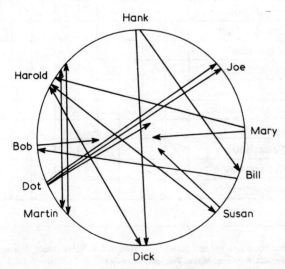

20. Four of these were made to the group as a whole, and so the arrows go only to the middle of the circle. Those with arrows at each end of a line show that the statement made by one person to another was responded to by the recipient.

We see that one person, Harold, had more statements directed toward him than did anyone else and that he responded or participated more than anyone else.

(2) Who makes what kinds of contributions (Table 1)?

Table 1

Member No.	1	2	3	4	5	6	7	8	9	10
1 Encourages										
2 Agrees, accepts										
3 Arbitrates										
4 Proposes action										
5 Asks suggestions										
6 Gives opinion										
7 Asks opinion										
8 Gives information										
9 Seeks information										
10 Poses problem										
11 Defines position										
12 Asks position										
13 Routine direction										
14 Depreciates self										
15 Autocratic manner										
16 Disagrees										
17 Self-assertion										
18 Active aggression										
19 Passive aggression										

(Based upon observational categories discussed in R.F. Bales (1950), *Interaction Process Analysis*. Reading, Mass., Addison-Wesley.)

This record makes possible the quick rating not only of who talked, but the type of contribution. Individuals in the group are given numbers which are listed at the top of the columns. At the end of a time period it is possible to note the frequency and type of participation by each member.

(3) What happens in the group?

Table 2

---

1. *What was the general atmosphere in the group?*
   Formal ....Informal ....
   Competitive ....Co-operative ....
   Hostile ....Supportive ....
   Inhibited ....Permissive ....
   Comments ....

2. *Quantity and quality of work accomplished*
   Accomplishment: High ....Low ....
   Quality of
   Production: High ....Low ....
   Goals: Clear ....Vague ....
   Methods: Clear ....Vague ....
   Comments ....

3. *Leadership behaviour*
   Attentive to group needs ....
   Supported others ....
   Concerned only with topic .... Took sides ....
   Dominated group .... Helped group ....
   Comments ....

4. *Participation*
   Most people talked .... Only few talked ....
   Members involved .... Members apathetic ....
   Group united .... Group divided ....
   Comments ....

This form (Table 2) can be used as a checklist by an observer to sum up his observations, or it can be filled out by all group members to start an evaluation discussion.

An example of the evaluation of a group using a very simple question-naire is given below. It is taken from 'Group for Mothers' by Brown and Smith (1972).

Evaluation

At the last session we distributed evaluation forms. Those who were not present or had previously dropped out were sent forms by post. A total of fifteen mothers were given forms. Of the seven most regular members, six returned them, and two of the other mothers who had dropped out returned theirs. Members were asked the following questions:

(1) Before you came to the group what did you expect it to be like?
(2) Was the group different from what you expected?
(3) Have you any suggestions for the leaders?
(4) Do you have any comments about meeting time, place, length of sessions, child-minding, or any other practical considerations?
(5) If another group were to start in the future would you be inter-ested in participating?

In summarising the evaluations we have used the following extracts.

One mother wrote that she expected the group to be 'rather formal with speakers and possibly visitors from the welfare department to talk to us'. Instead she found it 'far more informal and friendly. One feels one can bring into the open one's personal feelings and opinions'. Another who had had a very difficult time with the behaviour of her five year old subnormal son said 'I do not know quite why, but I thought the meetings might be very dull and felt attending them every week would be too often. I did not expect the lively and human discussions we did have.' In fact she found the meetings

> ... much more interesting than I had expected. I learnt a very great deal by attending the group meetings and derived much comfort and encouragement from the group. After the meetings, however, I must confess, I often felt sad and upset at the knowledge of some of the mothers' problems. I do feel strongly that although the group meetings are of very real value to mothers concerned, they should have the wider aim of establishing an effective link between parents, teachers and the children at school. Perhaps a Parent-Teacher Association is not appropriate at this stage, but certainly meetings of any future group should be mainly concerned with the problems of forwarding the children's progress both at school and at home ...

A third highly articulate mother, whose son regularly spends all the holidays at the subnormality hospital and who appeared to have made the 'perfect' adjustment to a handicapped child, expected 'a group of fairly inarticulate mothers airing their complaints about doctors and help offered from various sources', but found the mothers had a 'positive approach to their problem and not a negative one. They are able to discuss family emotions and compare methods of dealing with problems'. She felt the leaders' function was to 'control the group, as involved outsiders, and to help keep the thread of an interesting line of discussion'.

Another of the regular members, herself and her husband both artists and whose only child is autistic, wrote that she 'expected the group to be different — rather formal'. She found it 'very informal and a pleasant atmosphere'. She concluded 'I must stress that it gave me a tremendous satisfaction of being able to express my feelings about the problems that I have, or rather had, as it is easier now because I have shared it with others'.

One mother who is a nurse had very negative feelings towards the services and only attended two groups: she wrote that she wished the group had dealt with such things as times and places of coach pick-ups for school so that these could be more convenient for mothers.

Evaluating Information and Deciding about Change

Usually this has a number of steps:
(1) The members assess the observations, relate them to their experience, test to see whether they agree with the report.
(2) The group examines the reasons. What caused a thing to happen? Could we have recognised it earlier?
(3) The group moves to a decision on what to do. What can be done in future similar circumstances? What can individual members do earlier to help? What methods or procedures should be changed? What new directions sought?

It is very easy for the time of the discussion to be consumed by the first two steps in this procedure. The leader, as well as the members, needs to be sensitive to this danger and encourage the group to move into the third step of decision. A questionnaire like the 'Yardstick' can be used to facilitate this process.

A Yardstick for Measuring the Growth of a Group

As a group begins its life, and at several points during its growth, the leader and members might individually fill out the following scales (Table 3) and then spend some time sharing the data that is collected. Through these scales, it is possible to get a general picture of the perceptions which various members have about the group and how it is growing. It is also possible to pick up areas on which there may be some difficulties which are blocking progress.

> Evaluation of the progress of members is made more precise and easier for the worker if some plan is developed for tracing changes in attitudes, relationships, and behaviour periodically during the course of the group experience. Perhaps minimally summary reports should be made at the end of the first meeting, toward the end of the exploration phase, and when termination is being considered. The first report would include pertinent data about the individual; his characteristics, problems, capacities and motivations; goals as seen by the member, relevant others who may have referred him, and the worker; and an initial description and evaluation of the member's beginning in the group. As changes occur, these can be noted from week to week or periodically. These changes are usually those in attitudes toward self and others, changes in the quality and range of social relationships, and changes in problematic behaviour. Necessary data are then available for the practitioner to assist him to understand and evaluate the nature and extent of progress and regression. The movement of each individual is evaluated in relation to the trend of changes within the group, and the impact of environmental influences on it ... whenever termination is being considered, a thorough review and evaluation of what has or has not been accomplished, and the determinants thereof, is imperative. So, too, is a set of realistic goals for the periods of time that remain before the final termination. (Northen, 1969, pp. 224-5)

Recording

The recorder acts as a 'group memory', by recording important parts of the discussion, and by summarising its content.

He reminds the group what is under consideration when the

Table 3

---

1. *How clear are the group goals?*

1.	2.	3.	4.	5.
No apparent goals	Goal confusion, uncertainty or conflict	Average goal clarity	Goals mostly clear	Goals very clear

2. *How much trust and openness in the group?*

1.	2.	3.	4.	5.
Distrust, a closed group	Little trust, defensiveness	Average trust and openness	Considerable trust and openness	Remarkable trust and openness

3. *How sensitive and perceptive are group members?*

1.	2.	3.	4.	5.
No awareness or listening in the group	Most members self-absorbed	Average sensitivity and listening	Better than usual listening	Outstanding sensitivity to others

4. *How much attention was paid to process? (the way group was working)*

1.	2.	3.	4.	5.
No attention to process	Little attention to process	Some concern with group process	A fair balance between content and process	Very concerned with process

5. *How were group leadership needs met?*

1.	2.	3.	4.	5.
Not met, drifting	Leadership concentrated in one person	Some leadership sharing	Leadership functions distributed	Leadership needs met creatively and flexibly

6. *How were group decisions made?*

1.	2.	3.	4.	5.
No decisions could be reached	Made by a few	Majority vote	Attempts at integrating minority vote	Full participation and tested consensus

7. *How well were group resources used?*

1.	2.	3.	4.	5.
One or two contributed but deviants silent	Several tried to contribute but were discouraged	About average use of group resources	Group resources well used and encouraged	Group resources fully and effectively used

8. *How much loyalty and sense of belonging to the group?*

1.	2.	3.	4.	5.
Members had no group loyalty or sense of belonging	Members not close but some friendly relations	About average sense of belonging	Some warm sense of belonging	Strong sense of belonging among members

---

Source: Lippitt and Seashore (pamphlet).

discussion wanders and can assist communication between different groups.

He is a member of the group, and assists in the problem-solving task by working as a member of the team with the leader and co-leader. He also ensures that the group does not lose valuable material and he tends to free the leader from the very onerous task of record-keeping but this usually means reducing the effective contribution of the recorder as a member of the group. These points are elaborated upon below.

The recorder is in a sense an aid to the group memory. Everyone else in the group is freer to participate, if he knows that a specialized 'memory' is at work, seeing that the ideas and decisions that are being produced are stored up for later use. Every group needs a summary from time to time of what it has done, of where it stands in relation to the goals it has or the problem it has defined. Groups may wish to ask the recorder to make this kind of summary.

A group with continuing records of its various meetings may use these in the evaluation of its progress from meeting to meeting and in analysing and improving its productivity.

The records of ideas and decisions and their relation to each other are a significant and vital part of the resources of a group. The record of group thinking should be summarized in closely related para-graphs or outline units. Ideas developed over an extended period of discussion may be phrased in a simple pointed sentence or paragraph. Conflicting ideas should be reported as well as those showing consensus as these may be valuable in future deliberations on the group's problems. Verbatim records are rarely necessary but a clear exposition of the basic content of the group discussion is essential.

It is recommended that:

(a) recording should be made selectively.

(b) pages of the report might be kept for different areas of content e.g. Problems, Agreements, Decisions, Ideas, etc. Summaries, when required, are easier to make from organized source material.

(c) issues, points of assent and dissent, and what conclusion is arrived at should be clearly noted.

(d) the accuracy of the record should be checked out with the group.

(e) some such form of headings as the following should be used:

Date	Group Session	
Subject	Content	Decisions

(f) evaluation of the record by the group should be asked for along the lines of how much was left out, what was put in that was not needed and perhaps how the form of the record should be improved.

(g) organization of the record should take place as it is recorded in order to be available to the group when needed.

(h) underlining and other symbols should be used to distinguish various parts of the content.

(i) the recording should be available to the group whenever requested to check its progress.

(j) the recorder should stick to the content of the group's activities. 'Process' is the responsibility of the co-leader.

(k) the group should be asked to correct, amend, and check the record whenever doubt exists.

(l) the recorder should attempt to summarize for the group in the same terms as have already been used. Where semantic change occurs the recorder should check that the group's original meaning has not been changed.

(m) the recorder should be involved in the planning phases with leader and co-leader, especially over what records may be required.

References

Bales, R.F. (1950) *Interaction Process Analysis*, Addison-Wesley, Reading, Mass.

Bradford, L.P., Stock, D. and Morwitz, M. (1970), 'How to Diagnose Group Problems' in Robert T. Golembiewski and Arthur Blumberg, *Sensitivity Training and the Laboratory Approach: Readings about Concepts and Applications*, Peacock, Itasca, Illinois

Brown, L.K. and Smith, J. (1972) 'Group for Mothers', *Social Work Today 3 (10)*, 16

Lippitt, G.L. and Seashore, E.W., *The Leader looks at Group Effectiveness*, pamphlet

Northen, H. (1969) *Social Work with Groups*, Colorado Univ. Press, Boulder, Col.

Part 5

COMMUNITY LEARNING

The community as a setting and orientation for the education of
adults is not so easy to envisage as the individual or group, but has
nevertheless attracted increasing attention and controversy in
recent years. The first chapter in this section, by Michael
Newman, is, understandably, concerned with the definition of
'community'. Newman discusses six conceptions of community
commonly held amongst educators of adults — community equals
the working class, community equals quiescent poor, community
equals the disadvantaged, community equals the 'whole community', community equals acceptable community, community
equals society — before coming to the conclusion that 'if the adult
educator uses the word "community" correctly, ... he is indicating
his willingness to listen to, learn from and respond to minorities'.

Tom Lovett is also concerned in part by problems of definition
and interpretation. He examines two models of the role of adult
education in community action recently adopted in Britain, one
involving drawing the working class into a more effective
educational system, the other involving a radical critique of the
existing system and its potential for change, and the adoption of
an activist outreach approach to the educational needs of the
working class. He sees historical parallels to these differences of
approach in the Antigonish and Highlander movements in North
America, and then goes on to discuss more recent developments
in which he himself has been involved in Northern Ireland.

Reg Revans, on the basis of experience in management dating
back to the 1930s, suggests a rather different approach to
community education, advocating the application of action
learning (learning through doing) to the problems of the
inner cities and the unemployed. His approach might be
described as pragmatic, since it relies on the motivation provided

by economic circumstances, seeing the opportunities for the success of self-help community groups in their ability to survive, generate support and create wealth.

Finally, the chapter by Paulo Freire gives a Third World perspective on the problems and potential of education in and through the community. He outlines the practice and experience of the literacy groups which he helped to establish in Brazil. Freire sees the self-transformation or 'conscientization' of the individual in the community through education as being of central importance. Whilst his particular approach may be difficult to apply in other, particularly developed, countries, there are obvious parallels to be drawn between conscientization, the notion of perspective transformation expressed by Mezirow, and Tough's concern with major personal change (see the chapters by these authors, and also that by Bown, in this Reader).

COMMUNITY

Michael Newman

Source: *The Poor Cousin: A Study of Adult Education* (George Allen & Unwin, London, 1979). pp. 197-209.

The worry about whom the adult educator should approach or willingly respond to, the worry about priorities in the allocation of a centre's resources, is exacerbated and may even be caused by the continual confusion over the word 'community'. Adult education is being urged to increase its community provision, to cater more meaningfully for the community, to orient itself more realistically towards community needs, but who are we actually referring to when we use this imprecise, foggy word?

Here are six reasonably common ways in which adult educators interpret the concept of 'community':

Community Equals the Working Class

Often when adult educators use the word 'community' they are actually referring to the working class. 'We must establish closer links with the community' means 'we must get more working-class people into our classes'. 'Community education' means in effect more provision of activities on a working-class estate. 'Making adult education more representative of community values' means reducing the number of activities attended by the middle classes or that promote middle-class culture, and increasing the number of activities that promote working-class culture.

Some adult educators arrive at this equation of community with the working class simply because they realise that one of their branches in a working-class area is patronised almost completely by middle-class commuters or because they have noted that only a small number of working-class people make use of their facilities overall. Without going into the matter too deeply they feel that any extra effort should be directed to attracting more working-class people into their activities in order to achieve a more realistic social mix. And they take practical steps to do just that, redesigning their publicity,

241

reallocating classes to other branches, directing their outreach work towards recognisably working-class areas. They make no radical changes in their programme but simply seek to make the existing provision more accessible and tell more people about it.

Others make the equation of community with the working class because they see the working class consistently losing out both culturally and economically in a society controlled by middle-class institutions purveying middle-class values. These adult educators seek to reform their own institutions as a first step towards a more equitable education service. Frank Youngman, in *Planning Local Adult Education Provision,*[1] ends a section on establishing priorities with this uncompromising statement:

> The central problem remains that the Adult Education Service should offer recurrent educational opportunities to the majority of the nation that is failed by schools, yet it tends to attract only the minority who succeeded at school. I think the policies of Frobisher [Adult Education Institute] should be measured according to the success with which its service is made accessible or responsive to the working-class people within its area.

Others make the equation because of an unequivocal political commitment to the working class. They see adult education as a potential agent for raising working-class consciousness, an agency through which an attack on the maldistribution of educational, social and economic opportunities can begin to be mounted. They see adult education as an agent for social change. Keith Jackson, for example, interprets community development in terms of the conflict of class interests. In an article entitled 'The Marginality of Community Development — Implications for Adult Education'[2] he warns against the concept of community development as a process to integrate communities 'into the life of the nation'. He goes on:

> But this is politics, and why not say so? 'Neutral' community development workers are government agents at the local level. In industrial society this could only mean that the so-called 'communities' — usually in working-class areas — are to be integrated into the life of the ruling class, or elites.

To counter this he directs his attention to 'working-class activists', reaching this conclusion:

Evidence suggests that the alienation of working-class students from education results from their recognition that it does not reflect their values, and is not useful in pursuing their collective interests. Educationalists must therefore enter into a dialogue with working-class activists and 'students', from a position of solidarity with them, so that they may interpret their social situation, and the actions they take, in the light of their own values and interests.

And in summary he identifies three basic concerns for the adult educator involved in 'local social action':

Marginal reform of educational practices, a broader interpretation of significant resources, and a recognition of the need for economic strategies such as positive discrimination.

Political and social organisation involving co-option and alliances; both to release further resources and to shift power through changing relations with working-class activists, leading perhaps to more substantial reform.

Intervention to increase consciousness and awareness of social realities and of actions which are being taken, to alter these realities, leading perhaps to radical reform which cannot be contained within existing institutions.

Tom Lovett is equally clear about where his primary concern lies in his book *Adult Education, Community Development and the Working Class*,[3] and he is among the most outspoken critics of adult education's failure to cater for the working class:

The adult education movement in this country has never successfully tackled the problem of education for working-class communities. This is particularly true of that section of the working class to be found in EPAs (educational priority areas) — unskilled and semi-skilled workers suffering from a wide range of economic, social and educational deprivation. Certainly, the WEA and some of the university extra-mural departments have in recent years greatly extended their work with the trade union movement — mainly courses of a vocational nature for shop stewards — but it is generally accepted that those attending these classes are something of an elite amongst the working class. In fact, it is extremely doubtful if the adult education movement *ever* attracted students from the lower working class.[4]

There are still others who make the equation of community with the working class, not necessarily because of a sense of political solidarity with the working class, but because they see adult education as having a particular cultural mission to perform. These adult educators will argue that adult education is in part a guardian of our heritage; that with the passing of the village artisan, adult education now has an important role to play in keeping alive and passing on traditional skills and crafts. And they will argue that since middle-class culture is enshrined in most of our institutions, it is the duty of adult education to counter-balance this and orient a significant amount of its provision to maintaining and promoting working-class culture.

This commitment to getting the working class in or promoting specifically working-class activities can lead to an inverted snobbery. The new guard are particularly prone to this. Working-class becomes best and 'middle-class' a pejorative term. 'But did any real people come?' a community worker will ask of a meeting. Somehow the belief is fostered that to be working-class is to be more genuine, gutsier, straighter; and as a result of this prejudice certain subjects will become identified as middle-class activities and judged not worth supporting. Poor old badminton is one of these and so, ridiculously enough, is pottery.

Certainly there should be a reaction against the middle-class monopoly of adult education — and there seems to be a general consensus that this is the case — but it should not take the form of an over-reaction in which the middle classes are automatically found wanting, and so called middle-class subjects sent packing. 1977 saw the providers of community education in Coventry considering a plan to concentrate their provision in a working-class sector of the city and to make traditional adult education provision elsewhere in the city more financially self-supporting. But there are dangers in such a concentration of resources. The adult education service may very quickly lose its comprehensive character and the flexibility of response that goes with it. Dismiss middle-class support and the poor cousin may become even more marginal than it is at present. Dismiss middle-class support and a centre may lose its base of traditional provision from which it can reach out and engage in community development and action.[5]

Community Equals Quiescent Poor

Working-class people may not be satisfied in adult education terms with the provision of classes in pigeon fancying and dressmaking on a low budget. In an area where most of the wage earners work for one large employer the demand might just as easily be for a course on employment rights or Marxism or the politics and legalities of industrial action.

These harsh possibilities cause some adult educators, consciously or unconsciously, to shy away from the equation of community with the working class and limit themselves in their community work to the provision of 'non-controversial' activities such as keep-fit or arts and crafts classes in areas where people are poor and living in poor housing conditions. 'Community' in their terms now means 'quiescent poor only'.

The fact that some adult educators do make this equation was brought home to me in a discussion I had with two senior colleagues and my principal about the special studies courses at Addison. One of them had expressed reservations about some of our methods and my principal, perhaps to demonstrate to my critic that I was not all mad or totally bad, mentioned that I also went to a factory two mornings a week before the morning shift to teach English to a group of Asian women working there. My critic looked at me and said with very real feeling: 'Now that's what you *should* be doing!'

But this sort of attitude can imply an excessive paternalism. There is a danger of a throwback to the thinking of some Victorian good-works charity in which middle-class education is doled out to the working classes as long as they knuckle under. This may seem far-fetched when stated so baldly, but I detect something of this attitude in the way many of the new guard refer to working-class women. Spurred on by the pre-school playgroups movement and examples such as the Allfarthing family workshop, many adult educators have made very real efforts to provide activities for the parents of small children — arts and crafts groups, mothers and toddlers clubs, demonstration cookery classes with a makeshift crèche attached, and so on. The people responsible for this sort of provision have every right to be proud of it, but some seem to consider it the be-all and end-all of community education; and too many refer to the women making use of this sort of provision as 'working-class mums'.

The word 'mum' is a demeaning word, implying warmth and emotion but no imagination or thought. It deprives the person referred to of her individuality, turning her into a homely stereotype. When I hear adult educators referring to their 'working-class mums' I have a feeling that they are implying that the women are manipulable, and are taking comfort from their powerlessness.

Community Equals the Disadvantaged

Some adult educators see all their community work in terms of providing for the disadvantaged. The term 'disadvantaged' came into vogue in the early seventies replacing such terms as 'needy', 'underprivileged' and 'deprived', and was enshrined in a major recommendation in the *Russell Report* that 'more positive effort should be directed towards the disadvantaged' (page x, para. 3.6). But from the very beginning of its use in the adult education context the term was too broad to have any really useful meaning. Peter Clyne in his research for the Russell Committee, subsequently published in his book *The Disadvantaged Adult*, lists nine categories of people who can be regarded as disadvantaged:

Adult illiterates
Those in need of remedial education
Mentally ill
Mentally handicapped
Physically handicapped
Non-English-speaking immigrants
Deaf and hard of hearing
Blind and partially sighted
Elderly

— thus apparently lumping together in the same category an Indian immigrant whose only disability is his lack of fluent English, an Englishman confined to a wheelchair as a result of a car accident, and an adult who has been severely mentally handicapped since birth.

And from this very broad start, as the word has been used in policy statements, memoranda and reports, so its terms of reference have broadened. The *Russell Report* swept into the net 'the physically and mentally handicapped as well as those who, on account of their limited educational background, present cultural or social environment, age, location, occupation or status, cannot easily take part in adult education as normally provided' (para. 277). An ILEA circular added to the list 'those in hospitals, homes, prisons, etc., and other welfare groups; and the lonely and the shy'.[6] The 1976 ILEA report

493 added parents of handicapped children and women at maternity and child welfare centres . . . and so on, although the word had already attained its apotheosis of meaninglessness for me at a meeting about outreach work in late 1974 when this remark was made: 'But we are all disadvantaged in some way, aren't we?'

This over-use of the word would be laughable if it did not seriously mislead as well. Even Peter Clyne's list of nine categories[7] confuses the issue in that it blurs the distinction between people who, given access to the right kind of support, can help themselves, and those who, because of the kind or degree of their disability, are unable to help themselves. Adult education is subject to control by the users and is an experience in sharing among adults as equals. In any adult education activity, in effect, there is a large element of self-help. In the case of many of the groups listed under the blanket term of 'the disadvantaged' — the physically handicapped, the blind, the deaf, the socially deprived — such basic conditions can obtain. Some of the groups and some of the individuals within the groups will need intensive support, including special facilities, but they can still exert control over the educational provision they take part in. But there are some groups, or members of some groups, who through the severity of their disability are unable to exert control over the provision. In the case of the severely mentally ill, the severely mentally handicapped, some of the very elderly, the provision will have to be so specialised and so completely organised by the professional that it ceases to have much common ground with the rest of adult education.[8]

That is not to say that adult education should wash its hands of these groups. Adult education should seek to play a part in the educational activities of all groups within the community, but institutionalised and non-institutionalised groups should not be included in the same broad category. That might not matter if the lumping together of the institutionalised with the non-institutionalised meant that the adult educator then adopted non-institutionalised attitudes to everyone. But unfortunately the reverse tends to happen. The adult educator is led very easily into adopting a paternalistic, even authoritarian, approach to *all* groups he has denoted as disadvantaged.

The very word 'disadvantaged' helps compound this paternalistic approach. It suggests a lack, an emptiness, in the people so described which we, the purveyors of education with our 'body of knowledge', must set about filling. But many of the groups described as disadvantaged have a body of knowledge and a culture of their own. The elderly have a personal experience of the past that we younger people working with them only know at second hand. The blind have their own organisations, means of communication and a body of expertise — in relation to the complex techniques of blind mobility, for, example. And certain groups described as 'socially deprived' use a form of the language, adopt a life-style and interrelate in ways that mark them off from other sections of the community in a clear and positive way. Rather than being the empty vessels that the adult educator must rush to fill with his particular (usually middle-class) culture, many of the groups that are labelled 'disadvantaged' have a body of knowledge and culture to communicate or build upon themselves. If the adult educator is to provide something educationally valid, he must learn about this body of knowledge and become acquainted with the group's own culture first, and work from there.[9]

Because some of the groups under the disadvantage label are institutionalised and isolated from the rest of the community, the temptation is to consider the other groups as isolated by their particular disability too. Provision for the physically handicapped becomes a limited programme of arts and crafts classes at a local government lunch club. By providing for each group of the disadvantaged on their own institutional premises, the adult educator can avoid the arduous task of reordering his thinking and the facilities of his centre so that individuals suffering from particular disabilities can join in its general provision alongside non-disadvantaged members of the community. He can very easily fall into the trap of locating the blame for a group's non-use of his centre in that group's particular disability, rather than taking a long hard look at himself and his centre to see whether the reason for the group's non-use might be closer to home. The 'socially deprived' may stay away in their droves, not because that is the way with the socially deprived, but because of the centre's smugly superior atmosphere. The physically handicapped may stay away in their droves because the centre has never devised an uncomplicated and unembarrassing method of reception. And the elderly may stay away in their droves not just because they are elderly but because the authorities have chosen to locate daytime adult education facilities in that area (as they have at Addison) on the top floor of a building that has no lift!

Community Equals 'the Whole Community'

And then there is the 'whole community' brigade. Working together with the other sectors of the education service, they say, adult education should seek to provide an education service for the whole community. 'The whole community' is a seductive phrase, seemingly including every single one of us and broadly hinting at the de-schoolers' idea of the community as one large organic learning unit. But this, of course, would require a complete revolution in educational thinking, so not surprisingly the phrase usually implies something rather more modest.

So modest, in fact, that many of the projects that come under the banner of an education service for the whole community turn out, once the verbiage of the accompanying literature is stripped away, to be unadventurous exercises in parent education. Parent education varies from attempts to involve parents in the day-to-day running of their children's school, to a formal series of lectures under some such title as 'Your Child at Primary School', to parents coming to the school in the evening to experience the classroom activities their children engage in during the day. This involvement is valuable for the school and the few parents who do take part, but as a move towards an education service for the whole community it must be recognised as little more than tokenism. If we were to take parent education seriously, if we were seriously to recognise the extent to which a child's education is influenced by parental attitudes at home, then rather than setting up the occasional school-linked evening class we should be throwing major resources into equipping parents to play a full educational role in bringing up their children. We should be radically re-educating adults. We should be shifting resources from school education into adult education. This would involve a comprehensive system of day-release from work for working parents, grants, subsidies ... [10] But we are back to the idea of a revolution in our educational system — an all-out attempt to involve the whole community rather than the token classes on a couple of evenings a week for parents highly motivated enough to attend and not too tired after a full day's work.

Even when the advocates of an education service for the whole community look beyond parental involvement they are rarely talking about creating a recurrent education service literally available to everyone. More often the adult educator using the phrase is talking about achieving a mix of students in his centre that is representative of the population of his area. He may strive for a more accurate reflection of the social classes, or age groupings. Or a more even balance of the sexes. Or a representative number of people from ethnic minorities. Instead of conceiving of the community as a complex whole, he is more likely to think of the community in terms of a number of separate, clearly definable categories; and then judge his success in catering for 'the whole community' by the extent to which he manages to draw in a roughly proportional representation from each of these categories.

Community Equals Acceptable Community

Often the categories selected by the adult educator do not take in anything like the whole community. It is unusual for an adult educator to consider it part of his task to cater for dossers, or business people, or the unemployed, or homosexuals, for example. The idea of the whole community has certain understood limits, and nowhere is this more forcefully demonstrated than on the cover of an ILEA report, *An Education Service for the Whole Community* (1973). With such a title one would expect the cover to carry one of those staged photographs showing 50 or so people grouped together in the middle of a street all smiling up at the camera. They would be all ages, sizes and races. Some would look conventional and some extravagant and unconventional. There would be a city gent, a young drop-out, a policewoman, an office worker, a rasta, someone holding a football. In the background there might be some shops, a factory, a pub, houses, a field with a tractor in it, and so on and so on ... But no, the cover actually carries a photograph of a white, well-dressed, middle-class family standing outside a modern school building. The youngest, a boy of about twelve, is holding a book open and the others are admiring the work he has done in the building behind them. There are 13 other people in the background, all of them white and equally middle-class in appearance. Considering that the report states that 19.95 per cent of the resident population of the ILEA area in 1971 were born outside the UK, for the photographer to have found such an exclusively English group of people coming out of an ILEA school must be rated a notable achievement. In fact the report does recognise that ILEA's future provision 'must be based on the existence of a multi-racial society' (para. 11) but in all other respects the cover of the report sets the tone for what is inside. The community is seen in conventional terms, with the education service remaining institution-based. While arguing for an increased and interrelated use of existing institutions, an extension of resources to cater for certain sectors of society felt to be missed by current provision, and an increase in parent involvement and parent education, the report offers nothing to meet the radical promise of its title.

Community Equals Society

And so to a use of the word 'community' that contains no idea of community at all. Sometimes when using the word the adult educator is using it in the same way as a judge or a politician or a headmaster might use the word 'society'.

'Society requires that you be incarcerated for the remainder of your natural life.'

'Society requires laws and lawmakers.'

'Society rewards hard work.'

In the word 'society' there can reside a ringing, unquestionable authority. It suggests all the force of consensus opinion. The speaker will often be a person in authority himself who by virtue of his position claims the right to speak for the rest of us. And yet when we look at the pronouncements they often turn out to be based on assumptions and very little else. The judge who invokes society may in fact be expressing nothing more than a personal assessment, based perhaps on years of personal experience, but not less personal for that. He bases his judgement on what he 'knows' of society, although that knowledge may be limited to the artificial world of the courtroom and, outside that, his own class, age group, and personal circle. And even if the speaker is wise beyond the wisest judge or politician or headmaster, any appeal to the authority of society is based upon the further dubious assumption that society is a homogeneous whole that can be represented in clear, unequivocal statements without any great difficulty.

The community can be appealed to in the same way by an adult educator looking for an authority for his actions or policy.

'The community is not yet ready for such a course.'

'In any question of priorities, the community must come first.'

Ringing phrases but as unverifiable, as empty pieces of rhetoric, as an appeal to society. Indeed you could exchange 'the community' for 'society' without any great change in the meaning (or meaninglessness) of the phrases.

Multiplicity of Interests

There is probably no single, satisfactory definition of 'community'. But we misinterpret the word grossly if we appeal to the community as any kind of incontrovertible authority, or if we assume that the community can be represented by a single voice. One of the clues to the meaning of 'community' lies in its utter *lack* of any statutory authority.

'The community needs a new sports centre.'

The community may indeed need a new sports centre, but so what? The need may be screamingly obvious and there may be any number of local people and community organisations agitating for an increase in sporting facilities, but in the statement there is no hint of any external pressure such as a law or government or the education system obliging anyone actually to build the centre.

And although the word 'community' can be used apparently to encompass everyone, the concept does not imply a majority of people thinking, believing and behaving in unison. Rather it implies a multiplicity of interests. When not used synonymously with 'society', the word 'community' usually refers to minorities — lots of them bundled together and intersecting and interrelating in a myriad ways but minorities nevertheless. And if the adult educator uses the word 'community' correctly, I believe he is indicating his willingness to listen to, learn from and respond to minorities. [...]

Notes

1. Frank Youngman, *Planning Local Adult Education Provision* (Frobisher Resource Centre, Frobisher Adult Education Institute, London, 1975)

2. Keith Jackson, 'The Marginality of Community Development — Implications for Adult Education', *International Review of Community Development* (1973).

3. Tom Lovett, *Adult Education, Community Development and the Working Class* (Ward Lock, London, 1975).

4. Tom Lovett, 'EPAs — An Interim Report', *Adult Education*, vol. 43, no. 5 (1971).

5. The defenders of an adult education service for 'everybody' — senior executives, trade unionists, women, the working class, immigrants etc.,etc. — are Jennifer Rogers and Brian Groombridge in *Right to Learn* (Arrow, London, 1976). Their response to the Coventry proposals would probably be found on p. 110 of their book:

> But to spare money for those most in need, if it were to mean leaving the rest of society to its own devices, to random forms of self-help, to the caprices of the market, is in fact aristocratic, not democratic; philanthropy, not a policy for the common good.

6. As quoted by Frank Youngman in *Planning Local Adult Education Provision* (Frobisher Resource Centre, Frobisher Adult Education Institute, London, 1975). I have not seen the original circular but it is worth quoting because it seems to demonstrate, in its use of punctuation, the way additional groups were

simply tacked on to the end of the list as they came to people's minds.

7. In fairness to Peter Clyne, he does warn against the dangers of using a blanket term like 'disadvantaged': but his book, *The Disadvantaged Adult* (Longman, London, 1972), and the *Russell Report* between them have established the word as a blanket term in adult education parlance.

8. A thumbnail rule might be: if the clients can refuse the provision there may still be room for *education*, but if they are under such constraints that they cannot refuse, then what they are receiving is *treatment*.

9. In Part 3 of *The Disadvantaged Adult* (Longman, London, 1972) under the heading 'Adult education in culturally and socially poor communities' Peter Clyne gives a number of impressive examples of good adult education practice. But labels are fraught with dangers, and one needs to read this section of his book in the context of the arguments put forward in *Tinker, Tailor ... The Myth of Cultural Deprivation*, edited and introduced by Neil Keddie (Penguin, Harmondsworth, 1973).

10. See Terence Jackson, 'A new look at parent education', *Adult Education*, vol. 50, no. 5 (1978).

5.2

ADULT EDUCATION AND COMMUNITY ACTION

Tom Lovett

Source: Jane Thompson (ed.), *Adult Education For a Change* (Hutchinson, London, 1980), pp. 155-73.

The role of adult education in community action has aroused a great deal of debate and discussion amongst socially committed adult educators over the last decade.[1] On the one hand are those adult educators who see in it an exciting possibility to extend the concept of adult learning, to make it more relevant to the interests, needs and problems of the working class and to open up educational resources to the latter so that they can make the maximum use of the opportunities it offers them.[2] On the other hand are those who feel that 'adult educationists should be wary when they are offered the resplendent new garments of community development, intended to transform their perception of themselves and their possibilities as they sally forth as community adult educators'.[3] The latter argue that the concept of 'community' should not be taken too seriously and that the role of adult education in the community development/community action process is more limited than the enthusiasts might have us believe.[4] Theirs is a more sceptical, cautious analysis; highly critical of the political naivety of the former and a more explicitly Marxist analysis, locating the origins of local community problems in the larger economic and social inequalities of a class society.

In the first model the role of adult education in community action is seen as one of providing the working class with an effective educational service so that they can take full advantage of the educational system *and* make the best use of their individual talents and abilities. Adult education is viewed as a general, comprehensive, community adult education 'service' meeting a variety of needs and interests amongst the working class, encouraging personal growth and development, and supporting greater community awareness and involvement. It provides for the general educational interests and needs of individuals (for example, informal group work, O Levels, languages, keepfit, etc.) in working-class communities and offers

254

educational assistance to groups engaged in local community action. This was the approach of the adult education work in the Educational Priority Area Project in Liverpool.[5]

The second model has been closely associated with the work of Keith Jackson and his colleagues from the Liverpool Institute of Extension Studies in Vauxhall in the early 1970s. Throughout the literature on this work there is a consistent emphasis on the need to engage the residents in relevant education of a high standard which makes no concessions to informal community discussion methods or the 'learning through doing' approach. Working-class activists are to 'be given the chance to come to terms with a subject skill or field of knowledge so that they can understand its internal rules, become an expert as far as possible.'[6] This is regarded as an essential educational contribution to social action.

The distinction between these two positions presents a number of problems for those involved in adult education with working-class men and women. On the one hand there is an increasing emphasis in many adult education institutions and organizations on community education, or social and political education. It is now part of the conventional adult education wisdom. However, the practical implications are rarely understood or appreciated. If they were then there might not be so much enthusiasm for the concepts! On the other hand the radical critique characteristic of the Vauxhall approach, and the educational emphasis arising from it — whilst important — is , I believe, unnecessarily limited in scope and in many respects does less than justice to the complexity of the situation on the ground and the opportunities available for linking adult education constructively to social/community action whilst avoiding the danger of both educational elitism and 'informal' education.

In my own view the relationship between adult education and community development is neither the grand opportunity seen by the optimists nor the more restricted role outlined in the sceptics' approach. I believe adult education *has* an important role to play in community action, that it is not necessarily a restricted one and that the concept of community should be taken seriously. However, before elaborating on this I want to look at two historically important initiatives outside our tradition of socially committed adult education. Both were attempts to link adult education more closely to movements for social and political change. Both were committed to, and intensely involved in, the process itself drawing no fine distinctions between action and education. One was the Antigonish

Movement at the University of St Francis Xavier in Nova Scotia, Canada. The other was the Highlander Folk School in Tennessee, USA.

The Antigonish Movement

As with the Liverpool Institute experience, the Antigonish Movement was university based and initiated. It was also situated in a very economically depressed area. In this case a mainly rural, depopulated region on the eastern seaboard of Canada. It also emphasized the importance of the economic aspect of local community problems. However. the work took place in the 1920s and 1930s and it was initiated and directed by two Catholic priests, initially by Father Jimmy Tompkins and later by Father Moses Coady.

It was a programme of adult education, self-help and co-operative development which became world famous. It was far from being non-directive and, in fact, the leading figure in it, Coady, was a charismatic personality who passionately believed in the role of adult education as an agent for social change in society. To him adult education was an aggressive agent of change, a mass movement of reform.[7] [...]

Generally speaking there were two phases to the movement. One in the 1920s when Tompkins put a great deal of pioneering effort into persuading local people to tackle the social and economic problems in the community. And the second in the 1930s when, as a result of Tompkins's efforts, the University opened an extension department with Coady as Director. During this period there was more emphasis on training and education but both men regarded the whole process as essentially educational and drew no fine distinctions between action and education. The methods used ranged widely, for example, mass meetings, study clubs, radio listening groups, short courses, kitchen meetings, conferences, leadership schools and training courses.

The mass meeting was the place where the educators preached their message. They took the initiative because, although Coady believed that education should be concerned with the everyday problems facing people in the region, he did not believe in just responding to 'felt needs'. He put more emphasis on the creation of awareness explaining that 'a fish doesn't know he lives in water until he is taken out of it.'[8] He did not believe that the educator should avoid unfamiliar words and language.

After the mass meeting people were organized into study clubs or discussion groups. This was regarded as the key educational technique in the Antigonish Movement: 'the foundation of the people's programme for adult learning'.[9] Everyday problems were discussed and success depended on intelligent local leaders and proper study materials. The study clubs quickly advanced to direct action. A variation of the study club was the radio listening group which enabled the movement to reach a larger number of people with relevant learning material. This basic work was complemented by the more intensive work at conferences, short courses and training schemes on the university campus. It was in fact a comprehensive and extensive programme of adult education and social action which owed a great deal, not only to the charismatic quality of Coady's leadership and Tompkins's pioneering field work, but the basic philosophy behind the movement. This was simple and straightforward, understood and accepted by the network of voluntary workers (many of them clerics!) which formed the backbone of the movement. The basic principles were:

(i)   The needs of the individual must have primacy.
(ii) Social reform must come through education.
(iii) Education must begin with the economic situation.
(iv) Education must be through group action.
(v)   Effective social reform involves fundamental changes in social and economic institutions.
(vi) The ultimate objective of the movement is a full and abundant life for everyone in the community.[10]

It was a populist movement with a vision of a new society. Although it was strongly anti-communist it was nevertheless influenced by, and imbued with, certain co-operative and Christian socialist principles based on a critical analysis of the existing social order. It stressed the need not only for working people to build their own, alternative, co-operative society but for full participation in all the major institutions in society.

Although most of the literature on the movement is uncritical, and not particularly analytical, there are suggestions that this very public and active commitment to social change produced tensions between the movement and the local political and educational establishment. For instance in 1938, at the height of the movement, a university report stated that, 'It will be difficult for the University to continue to carry the burden of the Extension Department'[11] — apparently the latter was considered expendable!

When Coady died in 1959 the movement appears effectively to have died with him and it became institutionalized and enshrined in the establishment of a Coady International Institute. Little of the work remains and a recent analysis of the movement states:

> In Canso and Little Dover 50 years after Father Jimmy started his work there the people are still struggling with poverty and depriva-tion. Women working in the fish plant in the early 70s made $14 a night before taxes. In their efforts to organize the people here got help from Father Gerry Rodgers of the Extension Department of St Francis Xavier University, the living embodiment of the Antigonish Way. But he's a very lonely man.[12]

Antigonish believed that radical change would come about through education, public participation and the establishment of alt-ernative institutions, that is co-ops and credit unions, not explicit political action. It was not a revolutionary movement and it has been argued that it damped down radical political agitation, directed the attention of the workers from striving for a new social and political order and, 'removed the need for the political system to perform effi-ciently and to meet the needs of the people instead of the elite. It may have prevented its collapse'.[13]

Nevertheless, although the Antigonish Movement lacked any explicit class analysis or radical political philosophy it did succeed in engaging large numbers of workers in relevant education linked to social action with methods and techniques which even today would be regarded as too radical for many educational institutions. It drew no barriers between social action and adult education and was engaged on a number of fronts linking one to the other. Despite its limitations it is a good example of how such work can be developed from a committed adult education base.

Highlander

The Highlander Folk School in the USA was established in the 1930s by Myles Horton. Like Antigonish, it was situated in one of the most socially and economically depressed regions in North America, a mixture of mining and agricultural communities in Tennessee. Like

Antigonish its founder and leading figure throughout its early history was strongly imbued with Christian/socialist principles and deeply influenced by the Danish Folk High School Movement.[14] The latter was regarded by both as a prime example of how an educational movement could be linked effectively to movements for social change and the development of a sense of national pride and identity. Highlander also had a simple philosophy which was, however, based on a more explicit class analysis.

Highlander's basic philosophy is summed up well in the following extract from a letter written by Horton in 1933 shortly after the school was established:

> Our task is to make class-conscious workers who envision their roles in society and to furnish motivation as well as technicians for the achievement of this goal ... We have found that a very effective way to help students to understand the present social order is to throw them into conflict situations where the real nature of our society is projected in all its ugliness. To be effective, such exposure must be preceded, accompanied by and followed by efforts to help the observer appreciate and digest what he has seen. This keeps education from getting unrealistic. While this process is going on, students need to be given an inkling of the new society. Perhaps this can be done best by having our communal living at the school come into this picture as an important education factor.[15]

However, although committed to a revolution to alter basic political and economic relationships, Highlander was not ideologically rigid.[16] Like Antigonish the emphasis was on working with people on real issues and problems and emphasizing the importance of co-operation and acting in unison.

Unlike Antigonish, however, Highlander was an independent educational establishment with a more explicitly socialist philosophy and its approach was radically different. It did not *initiate* programmes of social action, like Antigonish. Instead it concentrated on identifying and working closely with emerging social movements thrown up by the times and people, providing them with practical advice and assistance on the ground as well as educational support in the form of workshops at Highlander. The latter generally fell into two distinct categories. As the particular movement gathered force the workshops were broad and loose in range, usually without a specific topic. As the movements gained momentum more concrete information was requested and greater use was made of experts.

In the 1930s Highlander played an active role in the bitter struggle to organize trade unions in Tennessee, not by providing classes and courses, but by being actively involved on the picket line and in the mass demonstrations and providing information and opportunities for discussions on strategies and tactics. Horton was arrested during one of the most bitter campaigns in a mining town called Wilder and charged with: 'coming here and getting information and going back and teaching it'.[17] It was the first of many such arrests. The strike had a powerful effect on the Highlander staff who were involved in it. They were themselves ideologically committed but realized that to accomplish their goals workers themselves would have to state their own beliefs and that Highlander had not only to serve the people but be of the people.

During the 1930s work with the unions meant this sort of active commitment and involvement, complemented by conferences and residential workshops at Highlander and study groups out in the local community. As the unions became more organized these increasingly developed into union training schools and Highlander became somewhat disillusioned by union conservatism. [...]

However, Highlander had always seen its work as a long-term process adapting to new movements and circumstances and, during the 1950s and 1960s, it turned its attention, increasingly, to the problems of black workers. It played an important supportive role in the growth of the Citizenship Schools (designed to assist illiterate negroes to read and write so that they could pass the voting test) and in the civil rights movement. As a result of this, and its earlier work with the trade unions, Highlander was labelled a communist training school by the racialist and reactionary forces in the south. Eventually in 1961 the State of Tennessee seized the school's property and revoked its charter. The idea and the institution were, however, quickly reorganized and rechartered under its present name, Highlander Research and Education Centre Inc.

Since 1964 Highlander has concentrated on the problems of poverty and inequality in Tennessee — still one of the most depressed regions in the USA. However, it has also attempted to unite the various depressed minorities throughout the United States. For example, in 1970 it held a workshop attended by militant blacks, Puerto Ricans, Indians from six nations, Mexican Americans and people from the Appalachians which, although it highlighted the antagonisms between the various groups, illustrated the fact that none of them were free to determine their own destiny and all were poor. This was one of numerous attempts by Horton and others to assist the growth of a bottom-up radical coalition in the USA.

Highlander's original purpose, educating for a revolution that would basically change economic and political power relationships to the advantage of the poor and powerless, has clearly not been achieved. That was obviously an impossible task for one Folk School! However, Highlander's educational methods and techniques are now used in various grassroots initiatives throughout the USA and there is evidence that a radical coalition is emerging.[18] Highlander has played a pioneering role in encouraging that process.

Northern Ireland

Much of the recent British debate about the theory and practice of adult education in the field of community development and community action finds an echo in the two North American examples discussed above. Many of the 'new' concepts and methods in community development and community education (and the related theories of radical educators like Freire), were understood and practised at Highlander and Antigonish over 40 years ago. As is so often the case in adult education it is not a matter of new theories and concepts but new arrangements responding to different circumstances and influenced by prevailing social/political and economic theories.

In some respects the situation facing Highlander and Antigonish was less complicated, more clear cut, than the situation facing radical committed adult educators today. The inequalities and the injustices were starker, more obvious, and the choices facing the educators concerned clearer than those facing their counterparts today. Maybe this accounts for their faith in the power of adult education; their simple message; their vision of the new society; their open, public sense of social commitment, dedication and active involvement in building that new society. They both paid a price for their radical commitment, however. Antigonish is now a lost dream. Highlander survived better probably because of its cranky independence, its non-institutional base, its ability to adapt to new movements and most important, its radical critique.

In terms of their *educational* contribution both took a broad view and did not seek to define too precisely what shape that contribution should take. They utilized a variety of methods and techniques ranging from the informal to the formal depending on the time, place and circumstances. Highlander placed more emphasis on educating leaders for emerging social movements whilst Antigonish sought to create and shape a 'movement' providing educational support at a variety of levels. Both, however, used real issues and problems as material for an educational process which — although it did not ignore the need for hard information and training — placed more emphasis on the development of the will, the imagination and creative human relationships than analytical skills. Highlander in particular stressed the important educational role of music and songs and other aspects of local culture in its work.

In their respective ideologies and strategies they reflect the two aspects of the contemporary debate about community development, community action and adult education mentioned earlier. On the one hand, Antigonish placed its faith in the creation of alternative social and economic institutions and structures at local, community level. On the other hand, Highlander placed its faith in providing educational support for emerging social movements which would fundamentally alter existing political and economic structures. [...] Generally speaking the former adopted a community development strategy with an emphasis on the creation of alternatives, whilst the latter adopted a community action strategy with an emphasis on conflict and radical political change. [...]

In Northern Ireland, at the Institute of Continuing Education, Highlander and Antigonish have been important influences, along with recent English initiatives, in deciding the educational strategies and methods the Community Action Research and Education project should adopt. Religion plays a large part in people's lives as it did in Nova Scotia and Tennessee. Many of the settlers in Tennessee were Ulster Irish and the music of that area has roots in Irish culture. Northern Ireland is a mixture of rural and urban communities and farming is still one of the most important industries in the province. There is still a traffic in evangelical ministers between Tennessee and Ulster. No wonder Northern Ireland has been described as Britain's Tennessee!

However, I do not want to push these comparisons too far. Northern Ireland is part of the economic and political structure of the United Kingdom — one of the most economically depressed regions in that economy with a long history of unemployment and poverty. It is a region which has not only gone through the pangs and torments of civil and military conflict but one which, within the last ten years, has witnessed great changes in its economic and social structure as a result of industrial decline, urbanization and redevelopment. [...][19]

A recent analysis suggests that it has a higher level of poverty than any other part of the United Kingdom.[20] It is a divided community. Its tragedy is that the conflict has often assumed the proportions of a civil war between Catholic and Protestant working class.

However, despite the conflict and the divisions between the working class, the social and economic changes referred to above have resulted in the growth of numerous community organizations throughout Northern Ireland in both Catholic and Protestant areas.[21] They have found common ground in the midst of communal conflict. This is the constituency we have decided to work and identify with, viewing it as the only hope for a united working-class movement which, through this common struggle, might find a solution to its larger political problems and divisions. In doing so we have had no option but to take the concept of 'community' seriously since it was one which is used by the people themselves to describe their work and to articulate their hopes and ideals. Thus 'community' is not a concept imposed from above but one which springs from the grass roots and is held sincerely and passionately by very articulate community leaders.

Our base is an institutional one. However, it is only recently established (1972) and initially had a public commitment to community education. In numerous public documents reference was made to the 'large-scale development of community oriented education'. This means putting 'educational resources at the disposal of the community'[22] to help in resolving the social and economic problems of the area. Such public statements of intent and purpose are always suspect until they are matched with practice. It's doubtful if the implications were understood or appreciated at the time. However, since it was a new institution with new staff, able to develop their own roles without any prior commitments to fulfil, it was possible to take these statements of intent seriously and to develop work in the community in the knowledge that it was official policy and a priority for the institution. Of course it soon became obvious that people had different views about what community should be served. Our emphasis on working-class communities and organizations has always been something of a minority interest and priority, but at least we have been able to pursue it, unencumbered initially by other responsibilities, free to develop and define our role. However, this proved to be a difficult situation and, until money was provided from outside sources, it was an uphill struggle.

Like Antigonish and Highlander we have over the years since then sought to support, and identify with, the two sections of the working class in their common struggles and to provide what resources and assistance we can, making a point of stressing the extent of university resources and our commitment to making them available.

This has not proved easy. On the one hand our practical interpretation of 'putting education resources at the disposal of the community' — which often meant simply using Institute premises for meetings and discussions about all sorts of social, economic and political problems facing working-class communities (they were one of the few neutral premises available) — was viewed with some suspicion by the Institute and meant that they had to be 'dressed up' as classes or seminars. On the other hand community activists were, and still are, suspicious of academics and their intentions. This is something which can only be resolved at a personal level, over time, by active involvement and it remains a 'personal' rather than an institutional solution to the problem.

Our work like Highlander has, generally speaking, fallen into two phases. During the first phase, when the community movement was gathering strength, we were involved in various local initiatives, such as setting up resource centres, organizing conferences on broad topics and issues and assisting in the creation of a province-wide federation. In the second phase we became more actively involved in running workshops and seminars on more specific topics and issues, providing opportunities to learn certain skills and obtain items of information.[23] At present we are engaged in producing radio discussion programmes;[24] organizing local study groups throughout Northern Ireland;[25] assisting in a programme of linked weekends for community activists; running a research workshop for local activists interested in the Derry economy; organizing a two-year extra-mural certificate in community studies in which we hope to link theory and practice, using materials arising out of the work here, as well as experiences and analysis from abroad.

In all this work we have taken a sympathetic but critical approach to the prevailing community ideology and the strategies arising from it. We have encouraged active discussion and debate about the latter and the role of socialists within it. This has taken the form of seminars and workshops at which a variety of activists presented their written views and opinions for discussion and debate. We have found, like

Antigonish and Highlander, that the people we are involved with are suspicious of what they regard as the cold clinical 'academic' approach. They tend to emphasize the practical, the affective, the imaginative, the need to create new structures out of new relationships. [...]

In some respects our task is both easier and harder than it is elsewhere in the UK. We do not have a strong Socialist/Labour/Trade Union tradition, although that can on occasions be a hindrance rather than a help! The changes of the last decade in Northern Ireland have, comparatively speaking, radicalized some sections of the working class here — including some sections of the Protestant working class.[26] This provides opportunities to engage in a dialogue about what shape a new society should take and the role of socialism in it. Our task is more difficult not only because of the divisions within community groups about their role but the divisions between them about the future of the state.[27] Many on both sides associate socialism with planning, bureaucracy and lack of freedom. That is what they know of the socialist dream. The struggle of the working class to achieve that dream is not, with some exceptions, seen as part of their heritage. We have thus placed some emphasis on finding ways of illustrating the common culture and problems of the Northern Irish working class, for example, through the radio discussion programmes, which are a sort of oral social history and material which helps to illustrate the similarities with working-class problems elsewhere in the UK and relates this to earlier working-class struggles — to develop in fact a sense of working-class history and culture. In all this work we have sought to combine the affective and the analytical, using aspects of the local culture as well as art, music and literature to help people articulate their dreams and aspirations, to investigate the major themes in their lives and to provide opportunities for serious analytical study and the acquisition of skills and information.

Freire sees this process in stages, that is, an initial stage of 'investigation' by the educator; a second stage in which learning material is produced which uses cultural artefacts familiar to the people, to explore major themes in their lives as reflected in the issues and problems they face. In the third stage, this material is discussed in cultural circles. [...] In the fourth stage Freire stresses the need to use specialists, like economists and sociologists, to assist in the more detailed analysis of the themes discovered in the third stage.[28]

We have found Freire's analysis and classification of this process helpful. However, his emphasis on *stages* does an injustice to the complexity of the evolving situation on the ground where different people, and different groups, are at various stages at the same time. We for example are involved on a number of fronts simultaneously, providing 'courses' for leading activists, whilst also involved in more informal work in workshops, seminars, study groups as well as practical action on the ground.

We are also aware that a simple 'economic' analysis and explanation of community problems does an injustice to the complexity of the 'themes' shaping and changing people's lives here. We have sought, therefore, not only to insert an economic perspective into the community debate, but also to include the political, the social and the cultural. Thus one of our radio discussion series was on religious stereotypes and another on changes in family and community life.

We feel, like Ralph Miliband,[29] that the search for a modern interpretation of the socialist dream, especially in the situation we find ourselves in here, entails a long search — a continuing dialogue which of necessity encompasses a wide variety of groups and individuals who are experiencing tremendous changes in their everyday lives and relationships. [...]

We hope in this way to assist in the creation of a radical social movement which will, of necessity, bring together people belonging to different groups and parties as well as individuals who belong to none. Like Miliband we visualize that some form of loose federation or alliance will be necessary and that it will attempt to articulate the 'themes' and visions implied in various aspects of the community struggle as well as to offer a radical critique of the existing order. Thus we have not concentrated specifically on community organizations but, through workshops and conferences, brought together activists from community groups, women's organizations, trade unions and those concerned with creating alternative institutions at local level. We have also assisted in organizing conferences on political options in Northern Ireland and the problem of human rights. All of this work has brought together not only Catholics and Protestants, but also supporters of various para-military groups in a debate which offers some hope for the future.

However, we realize there are dangers in over-emphasizing the need to establish links with organizations like the trade union movement. It can result in a form of educational elitism which, while providing classes in political economy and work on research, only reaches a tiny proportion of the working-class population. The need is to marry this form of social action with community action on the ground. Attempts by those involved in the latter to establish community control or work towards community 'development' should not be dismissed as they often are by those on the left. They have historical parallels in the history of the working class, that is the building up of local working-class organizations and informal social structures whilst engaged in wider social and political action.

They are two sides of the same coin and it is just not true to argue that all problems and issues facing the working class can *only* be resolved by mass movements for social and political change. The search for 'quality' in human relationships and convivial local institutions, a feature of the work of many local people involved in community development, tends to be ignored by political activists or dismissed as irrelevant. The mass movements' struggle is, however, long-term and new relationships and new structures at local level can be created which at least will illustrate what the new society might look like. It was done in the past in the most adverse conditions. It can be done today.

We have no illusions about that process but we believe radical educators must play a role in it whilst providing support for a social movement. It is doubtful if such a role will, or could be, undertaken by the formal adult educational system. [...] What is required is a new educational 'movement' based on existing independent initiatives — like the local resource centres. [...]

Our hope lies in the possibility of establishing a residential centre which would link in to the network of local resource centres to provide research and educational facilities, concentrating on weekend, and week-long workshops, with staff employed in the centre and in the field. It would be clear about its purpose and methods as the creation of the radical working-class movement, in which adult education would assist in encouraging a dialogue and analysis, not only about community action, but about wider social and political problems. Such a dialogue would seek to go beyond narrow Republican and Unionist stereotypes to a realization of the heritage and culture shared by both communities, an appreciation of the strengths in their different traditions, and the opportunities available to create a new future based on their common efforts and aspirations. That is the challenge for adult educators here in Northern Ireland. A similar challenge and opportunity faces all committed adult educators involved in community action.

Notes

1. J. Harrison, 'Community Work and Adult Education', *Studies in Adult Education*, vol. 6, no. 1 (April 1974). K.H. Lawson, 'Community Education — A Critical Assessment', in *Adult Education*, vol. 50, no. 1 (May 1977).

2. T. Lovett, *Adult Education, Community Development and the Working Class* (Ward Lock, 1975).

3. K. Jackson, 'The Marginality of Community Development — Implications for Adult Education', *International Review of Community Development* (Summer 1973).

4. Ibid.

5. Lovett, *Adult Education. Community Development and the Working-Class*.

6. Jackson, 'The Marginality of Community Development', p. 27.

7. M. Coady, *Masters of Our Destiny* (Harper and Bros., New York, 1939).

8. A.F. Laidlaw, *The Man from Margaree — Writings and Speeches of M.M. Coady* (McClelland and Stewart Ltd, Toronto, 1971), p. 57.

9. A.F. Laidlaw, *The Campus and the Community — The Global Impact of the Antigonish Movement* (Harvard House Ltd, Montreal, 1961), p. 116.

10. Ibid., p. 97.

11. Ibid., p. 90.

12. J. Lotz, 'The Antigonish Movement' in *Understanding Canada: Regional and Community Development in a New Nation* (N.C. Press Ltd, Toronto, 1977), ch. 10, p. 113.

13. Ibid., p. 112.

14. F. Adams, 'Highlander Folk School: Getting Information, Going Back and Teaching It', *Harvard Educational Review*, vol. 42, no. 4 (November 1972).

15. Ibid., p. 516.

16. F. Adams and M. Horton, *Unearthing Seeds of Fire — The Idea of Highlander* (J.F. Blair, N. Carolina, 1975), p. 206.

17. Ibid., p. 33.

18. J. Perlman, 'Grassrooting the System', *Social Policy* (Alan Gartner, New York; September/October, 1976).

19. For an analysis of these changes and how they have affected a Protestant working-class community in Belfast, see: R. Weiner, *The Rape and Plunder of the Shankill, Community Action: The Belfast Experience* (Notaems Press, Belfast, 1975).

20. E. Evason, 'Poverty: The Facts in N. Ireland', *Poverty Pamphlet*, no. 27 (Child Poverty Action Group, 1976).

21. T. Lovett and R. Percival, 'Politics, Conflict and Community Action in N. Ireland' in P. Curno (ed.), *Political Issues and Community Work* (Routledge & Kegan Paul Ltd, London, 1978).

22. 1973 Brochure — New University of Ulster (Institute of Continuing Education, Londonderry).

23. T. Lovett, 'Adult Education and Community Action — the N. Ireland Experience', *Community Education '77* (ed.), C. Fletcher (University of Nottingham, Department of Adult Education, 1977).

24. T. Lovett, 'Community Education and Local Radio' in *Collective Action — A Selection of Community Work Case Studies* in M. Pungate, P. Henderson and L. Smith (eds.) (Community Projects Foundation and Association of Community Workers, 1979).

25. L. Mackay and T. Lovett, 'Community Based Study Groups — N. Ireland Case Study', *Adult Education*, vol. 51, no. 1 (May 1978).

26. Weiner, *The Rape and Plunder of the Shankill.*

27. Lovett and Percival, 'Politics, Conflict and Community Action in N. Ireland'.

28. Paulo Freire, *Pedagogy of the Oppressed* (Penguin, Harmondsworth, 1972).

29. R. Miliband, 'The Future of Socialism in England', *The Socialist Register* (1977).

5.3

ACTION LEARNING AND THE INNER CITY

Reg Revans

Source: Copyright © Reg Revans 1981 (specially written for this volume).

Introduction

The most impressive quality of our times is the rate at which things are changing. Present speeds of travel and of computation suggest more increase in particular single years recently than in the previous century. One accompaniment of these changes is our army of unemployed; another is our urban decay.

Many explanations are given as to why things so continuously alter; many suggestions are made for getting people back to work. These arguments are not gone into in this paper, save to agree that much of our trouble is historically determined and will be with us a long time yet. How far we discover that there are no simplistic answers to our distress depends upon how closely we work together to escape from it, and cooperation is not easy for the British, with their separate and powerful institutions, some going back to Magna Carta or even King Alfred, and mostly very jealous of their own rights. An island people may forge a national alliance to fight a foreign war; it is not so easy to get our self-conscious bureaucracies to work together on totally new dangers arising from within. This note suggests a new get-together called action learning.

Brief Objective

One origin of this note is official: the motivation of the Manpower Services Commission; the other is personal: the writer's experience, going back to the 1930s, in local government, industry, education and public administration. It is argued that any useful course of action, to improve conditions for the unemployed in the inner cities, must be a substantial programme of learning for all involved, including members of parliament, local councillors, teachers, policemen and, above all, such experts as town planners and university

270

professors of urban development. It suggests that some local community puts up for support an action learning programme of its own devising, and calculated to advance its own recovery within three years. In every aspect, from first arousing interest to marketing its outputs or services three years later, it must strive after one condition: that all concerned will *learn from every move something that is worthwhile* for themselves and for the wider community. Given this, action learning suggests that:

(1) any delegation sufficiently stimulated to want to draw up its own proposed scheme will be eager to seek the advice of any other local delegation interested in drawing up proposals of its own; in this way, the ideas and experience of all become available to all and, almost overnight, a vast national store of lived experience becomes a new national asset;[1]

(2) such exchanges, by widening the vision of all, will start a national learning process; this will bring in local participants likely to have been unrecognised and local ideas likely to have been overlooked; that so few in authority showed any anticipation of their own coming disturbances, and that so many are now seeking expert (if not instant) solutions to their troubles, is proof that useful ideas must be sought from new quarters;[2]

(3) these proposed exercises in self-expression and mutual development will soon prove that any who begin them assuming the role of teacher or of expert will soon be forced by the hard facts of reality to change their outlook; any practical scheme will identify all who continue in it as *learners with and from each other* (the police, for example, howsoever grossly misjudged as an institution they may be, must learn with and from the local community how to improve their integration into it; the constable must be encouraged to learn from the adolescent no less than the adolescent is constrained to learn from the constable);[3]

(4) any local programme should be launched only by those who *genuinely care about* getting the unused assets (especially the human assets) of the local community more effectively used; it is vital that no scheme should be officially promoted by outsiders, howsoever expert or professional, unless it has been so thoroughly worked over by the local delegation as to be in effect the creation of the delegation itself; and in order not to remove responsibility and initiative from local agencies already existing, no local scheme should be promoted by any new bureaucracy set up for the purpose.[4]

Operational Moves

These four paragraphs express only the spirit of the new learning exercise; they say nothing about administration or finance. But, until a first attempt has been made to recruit the self-help, there is not much specifically that *can* be said about them. Nevertheless, granted that a common opinion has emerged, both on the streets as well as at national and local government levels, that it is worthwhile to marshal the talents and resources of the disadvantaged neighbourhoods, there are two preliminary stages to be worked through: first, we need to prepare a set of suggestions, put up by those with both action learning experience in other fields and also the conviction that it would help a few in the inner cities set out to arouse attention amongst other key persons in them; and, second, to give then all the encouragement and support to those key persons to motivate their own neighbours in designing their specific local programme.

Financial Implications

Existing special programmes of the Manpower Services Commission are a national investment in the potentials of individuals. The proposed action learning programme will still develop each participant, but also in a new fashion, since it aims to engender organisational strengths (synergy) as well as personal skill. Presumably, therefore, whatever investment per participant might seem reasonable under existing programmes would be acceptable for encouraging this experiment. But action learning does not merely suggest cooperation: it is cooperation and, with the prospect of semi-permanent unemployment to be removed, it is inevitable that many who participate in preparing their own programmes will have ideas about wealth creation that call for venture capital. Before specific proposals have been put up there is little virtue in going into the financial implications of an action learning programme in general, except to stress that, in designing any submission, the local delegation must clearly show how their scheme will become self-supporting at the earliest possible time; since any communal venture will be diverse, and some elements seem to make a profit while others make a loss, delegations should be encouraged to propose consolidated schemes. Since extending credit to enterprising persons goes back to the Middle Ages, it may be suggested that local delegations will not find it hard to get advice — even if money is harder to come by. Nevertheless, the magnitude and duration of our problems, unemployment coupled with urban decay, are bound to demand quite new methods for backing schemes of self-help and community growth. Such innovations will soon emerge from the interactions and exchanges of those comrades in adversity, a score of local delegations all seeking their own survival down the paths of action learning. The inevitable insights inspired by their misfortunes can be guaranteed to produce novel modes of financing. The extent to which, as in the deprived areas of New York today, the private banks will offer special terms to local enterprise; or to which, as in northern Spain, local residents might invest their savings; or to which resources now offered to Enterprise Workshops by the Manpower Services Commission may be available; or to which participant belief in their own ventures would lead to some self-financing (percentages of unemployment benefit as well as quotas from redundancy payment), or even grants to forthcoming local employers making special efforts to encourage the programme: none of this can be known until local proposals come forward.

Existing Authorities and Agencies

Action learning, displayed across the world in all sectors of its many economies, obliges participants to learn with and from each other how to use their present talents and resources more effectively. It holds up no textbook models of personal perfection and draws upon no treasure house of administrative theory. The scheme-making delegation must take the existing authorities as they are and seek all the cooperation they can. It will need to recruit the support of others — employers, shopkeepers, investors, residents, social services, police, education, welfare and job agencies, clubs, churches and so forth — by simple persuasion; progress will be made only if, as in all attempts at learning, those involved genuinely wish to learn. One cannot, in any legalistic sense, force those in one group to learn because it is in the interests of some other group to teach them. We learn of our own volition, not at the will of others. Thus the interest of participants must derive from the attractions of the scheme in the present and its promise for the future; its design will offer scope enough for the micro-political talents of the key organisers recruited at the start.

Elements of Operational Design

The cutting edge of action learning is the set of five or six participants, mostly unemployed, and their immediate associates; each set has a leader, and five or six sets form a consortium, whose set leaders also regularly meet each other as a higher-level set. Action learning requires the sets to be quite stable, so that the same individuals regularly meet to discuss their here-and-now needs with each other against a supportive background of here-and-now suggestions. Participants should not all be wholly unemployed, since variety among those who contribute ideas is the best guarantee of innovation; some should be in full-time employment. Granted that the working members of the sets, 150 or so in all, should (at least to begin with) be without a regular job, their set leaders need not all be full-time in the programme. Although, say a score of unemployed managers or other professional men and women would bring strength to those points in the programme where strength is most needed, a few key leaders, either to look after sets or to convene the higher-level sets composed of leaders, could be from those still in full-time work, giving up one day a week to ensure the integration of the programme into the economic and social life of the living community. One senior police officer should act, for example, as set leader or as a convener of set leaders; without this others in the programme will never learn to see the police as approachable and supportive. Nor, by the same token, will the police get that fresh vision of the unemployed adolescents essential to improving their relations with them. Only when both parties become interested in *the definition and solution of each other's troubles* can there be any realistic hope of better understanding. It will also be essential to bring into the sets, into their consortia and into the programme as a whole, a variety of unemployed older workers, skilled and unskilled, clerical and commercial, men and women, white and coloured, as set members alongside the adolescents and the younger unemployed, and also a vital leavening of trade union officials, teachers, staff of local authorities and of the social services, and above all, the most important class of employers and other apparent organisers of the real wealth-creating processes. Every participant must be aware that his set activities are supposed to be enhancing the tangible wealth of the community; if not, the whole effort is no more than academic fantasy. And if, as has been suggested, the local teachers are to join the programme, it is because they need to learn what should be done *within their own schools* if these (not unlike the police service) are to be brought back into the life of the community they were once expected to serve. Educators must no longer be afraid of a rethink.

The Conditions of Wealth Creation

To ask that the programme creates tangible wealth is simple realism. British unemployment and urban decay follow the collapse of manufacturing; only the restoration of our overseas trade can revive the chances of significantly more work for the majority. There is (particularly in Moss Side) no such thing as a free lunch. Although it is not supposed that 200 action learning pioneers in the back streets of what was the Cradle of the Industrial Revolution will, within a couple of days, be restocking the warehouses of San Francisco and the bazaars of Madras, their collective effort will bring a new drive to the use of the nation's most precious unused asset. Thus it is that those used to organising such effort shall be central to the programme, in order that they, too, may learn new forms of common employment, such as job sharing cooperatives, even community barter. A score of set leaders might be former managers or other professional men and women now out of a job themselves, and so no less charged than any others to interpret their experiences afresh. An ability to take the lead and to set the pace is not necessarily the shortest route to the hearts of one's fellows, but we face conditions in which what was once regarded as unfeeling brutality may now be seen as wholesome and constructive. Helping others to help themselves is often a thankless task, but it is also one from which the qualities of the single-minded go-getter may emerge with credit. If, moreover, the programme does succeed in bringing more closely together a large number of institutions skilled in minding their own business and proud to keep themselves to themselves (and for so laudable an objective as to prevent riots by creating wealth), we may set municipal life in Lancashire down the road to understanding.

Notes

1. Action learning brings together those with difficulties so profound and so unstructured that no solutions can be offered, even by experts; in such predicaments those who suffer the problems are obliged to ask themselves many questions

before useful and worthwhile courses of ameliorative action can be suggested. It is an experimental fact that those best able to help in the search for discriminating questions likely to lead to corrective measures are, not experts with predispositions towards their own available solutions, but others embarrassed by profound and unstructured problems of their own.

Action learning (although first practised in NCB collieries in the 1950s and London hospitals in the 1960s) has become well known and widely applied only in the past few years. The growing complexity of current problems, whether in industry and commerce, banking and international trade, government and the social services, coupled with a growing disillusion over the remedies offered by the business schools and the professional consultants, are encouraging those with the troubles discussed to work together among themselves on collective programmes of diagnosis and therapy. There is now an extensive literature, produced by the managers themselves rather than by professional advisers, upon action learning. Particularly relevant articles are those about improving the coordination of the services for the mentally handicapped, an action learning programme organised between 1971 and 1974 by The King Edward Fund for London, and involving parents and general practitioners no less than health visitors, mental welfare officers and other professionals. More recently (1979-81), the success of action learning in improving the running of the Victoria State Housing Commission (in Australia), bringing in on equal terms the tenants and maintenance men beside the management and the leasing agents, has led to its chief general manager (Dr Roy V. Gilbert) being invited to Ulster to help the Northern Ireland Housing Authority apply more effectively the experience of all concerned with it. This is true action learning — or will become so when the officers in Ulster are invited to take their newly-gained insights out to Melbourne.

2. One of the more singular features of the Bristol, Brixton, Toxteth and Moss Side riots were their unexpectedness to most persons, especially those in positions of power and authority in the districts themselves. Action learning accepts that those who grow familiar with such-and-such conditions eventually become all but unable to ask questions about what, if anything, may be going on around them; the most fertile stimulant of fresh questions is the comrade in parallel adversity suddenly awakened to his own need to think afresh. In the words of Gp/Capt Leonard Cheshire: 'The best way to deal with your own troubles is to go to somebody else's help.' — provided always that the somebody else is also ready to lend a hand with one's own. There is a profound difference between the search for discriminating questions, carried out among equal colleagues, and the application of programmed solutions drawn up by experts. The first is without preconceived boundaries and will uncover the unsuspected (and if there is one urgent need in trying to treat the urban riots of 1981 it is to identify more clearly their *causes* rather than to describe their immediate *occasions*), while the second may very well focus attention upon quite the most inappropriate opinions. For example, it is not generally known (and by interested parties will probably be denied) that adolescent violence is engendered by the secondary school system as such, irrespective of colour, affluence and likelihood of employment; Japanese youth, with all the security that their counterparts in Toxteth and Moss Side could wish for, are responding to their educational experiences by knifing the teachers whom they do not like. Just as Ulster may learn a little about housing from Australia, so action learning suggests that Liverpool and Tokyo might usefully exchange thoughts about schooling. Nothing could be more disastrous at the present moment than that those responsible for improving the quality of life in Britain's inner cities should seek the advice of educational experts ready with treatments expressing ideas drawn wholly from the dead and from the past.

3. Action learning by its acknowledged successes demonstrates that insight is a

social process: as Gp/Capt Cheshire implies, one learns from the other only if the other also learns from the one: the very first action learning programme (among sets of colliery managers struggling with the rehabilitation of Britain's mines after decades of neglect brought on by underinvestment) showed the dangers of mixing experts with prefabricated solutions in among the more open-minded managers anxious to diagnose as fully as possible what might be wrong before being hustled into accepting ready-made remedies. Unless all parties to an action learning programme — or, for that matter, to any enquiry into affairs that have gone seriously and inexplicably amiss — are ready to join it as acknowledged learners, it is better to give in at once to the experts and to waste no further time in delaying the next disaster. Thus those concerned with inner city problems will be interested to hear that there is a precedent (long before the riots of 1981) of employers, education authorities and police working together on their own and each other's involvements with the adolescents of their particular city.

4. Action learning is not primarily a professional technique on sale by experts — although there will now be plenty in the field making offers to provide it at a suitable fee. Naturally enough those in Manchester, say, who have never heard of what action learning has achieved in solving the housing problems of the immigrant population of Melbourne (a city with three times as many inhabitants as Manchester), nor in helping the parents of that most disadvantaged class of all, the mentally handicapped, to come to terms with neighbourly judgments and even guilty consciences, must at least be introduced to its primary ideas. All the same, a handful of managers or of social workers who have themselves been actively engaged in an action learning programme can soon explain to others interested in tackling their own afflictions at first hand what action learning may be; they might also offer to run some introductory seminars to enter more deeply into the practice of diagnosis and therapy. What must certainly be avoided, and at any cost, is that the members of the local programme become dependent upon the experts who offer to run action learning exercises, whether in sets, consortia or whole local schemes. Most of the current problems of the British nation can with a little imagination, be traced back to the dependency upon professors, lecturers, teachers and academic experts of other kinds which is not only the accepted tradition of scholarship and the foundation of all elitism, but which deprives the majority of the population from ever finding out who they are while still young enough to preserve the curiosity to do so. We need forms of self-discovery that may help the great crisis in identity among the major part of the British to be resolved, and action learning by forcing people to work together in treating their own here-and-now troubles, is one such form. It must never be permitted to degenerate into the educational tradition of teacher knowing best and telling the pupil what to do.

References

R.W. Revans (1976) *Action Learning in Hospitals*, McGraw-Hill, London. This gives an account (with statistical evidence for its success) of the consortium of London hospitals working together on their own problems and on those of the other participants; it also describes the consortium of seven local authorities working together on the problems of domiciliary care for the mentally handicapped.

_____ (1980) *Action Learning*, Blond & Briggs, London. This describes the application of action learning across the world, from 1950 until the present. It has a report by Dr R.V. Gilbert upon the action learning programmes of the Australian civil services.

_____ _ (1982) *The Origins and Growth of Action Learning*, Studentlitteratur, Lund, Sweden. An extensive selection of articles on action learning in many different fields.

G.F. Wieland (1981) *Improving Health Care Management*, Health Administration Press, Ann Arbor, Mich. 48109, USA. This is a second evaluation of the London hospitals project by the same critic; it gives a most rigorous proof of the success of action learning.

5.4

EDUCATION AND CONSCIENTIZAÇÃO

Paulo Freire

Source: *Education For Critical Consciousness* (Sheed and Ward, London, 1973)
pp. 41-58. Pbk. edn: *Education: The Practice of Freedom* (The Writers and
Readers Publishing Cooperative).

[...] For more than 15 years I had been accumulating experiences in
the field of adult education, in urban and rural proletarian and
subproletarian areas. Urban dwellers showed a surprising interest in
education, associated directly to the transitivity of their consciousness; the inverse was true in rural areas. (Today, in some areas, that
situation is already changing.) I had experimented with — and
abandoned — various methods and processes of communication.
Never, however, had I abandoned the conviction that only by
working with the people could I achieve anything authentic on their
behalf. Never had I believed that the democratization of culture
meant either its vulgarization or simply passing on to the people
prescriptions formulated in the teacher's office. I agreed with
Mannheim that 'as democratic processes become widespread, it
becomes more and more difficult to permit the masses to remain in a
state of ignorance.'[1] Mannheim would not restrict his definition of
ignorance to illiteracy, but would include the masses' lack of experience at participating and intervening in the historical process.

Experiences as the Coordinator of the Adult Education Project of
the Movement of Popular Culture in Recife led to the maturing of my
early educational convictions. Through this project, we launched a
new institution of popular culture, a 'culture circle', since among us a
school was a traditionally passive concept. Instead of a teacher, we
had a coordinator; instead of lectures, dialogue; instead of pupils,
group participants; instead of alienating syllabi, compact programs
that were 'broken down' and 'codified' into learning units.

In the culture circles, we attempted through group debate either to
clarify situations or to seek action arising from that clarification. The
topics for these debates were offered us by the groups themselves.
Nationalism, profit remittances abroad, the political evolution of
Brazil, development, illiteracy, the vote for illiterates, democracy,

279

were some of the themes which were repeated from group to group. These subjects and others were schematized as far as possible and presented to the groups with visual aids, in the form of dialogue. We were amazed by the results.

After six months of experience with the culture circles, we asked ourselves if it would not be possible to do something in the field of adult literacy which would give us similar results to those we were achieving in the analysis of aspects of Brazilian reality. We started with some data and added more, aided by the Service of Cultural Extension of the University of Recife, which I directed at the time and under whose auspices the experiment was conducted.

The first literacy attempt took place in Recife, with a group of five illiterates, of whom two dropped out on the second or third day. The participants, who had migrated from rural areas, revealed a certain fatalism and apathy in regard to their problems. They were totally illiterate. At the twentieth meeting, we gave progress tests. To achieve greater flexibility, we used an epidiascope. We projected a slide on which two kitchen containers appeared. 'Sugar' was written on one, 'poison' on the other. And underneath, the caption: 'Which of the two would you use in your orangeade?' We asked the group to try to read the question and to give the answer orally. They answered, laughing, after several seconds, 'Sugar.' We followed the same procedure with other tests, such as recognizing bus lines and public buildings. During the twenty-first hour of study, one of the participants wrote, confidently, 'I am amazed at myself.'

From the beginning, we rejected the hypothesis of a purely mechanistic literacy program and considered the problem of teaching adults how to read in relation to the awakening of their consciousness. We wished to design a project in which we would attempt to move from naîveté to a critical attitude at the same time we taught reading. We wanted a literacy program which would be an introduction to the democratization of culture, a program with men as its subjects rather than as patient recipients,[2] a program which itself would be an act of creation, capable of releasing other creative acts, one in which students would develop the impatience and vivacity which characterize search and invention.

We began with the conviction that the role of man was not only to be in the world, but to engage in relations with the world — that through acts of creation and re-creation, man makes cultural reality and thereby adds to the natural world, which he did not make. We were certain that man's relation to reality, expressed as a Subject to an object, results in knowledge, which man could express through language.

This relation, as is already clear, is carried out by men whether or not they are literate. It is sufficient to be a person to perceive the data of reality, to be capable of knowing, even if this knowledge is mere opinion. There is no such thing as absolute ignorance or absolute wisdom.[3] But men do not perceive those data in a pure form. As they apprehend a phenomenon or a problem, they also apprehend its causal links. The more accurately men grasp true causality, the more critical their understanding of reality will be. Their understanding will be magical to the degree that they fail to grasp causality. Further, critical consciousness always submits that causality to analysis; what is true today may not be so tomorrow. Naïve consciousness sees causality as a static, established fact, and thus is deceived in its perception.

Critical consciousness represents 'things and facts as they exist empirically, in their causal and circumstantial correlations ... naïve consciousness considers itself superior to facts, in control of facts, and thus free to understand them as it pleases.'[4]

Magic consciousness, in contrast, simply apprehends facts and attributes to them a superior power by which it is controlled and to which it must therefore submit. Magic consciousness is characterized by fatalism, which leads men to fold their arms, resigned to the impossibility of resisting the power of facts.

Critical consciousness is integrated with reality; naïve consciousness superimposes itself on reality; and fanatical consciousness, whose pathological naïveté leads to the irrational, adapts to reality.

It so happens that to every understanding, sooner or later an action corresponds. Once man perceives a challenge, understands it, and recognizes the possibilities of response, he acts. The nature of that action corresponds to the nature of his understanding. Critical understanding leads to critical action; magic understanding to magic response.

We wanted to offer the people the means by which they could supersede their magic or naïve perception of reality by one that was predominantly critical, so that they could assume positions appropriate to the dynamic climate of the transition. This meant that we must take the people at the point of emergence and, by helping them move from naïve to critical transitivity, facilitate their intervention in the historical process.

But how could this done?

The answer seemed to lie:
(a) in an active, *dialogical,* critical and criticism-stimulating *method*;
(b) in changing the *program content* of education;
(c) in the use of *techniques* like thematic 'breakdown' and 'codification'.[5]

Our method, then, was to be based on dialogue, which is a horizontal relationship between persons. Born of a critical matrix,
dialogue creates a critical attitude (Jaspers). It is nourished by love,
humility, hope, faith, and trust. When the two 'poles' of the dialogue
are thus linked by love, hope, and mutual trust, they can join in a
critical search for something. Only dialogue truly communicates.

Dialogue is the only way, not only in the vital questions of the
political order, but in all the expressions of our being. Only by
virtue of faith, however, does dialogue have power and meaning:
by faith in man and his possibilities, by the faith that I can only
become truly myself when other men also become themselves.[6]

And so we set dialogue in opposition with the anti-dialogue which
was so much a part of our historical-cultural formation, and so
present in the climate of transition. It involves vertical relationships
between persons. It lacks love, is therefore acritical, and cannot
create a critical attitude. It is self-sufficient and hopelessly arrogant.
In anti-dialogue the relation of empathy between the 'poles' is
broken. Thus, anti-dialogue does not communicate, but rather issues
communiqués.[7]
    Whoever enters into dialogue does so with someone about
something; and that something ought to constitute the new content of
our proposed education. We felt that even before teaching the
illiterate to read, we could help him to overcome his magic or naïve
understanding and to develop an increasingly critical understanding.
Toward this end, the first dimension of our new program content
would be the anthropological concept of culture — that is, the distinction between the world of nature and the world of culture; the
active role of men *in* and *with* their reality; the role of mediation
which nature plays in relationships and communication among men;
culture as the addition made by men to a world they did not make;
culture as the result of men's labor, of their efforts to create and re-
create; the transcendental meaning of human relationships; the

humanist dimension of culture; culture as a systematic acquisition of human experience (but as creative assimilation, not as information-storing); the democratization of culture; the learning of reading and writing as a key to the world of written communication. In short, the role of man as Subject in the world and with the world.

From that point of departure, the illiterate would begin to effect a change in his former attitudes, by discovering himself to be a maker of the world of culture, by discovering that he, as well as the literate person, has a creative and re-creative impulse. He would discover that culture is just as much a clay doll made by artists who are his peers as it is the work of a great sculptor, a great painter, a great mystic, or a great philosopher; that culture is the poetry of lettered poets and also the poetry of his own popular songs — that culture is all human creation.

To introduce the concept of culture, first we 'broke down' this concept into its fundamental aspects. Then, on the basis of this breakdown, we 'codified' (i.e., represented visually) ten existential situations. Each representation contained a number of elements to be 'decoded' by the group participants, with the help of the coordinator. Francisco Brenand, one of the greatest contemporary Brazilian artists, painted these codifications, perfectly integrating education and art.

It is remarkable to see with what enthusiasm these illiterates engage in debate and with what curiosity they respond to questions implicit in the codifications. In the words of Odilon Ribeiro Coutinho, these 'detemporalized men begin to integrate themselves in time.' As the dialogue intensifies, a 'current' is established among the participants, dynamic to the degree that the content of the codifications corresponds to the existential reality of the groups.

Many participants during these debates affirm happily and self-confidently that they are not being shown 'anything new, just remembering.' 'I make shoes,' said one, 'and now I see that I am worth as much as the Ph.D. who writes books.'

'Tomorrow,' said a street-sweeper in Brasília, 'I'm going to go to work with my head high.' He had discovered the value of his person. 'I know now that I am cultured,' an elderly peasant said emphatically. And when he was asked how it was that now he knew himself to be cultured, he answered with the same emphasis, 'Because I work, and working, I transform the world.'[8]

Once the group has perceived the distinction between the two worlds — nature and culture — and recognized man's role in each, the coordinator presents situations focusing on or expanding other aspects of culture.

The participants go on to discuss culture as a systematic acquisition of human experience, and to discover that in a lettered culture this acquisition is not limited to oral transmission, as is the case in unlettered cultures which lack graphic signs. They conclude by debating the democratization of culture, which opens the perspective of acquiring literacy.

All these discussions are critical, stimulating, and highly motivating. The illiterate perceives critically that it is necessary to learn to read and write, and prepares himself to become the agent of this learning.

To acquire literacy is more than to psychologically and mechanically dominate reading and writing techniques. It is to dominate these techniques in terms of consciousness; to understand what one reads and to write what one understands; it is to *communicate* graphically. Acquiring literacy does not involve memorizing sentences, words, or syllables — lifeless objects unconnected to an existential universe — but rather an attitude of creation and re-creation, a self-transformation producing a stance of intervention in one's context.

Thus the educator's role is fundamentally to enter into dialogue with the illiterate about concrete situations and simply to offer him the instruments with which he can teach himself to read and write. This teaching cannot be done from the top down, but only from the inside out, by the illiterate himself, with the collaboration of the educator. That is why we searched for a method which would be the instrument of the learner as well as of the educator, and which, in the lucid observation of a young Brazilian sociologist,[9] 'would identify learning *content* with the learning *process*.'

Hence, our mistrust in primers,[10] which set up a certain grouping of graphic signs as a gift and cast the illiterate in the role of the *object* rather than the *Subject* of his learning. Primers, even when they try to avoid this pitfall, end by *donating* to the illiterate words and sentences which really should result from his own creative effort. We opted instead for the use of 'generative words,' those whose syllabic elements offer, through re-combination, the creation of new words. Teaching men how to read and write a syllabic language like Portuguese means showing them how to grasp critically the way its words are formed, so that they themselves can carry out the creative play of combinations. Fifteen or eighteen words seemed sufficient to present the basic phonemes of the Portuguese language.

The program is elaborated in several phases:

Phase 1. Researching the vocabulary of the groups with which one is working. This research is carried out during informal encounters with the inhabitants of the area. One selects not only the words most weighted with existential meaning (and thus the greatest emotional content), but also typical sayings, as well as words and expressions linked to the experience of the groups in which the researcher participates. These interviews reveal longings, frustrations, disbeliefs, hopes, and an impetus to participate. During this initial phase the team of educators form rewarding relationships and discover often unsuspected exuberance and beauty in the people's language.

The archives of the Service of Cultural Extension of the University of Recife contain vocabulary studies of rural and urban areas in the Northeast and in southern Brazil full of such examples as the following: 'The month of January in Angicos,' said a man from the backlands of Rio Grande do Norte, 'is a hard one to live through, because January is a tough guy who makes us suffer.' (*Janeiro em Angicos é duro de se viver, porque janeiro é cabra danado para judiar de nós.*)

'I want to learn to read and write,' said an illiterate from Recife, 'so that I can stop being the shadow of other people.'

A man from Florianópolis: 'The people have an answer.'

Another, in an injured tone: 'I am not angry (*não tenho paixão*) at being poor, but at not knowing how to read.'

'I have the school of the world,' said an illiterate from the southern part of the country, which led Professor Jomard de Brito to ask in an essay, 'What can one presume to "teach" an adult who affirms "I have the school of the world"?'[11]

'I want to learn to read and to write so I can change the world,' said an illiterate from São Paulo, for whom *to know* quite correctly meant *to intervene* in his reality.

'The people put a screw in their heads,' said another in somewhat esoteric language. And when he was asked what he meant, he replied in terms revealing the phenomenon of popular emergence: 'That is what explains that you, Professor, have come to talk with me, the people.'

Such affirmations merit interpretation by specialists, to produce a more efficient instrument for the educator's action.[12] The generative words to be used in the program should emerge from this field vocabulary research, not from the educator's personal inspiration, no matter how proficiently he might construct a list.

Phase 2. Selection of the generative words from the vocabulary which was studied. The following criteria should govern their selection:
   (a) phonemic richness;
   (b) phonetic difficulty (the words chosen should correspond to the phonetic difficulties of the language, placed in a sequence moving gradually from words of less to those of greater difficulty);
   (c) pragmatic tone, which implies a greater engagement of a word in a given social, cultural and political reality. [...]

Phase 3. The creation of the 'codifications': the representation of typical existential situations of the group with which one is working. These representations function as challenges, as coded situation-problems containing elements to be decoded by the groups with the collaboration of the coordinator. Discussion of these codifications will lead the groups toward a more critical consciousness at the same time that they begin to learn to read and write. The codifications represent familiar local situations — which, however, open perspectives for the analysis of regional and national problems. The generative words are set into the codifications, graduated according to their phonetic difficulty. One generative word may embody the entire situation, or it may refer to only one of the elements of the situation.

Phase 4. The elaboration of agendas, which should serve as mere aids to the coordinators, never as rigid schedules to be obeyed.

Phase 5. The preparation of cards with the breakdown of the phonemic families which correspond to the generative words.
   A major problem in setting up the program is instructing the teams of coordinators. Teaching the purely technical aspect of the procedure is not difficult; the difficulty lies rather in the creation of a new attitude — that of dialogue, so absent·in our own upbringing and education. The coordinators must be converted to dialogue in order to carry out education rather than domestication. Dialogue is an I-Thou relationship, and thus necessarily a relationship between two Subjects. Each time the 'thou' is changed into an object, an 'it', dialogue is subverted and education is changed to deformation. The

period of instruction must be followed by dialogical supervision, to avoid the temptation of anti-dialogue on the part of the coordinators.

Once the material has been prepared in the form of slides, film-strips, or posters, once the teams of coordinators and supervisors have been instructed in all aspects of the method and have been given their agendas, the program itself can begin. It functions in the following manner:

The codified situation is projected, together with the first generative word, which graphically represents the oral expression of the object perceived. Debate about its implications follows.

Only after the group, with the collaboration of the coordinator, has exhausted the analysis (decoding) of the situation does the coordinator call attention to the generative word, encouraging the participants to visualize (not memorize) it. Once the word has been visualized, and the semantic link established between the word and the object to which it refers, the word is presented alone on another slide (or poster or photogram) without the object it names. Then the same word is separated into syllables, which the illiterate usually identifies as 'pieces.' Once the 'pieces' are recognized, the coordinator presents visually the phonemic families which compose the word, first in isolation and then together, to arrive at the recognition of the vowels. The card presenting the phonemic families has been called the 'discovery card'.[13] Using this card to reach a synthesis, men discover the mechanism of word formation through phonemic combinations in a syllabic language like Portuguese. By appropriating this mechanism critically (not learning it by rote), they themselves can begin to produce a system of graphic signs. They can begin, with surprising ease, to create words with the phonemic combinations offered by the breakdown of a trisyllabic word, on the first day of the program.[14]

For example, let us take the word *tijolo* (brick) as the first generative word, placed in a 'situation' of construction work. After discussing the situation in all its possible aspects, the semantic link between the word and the object it names is established. Once the word has been noted within the situation, it is presented without the object: *tijolo*.

Afterwards: *ti-jo-lo*. By moving immediately to present the 'pieces' visually, we initiate the recognition of phonemic families. Beginning with the first syllable, *ti*, the group is motivated to learn the whole phonemic family resulting from the combination of the initial consonant with the other vowels. The group then learns the second family through the visual presentation of *jo*, and finally arrives at the third family.

When the phonemic family is projected, the group at first recognizes only the syllable of the word which has been shown:

(ta-te-*ti*-to-tu), (ja-je-ji-*jo*-ju), (la-le-li-*lo*-lu)

When the participants recognize *ti*, from the generative word *tijolo*, it is proposed that they compare it with the other syllables; whereupon they discover that while all the syllables begin the same, they end differently. Thus, they cannot all be called *ti*.

The same procedure is followed with the syllables *jo* and *lo* and their families. After learning each phonemic family, the group practices reading the new syllables.

The most important moment arises when the three families are presented together:

ta-te-ti-to-tu
ja-je-ji-jo-ju   THE DISCOVERY CARD
la-le-li-lo-lu

After one horizontal and one vertical reading to grasp the vocal sounds, the group (*not* the coordinator) begins to carry out oral synthesis. One by one, they all begin to 'make' words with the combinations available:[15]

tatu (armadillo), *luta* (struggle), *lajota* (small flagstone), *loja* (store), *jato* (jet), *juta* (jute), *lote* (lot), *lula* (squid), *tela* (screen), etc. There are even some participants who take a vowel from one of the syllables, link it to another syllable, and add a third, thus forming a word. For example, they take the *i* from li, join it to *le* and add *te: leite* (milk).

There are others, like an illiterate from Brasília, who on the first night he began his literacy program said, '*tu já lê*' ('you already read').[16]

The oral exercises involve not only learning, but recognition (without which there is no true learning). Once these are completed, the participants begin — on that same first evening — to write. On the following day they bring from home as many words as they were able to make with the combinations of the phonemes they learned. It doesn't matter if they bring combinations which are not actual words — what does matter is the discovery of the mechanism of phonemic combinations.

The group itself, with the help of the educator (*not* the educator with the help of the group), should test the words thus created. A group in the state of Rio Grande do Norte called those combinations which were actual words 'thinking words' and those which were not, 'dead words'.

Not infrequently, after assimilating the phonemic mechanism by using the 'discovery card', participants would write words with complex phonemes (*tra, nha*, etc.), which had not yet been presented to them. In one of the Culture Circles in Angicos, Rio Grande do Norte, on the fifth day of discussion, in which simple phonemes were being shown, one of the participants went to the blackboard to write (as he said) 'a thinking word'. He wrote: '*o povo vai resouver os poblemas do Brasil votando conciente*'[17] ('the people will solve the problems of Brazil by informed voting'). In such cases, the group discussed the text, debating its significance in the context of their reality.

How can one explain the fact that a man who was illiterate several days earlier could write words with complex phonemes before he had even studied them? Once he had dominated the mechanism of phonemic combinations, he attempted — and managed — to express himself graphically, in the way he spoke.[18]

I wish to emphasize that in educating adults, to avoid a rote, mechanical process one must make it possible for them to achieve critical consciousness so that they can teach themselves to read and write.

As an active educational method helps a person to become consciously aware of his context and his condition as a human being as Subject, it will become an instrument of choice. At that point he will become politicized. When an ex-illiterate of Angicos, speaking before President João Goulart and the presidential staff,[19] declared that he was no longer part of the *mass*, but one of the *people*, he had done more than utter a mere phrase; he had made a conscious option. He had chosen decisional participation, which belongs to the people, and had renounced the emotional resignation of the masses. He had become political.

The National Literacy Program of the Ministry of Education and Culture, which I coordinated, planned to extend and strengthen this education work throughout Brazil. Obviously we could not confine that work to a literacy program, even one which was critical rather than mechanical. With the same spirit of a pedagogy of communication, we were therefore planning a post-literacy stage which would vary only as to curriculum. If the National Literacy Program had not been terminated by the military coup, in 1964 there would have been more than 20,000 culture circles functioning throughout the country. In these, we planned to investigate the themes of the Brazilian people. These themes would be analyzed by specialists and broken down into learning units, as we had done with the concept of culture and with the coded situations linked to the generative words. We would prepare filmstrips with these breakdowns as well as simplified texts with references to the original texts. By gathering this thematic material, we could have offered a substantial post-literacy program. Further, by making a catalog of thematic breakdowns and bibliographic references available to high schools and colleges, we could widen the sphere of the program and help identify our schools with our reality.

At the same time, we began to prepare material with which we could carry out concretely an education that would encourage what Aldous Huxley has called the 'art of dissociating ideas'[20] as an antidote to the domesticating power of propaganda.[21] We planned filmstrips, for use in the literacy phase, presenting propaganda — from advertising commercials to ideological indoctrination — as a 'problem-situation' for discussion.

For example, as men through discussion begin to perceive the deceit in a cigarette advertisement featuring a beautiful, smiling woman in a bikini (i.e., the fact that she, her smile, her beauty, and her bikini have nothing at all to do with the cigarette), they begin to discover the difference between education and propaganda. At the same time, they are preparing themselves to discuss and perceive the same deceit in ideological or political propaganda; they are arming themselves to 'dissociate ideas'. In fact, this has always seemed to me to be the way to defend democracy, not a way to subvert it.

One subverts democracy (even though one does this in the name of democracy) by making it irrational; by making it rigid in order 'to defend it against totalitarian rigidity'; by making it hateful, when it can only develop in a context of love and respect for persons; by closing it, when it only lives in openness; by nourishing it with fear when it must be courageous; by making it an instrument of the powerful in the oppression of the weak; by militarizing it against the people; by alienating a nation in the name of democracy.

One defends democracy by leading it to the state Mannheim calls 'militant democracy' — a democracy which does not fear the people, which suppresses privilege, which can plan without becoming rigid, which defends itself without hate, which is nourished by a critical spirit rather than irrationality.

Notes

1. Karl Mannheim, *Freedom, Power, and Democratic Planning* (Oxford University Press, New York, 1950).

2. In most reading programs, the students must endure an abysm between their own experience and the contents offered for them to learn. It requires patience indeed, after the hardships of a day's work (or of a day without work), to tolerate lessons dealing with 'wing'. 'Johnny saw the wing.' 'The wing is on the bird.' Lessons talking of Graces and grapes to men who never knew a Grace and never ate a grape. 'Grace saw the grape.'

3. No one ignores everything, just as no one knows everything. The dominating consciousness absolutizes ignorance in order to manipulate the so-called 'cultured'. If some men are 'totally ignorant', they will be incapable of managing themselves, and will need the orientation, the 'direction', the 'leadership' of those who consider themselves to be 'cultured' and 'superior'.

4. Alvaro Vieira Pinto, *Consciência e Realidade Nacional* (Rio de Janeiro, 1961).

5. 'Breakdown': a splitting of themes into their fundamental nuclei. See *Pedagogy of the Oppressed*, p. 113 ff. 'Codification': the representation of a theme in the form of an existential situation. See *Pedagogy*, pp. 106-7 and pp. 114-15 (translator's note).

6. Karl Jaspers, *The Origin and Goal of History* (New Haven, 1953); Karl Jaspers, *Reason and Anti-reason in our Time* (New Haven, 1952).

7. See Jaspers, ibid.

8. Similar responses were evoked by the programs carried out in Chile.

9. Celso Beisegel, in an unpublished work.

10. I am not opposed to reading texts, which are in fact indispensable to developing the visual-graphic channel of communication and which in great part should be elaborated by the participants themselves. I should add that our experience is based on the use of multiple channels of communication.

11. 'Educação de Adultos e Unificação de Cultura,' Estudos Universitários, *Revista de Cultura*, Universidade de Recife, 2-4, 1963.

12. Luis Costa Lima, Professor of Literary Theory, has analysed many of these texts by illiterate authors.

13. Aurenice Cardoso, 'Conscientização e Alfabetização — Visão Prática do Sistema Paulo Freire de Educação de Adultos,' Estudos Universitários, *Revista de Cultura*, Universidade do Recife, No. II, 1963.

14. Generally, in a period of six weeks to two months, we could leave a group of 25 persons reading newspapers, writing notes and simple letters, and discussing problems of local and national interest.

15. In a television interview, Gílson Amado observed lucidly, 'They can do this, because there is no such thing as oral illiteracy.'

16. In correct Portuguese, *tu já lês*.

17. *Resouver* is a corruption of *resolver*; *poblemas* a corruption of *problemas*; the letter *s* is lacking from the syllable *cons*.

18. Interestingly enough, as a rule the illiterates wrote confidently and legibly, largely overcoming the natural indecisiveness of beginners. Elza Freire thinks this may be due to the fact that these persons, beginning with the discussion of the anthropological concept of culture, discovered themselves to be more fully human, thereby acquiring an increasing emotional confidence in their learning which was reflected in their motor activity.

19. I wish to acknowledge the support given our efforts by President Goulart, by Ministers of Education Paulo de Tarso and Júlio Sambaquy, and by the Rector of the University of Recife, Professor João Alfredo da Costa Lima.

292   *Education and Conscientização*

20. *Ends and Means* (New York and London, 1937), p. 252.

21. I have never forgotten the publicity (done cleverly, considering our acritical mental habits) for a certain Brazilian public figure. The bust of the candidate was displayed with arrows pointing to his head, his eyes, his mouth, and his hands. Next to the arrows appeared the legend:

You don't need to think, he thinks for you!
You don't need to see, he sees for you!
You don't need to talk, he talks for you!
You don't need to act, he acts for you!

INDEX